图解 汽车专业英语

Illustrated Professional
English of
Automotive Industry

朱派龙　主　编
何健斌　唐电波　副主编

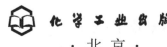
化学工业出版社
·北京·

图书在版编目（CIP）数据

图解汽车专业英语/朱派龙主编. —北京：化学工业出版社，2017.6 （2022.11重印）
ISBN 978-7-122-29598-9

Ⅰ.①图… Ⅱ.①朱… Ⅲ.①汽车工程-英语-图解 Ⅳ.①U46-64

中国版本图书馆 CIP 数据核字（2017）第 096177 号

责任编辑：贾　娜　　　　　　　　　　　　　　装帧设计：王晓宇
责任校对：边　涛

出版发行：化学工业出版社（北京市东城区青年湖南街13号　邮政编码100011）
印　　装：北京天宇星印刷厂
787mm×1092mm　1/16　印张17¾　字数485千字　2022年11月北京第1版第7次印刷

购书咨询：010-64518888　　　　　　　　售后服务：010-64518899
网　　址：http://www.cip.com.cn
凡购买本书，如有缺损质量问题，本社销售中心负责调换。

定　价：69.00元　　　　　　　　　　　　　　　　　　　版权所有　违者必究

前言
Foreword

  China on wheels, 高速发展的中国最显著的标志就是汽车遍布, 与汽车相关的行业蓬勃发展, 诸多省市都将汽车工业作为自己的支柱产业。 汽车的产生源于国外, 但是近十年来, 中国的汽车产销量排列世界第一。 特别是国产 SUV 汽车发展迅猛, 2016 年销量前三位均为纯国产品牌, 其中第一位的长城哈弗 H6 单品牌销量达到 58 万多辆, 远超合资品牌 (第 4 名只有 27 万多辆)。

  汽车是一种结构复杂的产品, 一辆普通的汽车包含的零件数量就达万件以上, 可以说汽车技术及其产品或零部件涉及面十分宽泛、复杂。 随着汽车技术的提高及我国进出口贸易的发展, 掌握一定的专业英语成为汽车领域从业人员的必备技能。考虑到汽车结构及汽车专业的特点, 辅以图形会使专业内容更加直观、形象、具体、生动, 基本达到"望图知意"的程度, 所以我们收集整理了国外的汽车技术原版专著、外文教材以及国内的汽车技术资料, 精心编写了《图解汽车专业英语》一书, 将中文名称、英文表达和相关图形有机结合, 力求做到"有图有真相", 使读者在学会专业词汇英语表达的同时, 进一步巩固、加深对汽车本身专业术语的理解。

  本书主编朱派龙就是汽车运用不折不扣的践行者, 十年来自驾游览了神州大地的每一个省份。 为了使本书内容更切合生产实际和行业动态, 特邀请广汽日野汽车有限公司的技术部副部长何健斌担任副主编, 负责审核图书结构并提供实用资料。 唐电波也担任了本书的副主编。

  本书编写工作具体分工为: 何健斌编写 Chapter1、Chapter2 中的 2.1~2.4; 朱派龙编写 Chapter2 中的 2.5~2.12、Chapter3、Chapter5 中的 5.20~5.24、Chapter6、Chapter7 并负责全书统稿协调; 唐电波编写 Chapter4; 吴锦传编写 Chapter5 中的 5.1~5.4; 谢建周编写 Chapter5 中的 5.5~5.10; 余尚行编写 Chapter5 中的 5.11~5.19。

  本书内容直观明了, 形象生动, 不仅可作为大中专院校汽车相关专业的英语教材, 还有助于汽车行业的工程师、技术员识读英文图纸和技术资料, 同时也适合从事汽车进出口贸易、零部件供应的从业人士, 特别是非工科背景的从业人员学习参考。 本书在一定程度上还可以作为简明的汽车词汇手册供读者查阅使用。

编 者

目录 Contents

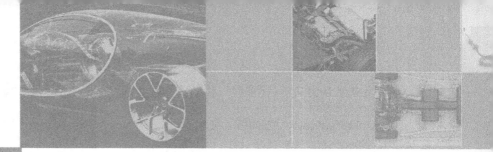

Chapter 1 Perspective view 汽车外观 / 1

Chapter 2 Engine 发动机 / 5

 2.1 Principle and types of engine 发动机工作原理和类型 6
 2.2 Structure of engine 发动机的构造 7
 2.3 Fuel supply system 燃油（气）供给系统 9
 2.4 Ignition system 点火系统 36
 2.5 Intake & exhaust control 进/排气控制 38
 2.6 Piston, connecting rod and crankshaft 活塞、连杆和曲轴机构 44
 2.7 Block group 机体组 47
 2.8 Valve train 配气机构 48
 2.9 Starter 启动机 49
 2.10 Lubrication system 润滑系统 50
 2.11 Cooling system 冷却系统 51
 2.12 Engine mounting 发动机安装垫 52

Chapter 3 Body 车身 / 55

 3.1 Types and structure of car bodies 车身类型与结构 56
 3.2 Vehicle body aerodynamics 车身空气动力学 59

Chapter 4 Chassis 底盘 / 67

 4.1 Overall structure 总体构成 68
 4.2 Chassis 底盘 69
 4.3 Axle 车桥（轴） 71
 4.4 Suspension 悬架 77
 4.5 Shock absorber 减振装置 99
 4.6 Fifth wheel coupling 半挂牵引装置 104

Chapter 5 Functional components 功能部件 / 111

 5.1 Refrigeration devices 制冷装置 112
 5.2 Clutch 离合器 118
 5.3 Transmission 变速器 123
 5.4 Fluid coupling and torque convertor 液力偶合器和变矩器 134
 5.5 Synchronizer 同步（离合）器 142
 5.6 Differential 差速器 147

5.7　Speed reducer　减速器　152
5.8　Drive shaft　传动轴　155
5.9　Universal joint　万向节　155
5.10　Steering gear　转向器　158
5.11　Brake　制动器　170
5.12　Parking brake　驻车制动器　187
5.13　Tyre　轮胎　189
5.14　Distributor　分电器　193
5.15　Alternator　发电机　193
5.16　Belt tensioner　安全带张紧器　194
5.17　Instrument panel　汽车仪表盘　195
5.18　Electronic control system　电子控制系统　196
5.19　Door lock control system　门锁控制系统　198
5.20　ABS and EBD　防抱死与电子动力分配　199
5.21　Airbag　安全气囊　201
5.22　Traction control system　牵引力控制系统　202
5.23　Exhaust gas control　废气控制　206
5.24　Apparatus for automotive service and maintenance　汽车维护工具（仪器）　210

Chapter 6　Special-purpose vehicles　特种车辆 ／ 215

Chapter 7　Electric vehicles　电动汽车 ／ 219

7.1　Types and structure of EV　电动车类型及其结构　220
7.2　Battery system　电池系统　222
7.3　Motor　电机　226
7.4　Hybrid vehicle　混合动力车　227

Vocabulary with Figure Index　词汇及图形索引（英中对照） ／ 230

Vocabulary with Figure Index　词汇及图形索引（中英对照） ／ 253

参考文献 ／ 276

Chapter 1
Perspective view
汽车外观

Chapter 2
Engine
发动机

Chapter 3
Body
车身

Chapter 4
Chassis
底盘

Chapter 5
Functional components
功能部件

Chapter 6
Special-purpose vehicles
特种车辆

Chapter 7
Electric vehicles
电动汽车

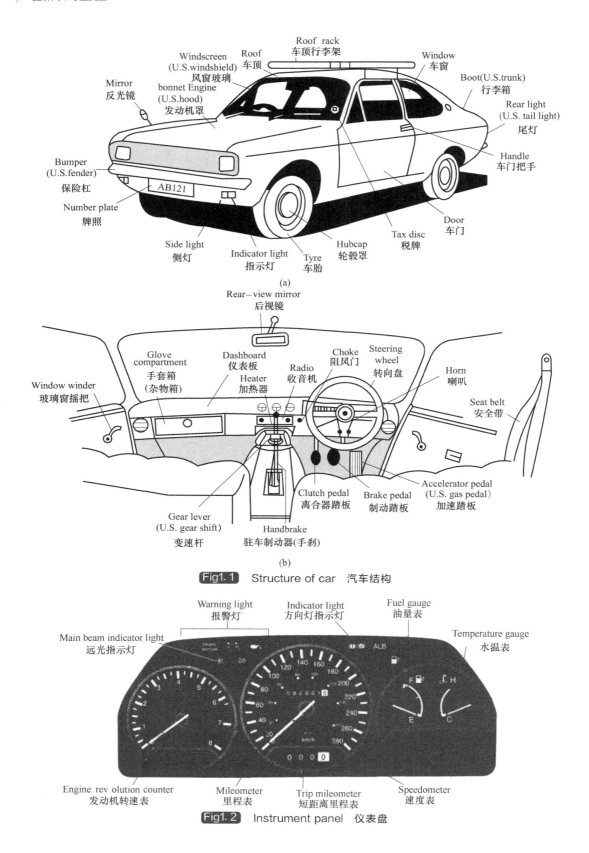

Fig1.1　Structure of car　汽车结构

Fig1.2　Instrument panel　仪表盘

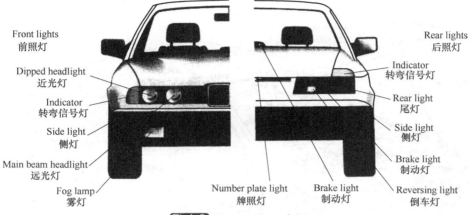

Fig1.3　Car lights　车灯

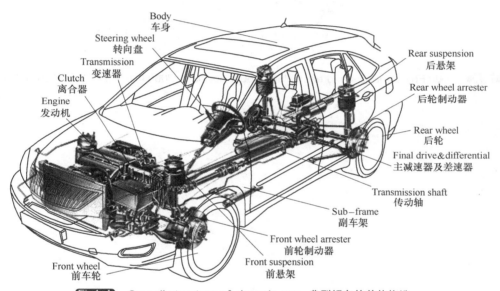

Fig1.4　Overall structure of classsic car　典型轿车的总体构造

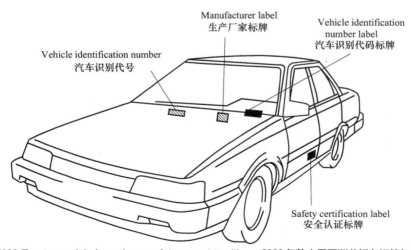

Fig1.5　2000 Toyota car labels and nameplate mount position　2000年款丰田亚洲龙轿车标签与铭牌贴装位置

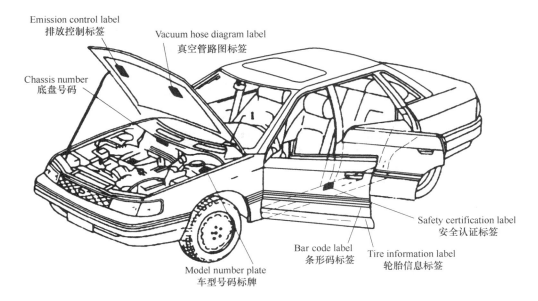

Fig1.6　2000 Fuji car labels and nameplate mount position　2000年款富士轿车标签与铭牌贴装位置

Chapter 1
Perspective view
汽车外观

Chapter 2
Engine
发动机

Chapter 3
Body
车身

Chapter 4
Chassis
底盘

Chapter 5
Functional components
功能部件

Chapter 6
Special-purpose vehicles
特种车辆

Chapter 7
Electric vehicles
电动汽车

2.1 Principle and types of engine
发动机工作原理和类型

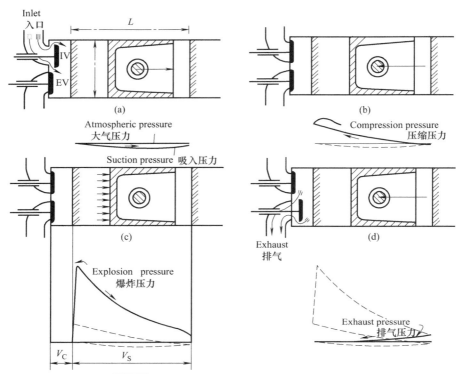

Fig2.1　The four-stroke cycle　四个冲程循环

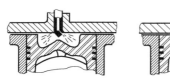

(a) Direct injection or open chamber type of combustion chamber
直喷式或开式燃烧室

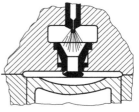

(b) Pre-combustion chamber
预燃烧的燃烧室

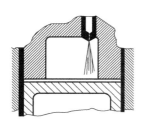

(c) Vortex combustion chamber
涡流燃烧室

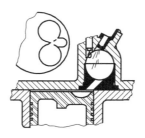

(d) Comet combustion chamber
彗星燃烧室

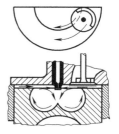

(e) Saurer combustion chamber
索雷尔燃烧室

Fig2.2　Types of chamber　燃烧室类型

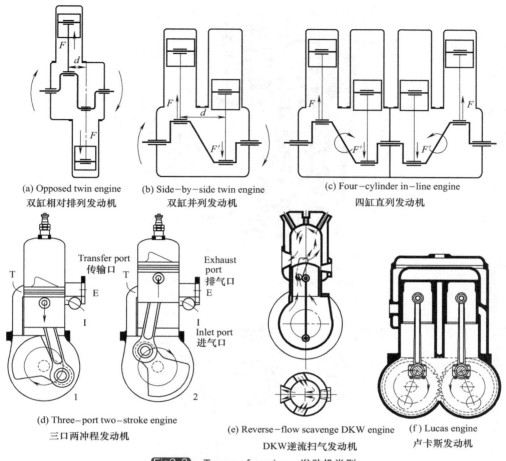

Fig2.3　Types of engine　发动机类型

(a) Opposed twin engine 双缸相对排列发动机
(b) Side-by-side twin engine 双缸并列发动机
(c) Four-cylinder in-line engine 四缸直列发动机
(d) Three-port two-stroke engine 三口两冲程发动机
(e) Reverse-flow scavenge DKW engine DKW逆流扫气发动机
(f) Lucas engine 卢卡斯发动机

2.2　Structure of engine　发动机的构造

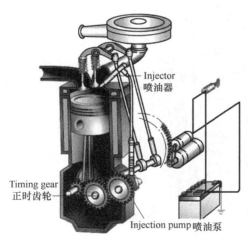

Fig2.4　Diesel engine appearance structure
柴油机外形结构

The Cummins 10-litre diesel engine is characterized by a clear rectangular line, and the panelling of the crankcase reduces noise output
康明斯10L柴油发动机特征是清晰的矩形线条，镶嵌的曲轴箱可减少噪声的输出

Fig2.5　Cummins 10-litre diesel engine
康明斯 10L 柴油发动机

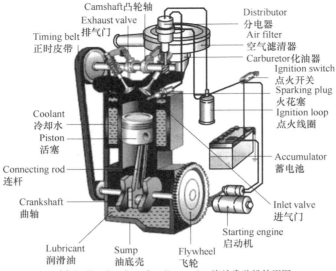
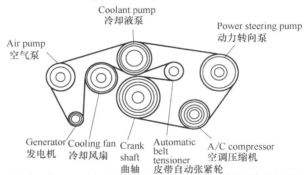

(a) Outline drawing of gasline engine 汽油发动机外形图

(b) Winding diagram of shake-like belts for engine 发动机蛇形皮带盘绕图

Fig2.6　Construct of gasline engine　汽油发动机结构

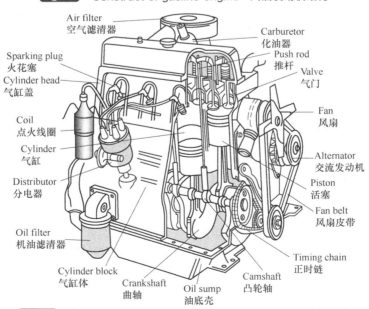

Fig2.7　Construct of internal combustion engine　内燃机结构

2.3 Fuel supply system 燃油（气）供给系统

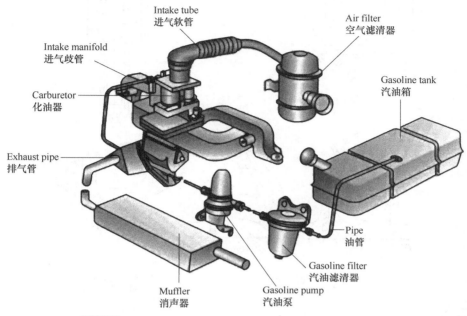

Fig2.8　Fuel system of gasoline engine　汽油机燃油系统

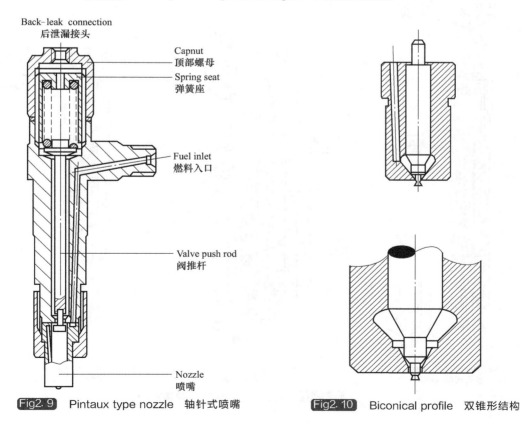

Fig2.9　Pintaux type nozzle　轴针式喷嘴

Fig2.10　Biconical profile　双锥形结构

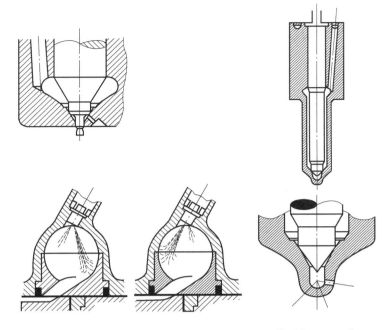
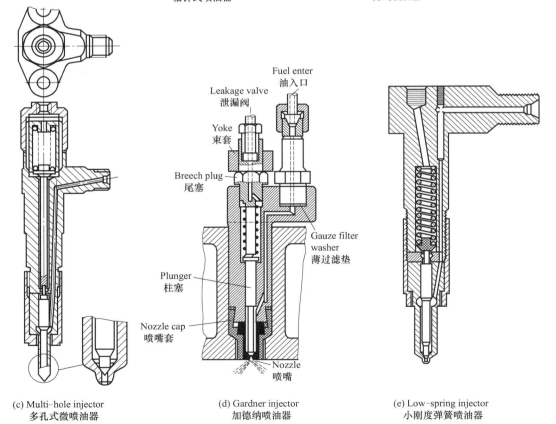

Fig2.11　Types of injector　喷油器类型

Chapter 2　Engine　发动机

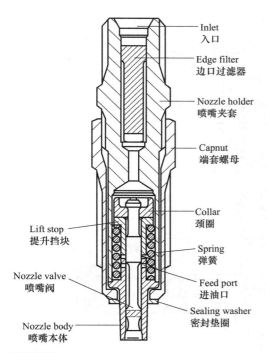

Fig2.12　General arrangement of microjector
微喷油器的通用设计

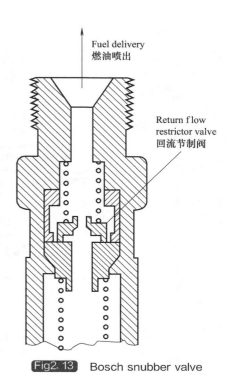

Fig2.13　Bosch snubber valve
博世减振阀

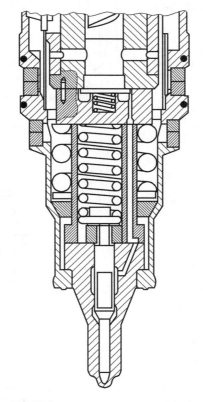

Fig2.14　Direct injection　直喷装置

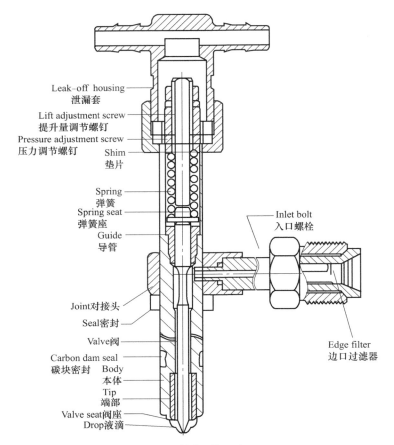
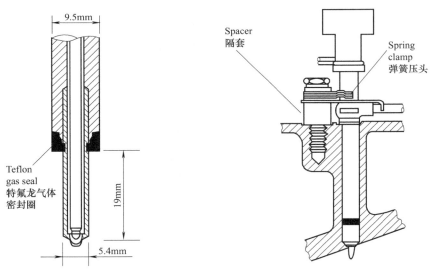

Fig2.15　Three types of nozzles　三种喷嘴

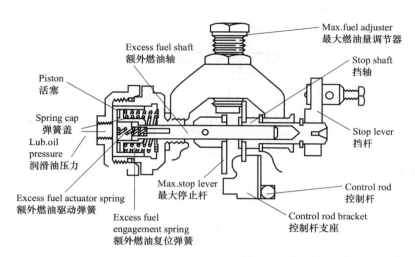

Fig2.16　A hydraulic actuator unit increases the oil pressure, which causes the piston to move to the right, and the excess fuel oil is discharged for the engine to start
液压启动单元增加油压使活塞右移排出额外燃油供发动机启动用

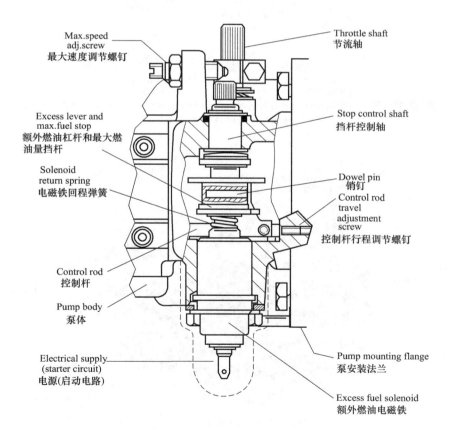

Fig2.17　The solenoid-actuated system for resetting the stop so that the fuel rack can move further to provide excess fuel for starting
电磁铁驱动重置燃油挡杆以便燃油齿条进一步移动额外供油用于启动

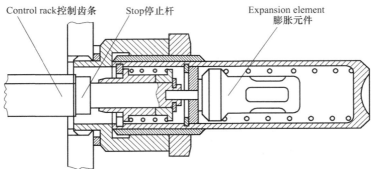

Fig2.18　The Bosch thermostatically actuated device for terminating cold start fuelling
结束冷启动供油的博世热启动装置

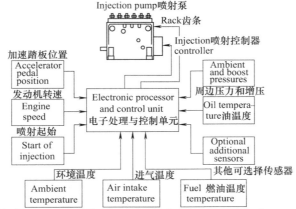

Fig2.19　Block diagram of the Bosch electronic control system and its sensors
博世电控系统及传感器框图

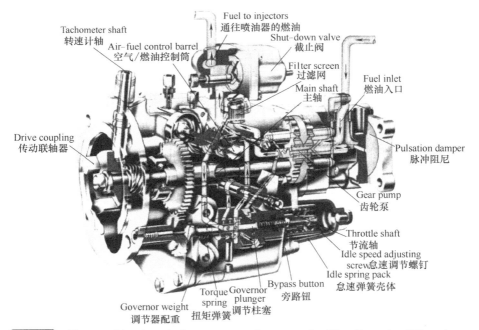

Fig2.20　The combined control, governor and pump unit of the Cummins PT system
集控制、调节器和泵单元于一体的康明斯PT系统

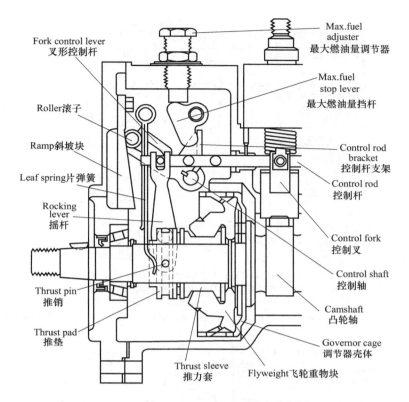

(a) To have a leaf spring 具有片弹簧

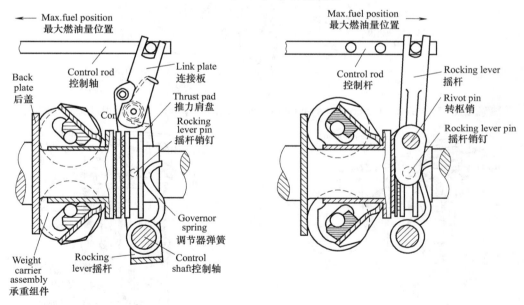

(ⅰ) Governor with normal linkage 普通连杆调节器

(ⅱ) Governor with reverse linkage 反向连杆调节器

(b) A minimec governor with a coil spring loaded in tension 线圈弹簧张紧时的微机械调节器

Fig2.21 Minimec governor 微机械调节器

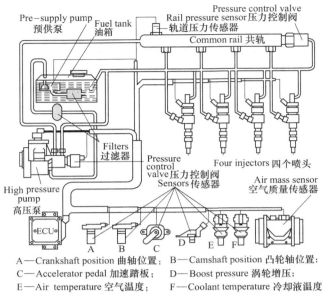

Fig2.22　Main components of the Bosch common rail injection system　博世共轨喷射系统的主要部件

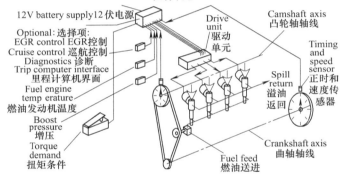

Fig2.23　The electronic control system of unit injection system　单元喷射系统的电控系统

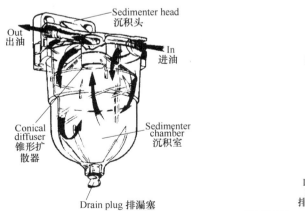

Fig2.24　The simple water separator of sedimenter
（it generally has a glass bowl, so that accumulation
of water or sediment can be easily observed）
简易分水器或沉积器（通常有一个玻璃器皿以
便沉积水或沉积物能够易于观察）

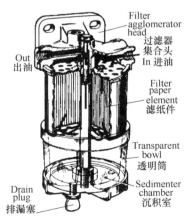

Fig2.25　Water droplets agglomerate on the clean side
of a filter element and, together with heavy particles
of sediment, drop down into the sedimenter below
水滴及沉积颗粒重物聚合在过滤元件的洁净边，
掉落在下边的沉积室里

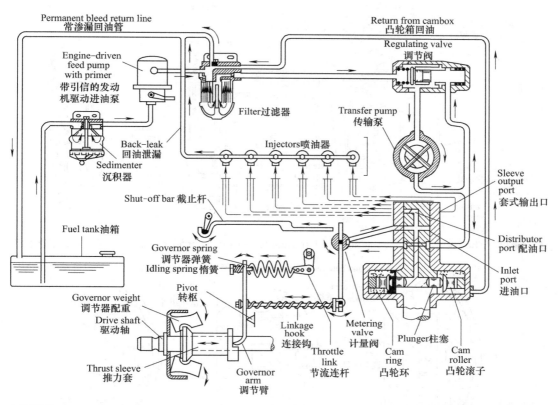

Fig2.26 Fuel system with DPA pump and mechanical governor 带 DPA 泵和机械调节器的燃油系统

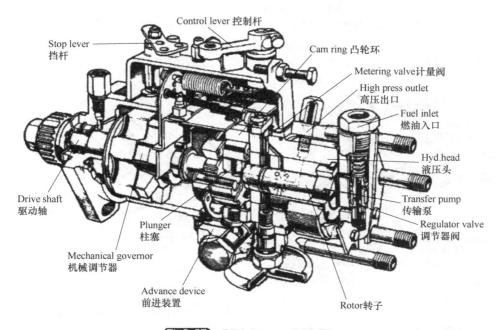

Fig2.27 DPA Pump DPA 泵

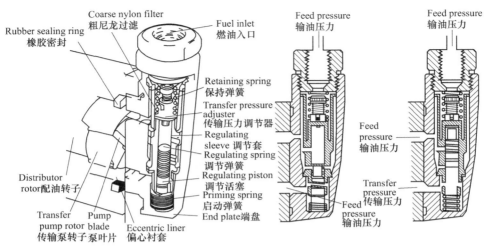

Fig2.28　The regulating valve is screwed into the top of the transfer pump　调节阀拧入传输泵顶部

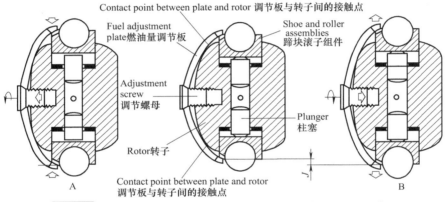

Fig2.29　Maximum fuel adjustment device　最大燃油量调节装置

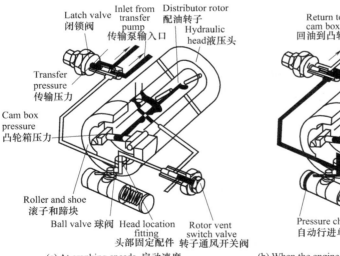
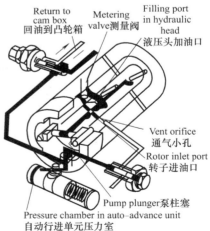

(a) At cranking speeds　启动速度

(b) When the engine fires and runs under its own power. the ducts in the distributor rotor are under metering pressure
发动机点火并靠自己动力运转,配油器转子导管处于测量压力

Fig2.30　Diagram of fuel distribution system for latch valve and rotor vent switch valve
闭锁阀和转子开关通风阀的燃油分配系统图解

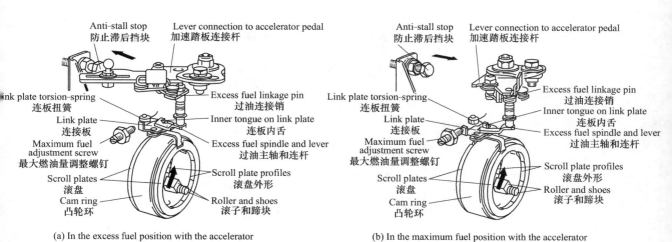

Fig2.31 In the DPS pump, the maximum fuel delivery is controlled by scroll plates
DPS 泵的最大燃油输出受到滚盘的控制

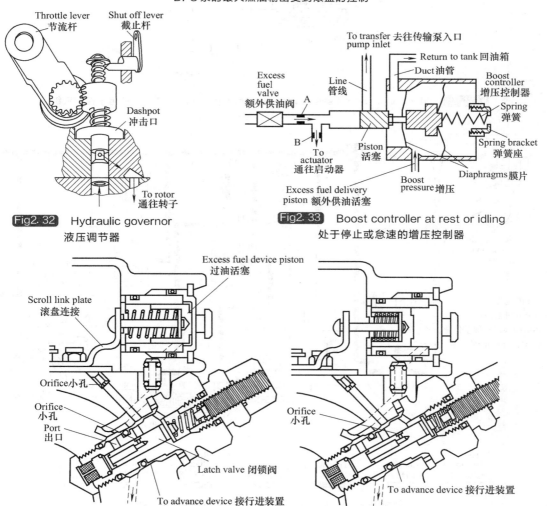

Fig2.32 Hydraulic governor 液压调节器

Fig2.33 Boost controller at rest or idling 处于停止或怠速的增压控制器

Fig2.34 Hydraulic excess fuel unit 液压过油单元

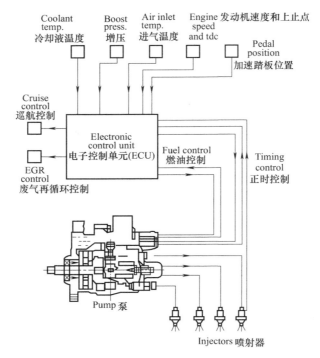

Fig2.35　Electronic control system for indirect injection　间接喷射的电子控制系统

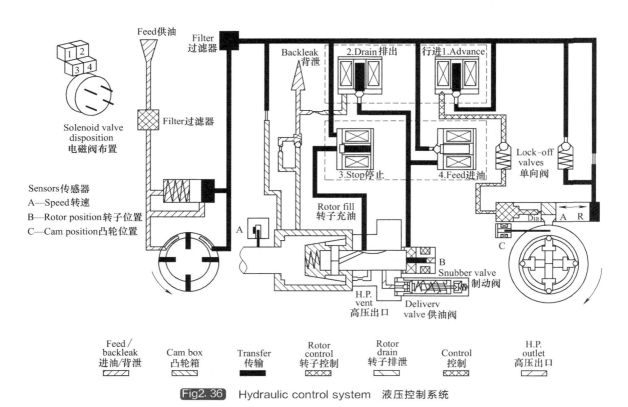

Fig2.36　Hydraulic control system　液压控制系统

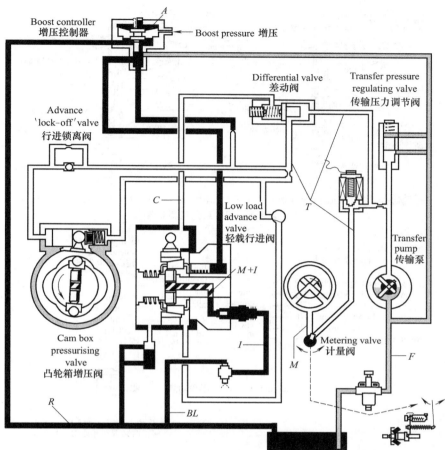

Fig2.37 Diagram illustrating the DPC distributor type pump system incorporating a boost controller (To the left of and below the transfer pressure regulating valve is a solenoid-actuated low load delivery valve) DPC 分电类泵系统（采用了增压控制器传输压力调节阀的左端和下端是电磁铁启动的轻载供油阀）

The key letters under different pressures in the system are as follows 系统不同压力标识字母如下：
A—Atmospheric 大气压；BL—Back leakage 背部泄漏压力；C—Cam box 凸轮箱压力；F—Fuel feed 燃油供给压力；
I—Injection 喷射压力；M+I—Alternately metering and injection 交替的计量和喷射压力；
R—Return to tank 返回油箱压力；T—Transfer pressure 传输压力

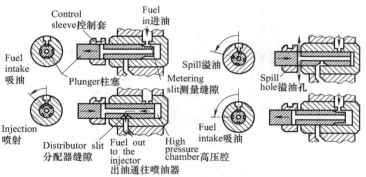

(a) In the delivery 供油状态　　(b) In the spill condition control 溢油条件控制

Fig2.38 Elevation design of the plunger and control sleeve of the Bosch VE type pump (by the governor, over the fuelling is effected by axial movement of the control sleeve to vary the spill point) 调节器对博世分配型泵的柱塞和控制套的提升设计（控制套轴向移动改变溢油点从而影响供油量）

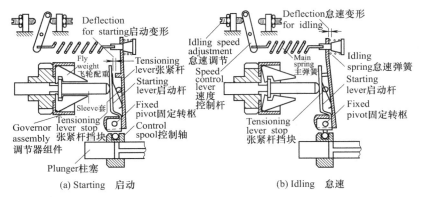

Fig2.39　All-speed version of the Bosch governor for the VE series pumps
博世全速版分配式系列泵调节器

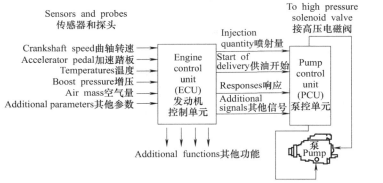

Fig2.40　Arrangement of the ECU and PCU in relation to the pump
电控单元和泵控单元与泵的对应布局

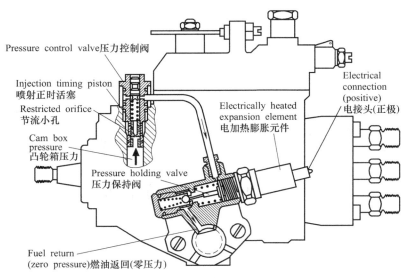

Fig2.41　Arrangement of the Bosch KSB hydraulic cold start injection advance device
博世 KSB 液压冷启动喷射行进装置

Chapter 2 Engine 发动机

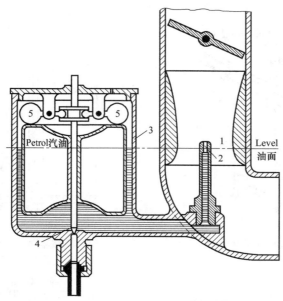

Fig2. 42 Elementary carburettor with only a single jet, together with the bottom feed needle valve and its actuation mechanism 单喷嘴化油器及其底部进油针阀和启动机构

1—The throat of the venturi, or choke (air orifice) 文丘里管喉部，即阻风门（进气孔）；2—Fuel jet (fuel orifice) 燃油喷嘴（燃油小孔）；3—Float chamber 浮子室；4—Needle valve 针阀；5—Levers translating upward motion of the float to downward motion of the needle valve, and vice versa 杠杆将浮子的向上运动转换为针阀的向下运动，反之亦然

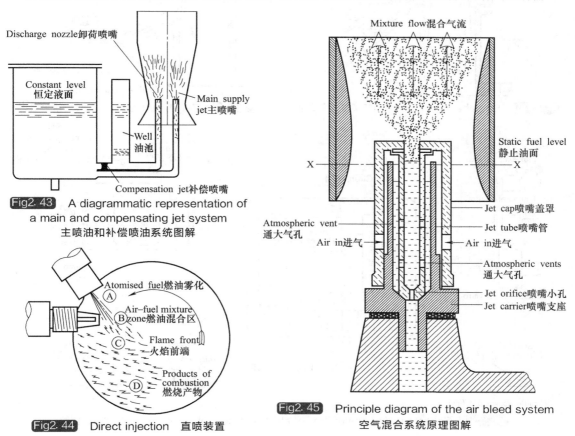

Fig2. 43 A diagrammatic representation of a main and compensating jet system 主喷油和补偿喷油系统图解

Fig2. 44 Direct injection 直喷装置

Fig2. 45 Principle diagram of the air bleed system 空气混合系统原理图解

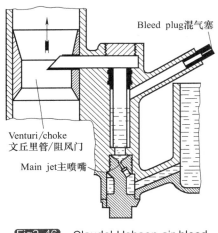

Fig2.46　Claudel-Hobson air bleed 克劳德-霍森混气装置

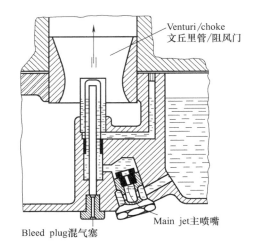

Fig2.47　Solex 'assembly 20' 索莱克斯20组件混气装置

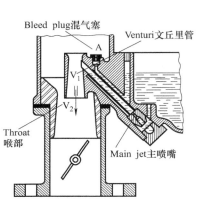

Fig2.48　Stromberg air bleed　斯托贝格混气装置

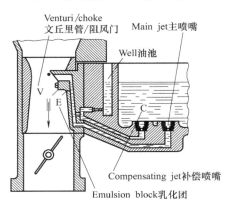

Fig2.49　Zenith air bleed　"顶峰"混气装置

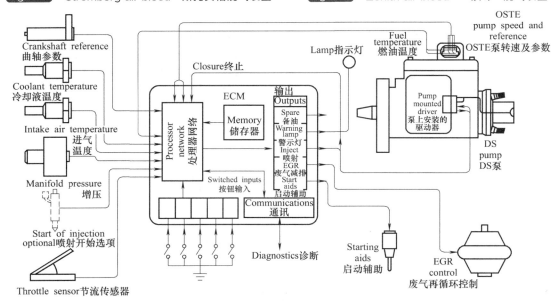

Fig2.50　Schematic diagram of the DS electronic control system　DS电控系统图解

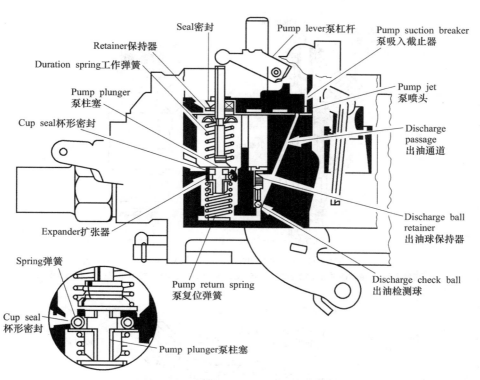

Fig2.51　Acceleration pump system with, in the scrap view, details of the head of the plunger and its seal
加速泵系统及其拆解图和柱塞、密封放大图

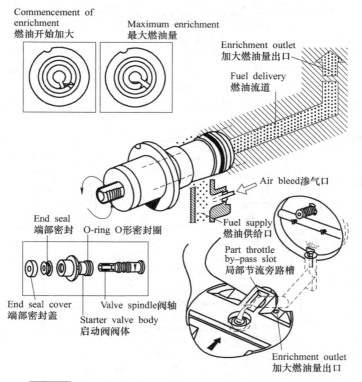

Fig2.52　Cold start enrichment device　冷启动补油装置

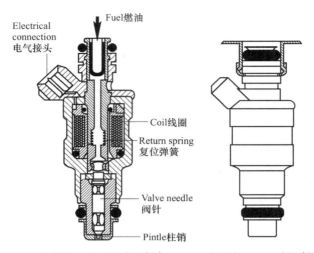

Fig2.53 Injector for the Bosch K-Jetronic system 博世 K 系燃油电喷系统

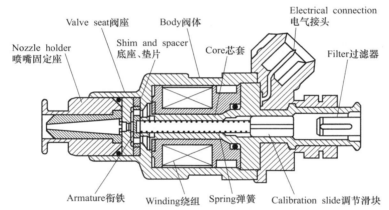

Fig2.54 In the Lucas-D-Series injector, alternative nozzles, for delivering single, twin or three sprays, can be fitted in the nozzle holder 可以安装在喷嘴座里的具有多种喷嘴（单头、双头和三头）可选的卢卡斯 D 系列喷油器

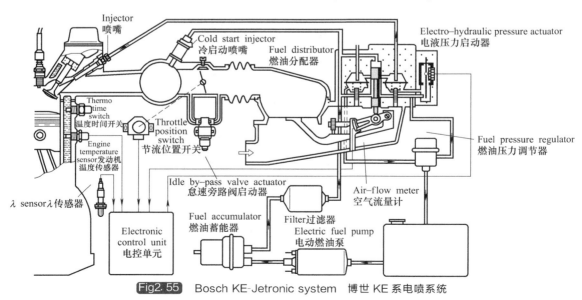

Fig2.55 Bosch KE-Jetronic system 博世 KE 系电喷系统

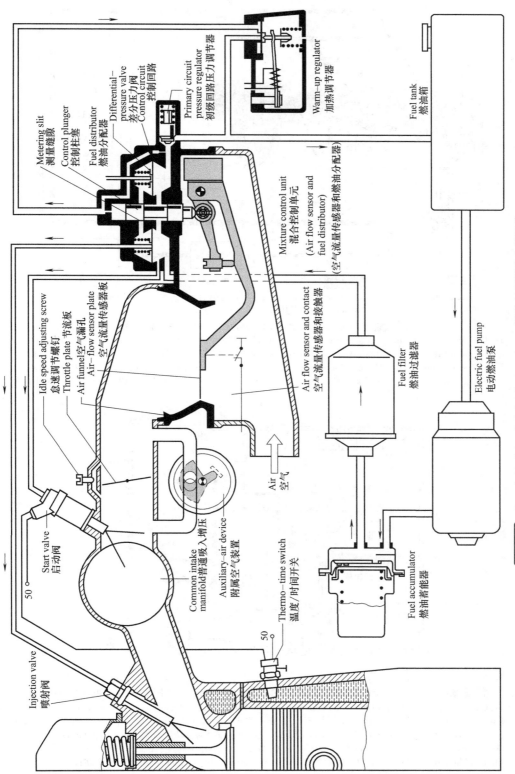

Fig2.56 Bosch K-Jetronic injection system 博世K系燃油电喷系统

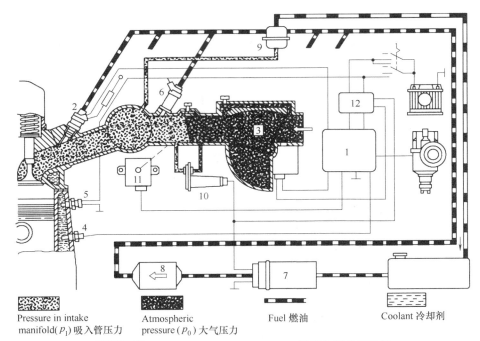

Pressure in intake manifold(p_1) 吸入管压力   Atmospheric pressure(p_0) 大气压力   Fuel 燃油   Coolant 冷却剂

Fig2.57 Bosch L-Jetronic system 博世 L 系电喷系统

1—Electronic control unit 电控单元；2—Injection valve 喷射阀；3—Air-flow sensor 空气流传感器；
4—Temperature sensor 温度传感器；5—Thermo-time switch 温度时间开关；6—Start valve 启动阀；
7—Electric pump 电动泵；8—Fuel filter 燃油过滤器；9—Pressure regulator valve 压力调节阀；
10—Auxiliary-air device 空气附属装置；11—Throttle-valve switch 节流阀开关；12—Relay set 延时装置

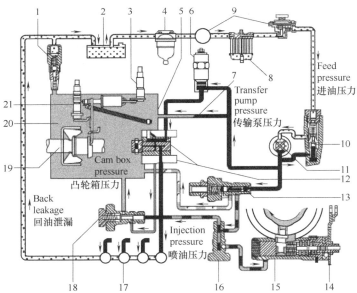

Fig2.58 Fuel system of the Lucas DPS injection pump 卢卡斯 DPS 喷油泵燃油系统

1—Pressurising valve 压力阀；2—Fuel tank 燃油箱；3—Throttle shaft 节流轴；4—Sedimenter or water stop 沉积器/积水器；
5—Metering valve 计量阀；6—Shut-off solenoid 截止电磁铁；7—Vent orifice 通风小孔；8—Filter 过滤器；
9—Feed pump (when fitted) or hand primer (when fitted) 输油泵或手动启动注油器；10—Regulating valve 调节阀；
11—Transfer pump 传输泵；12—Hydraulic head and rotor 液压头和转子；13—Latch valve 闭锁阀；
14—Manual idle advance lever 手动急速调节杆；15—Automatic advance and retard unit 自动行进和阻滞单元；
16—Head locating fitting 头部固定配合；17—Injector 喷油器；18—Rotor vent switch valve 转子通风开关阀；
19—Two-speed mechanical governor and control linkage 两速度机械调节器和控制连接；20—Cam box 凸轮箱；21—Idle shaft 惰轴

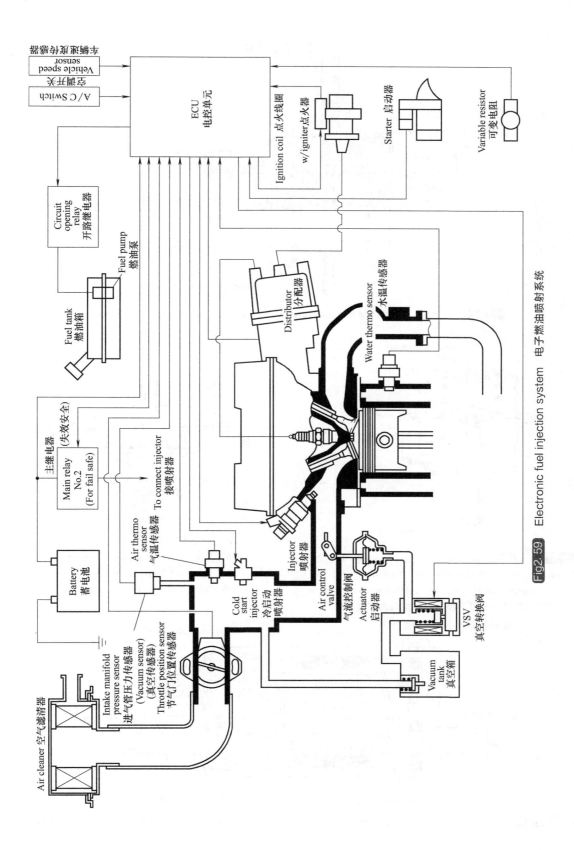

Fig2-59　Electronic fuel injection system　电子燃油喷射系统

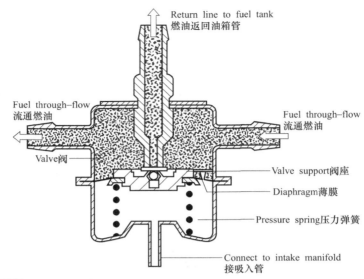

Fig2.60 Cross-section of the fuel-pressure regulator 燃油压力调节器剖视图

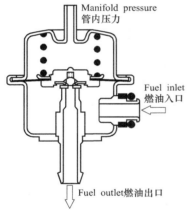

Fig2.61 A Bosch diagrammatic representation of the pressure regulator for their Motronic injection and ignition control system
博世压力调节器用于协同喷射和点火控制图解

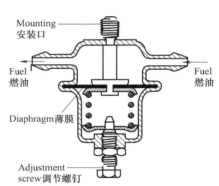

Fig2.62 Bosch pulsation damper for the Motronic system
博世发动机协同管理的脉冲阻尼器

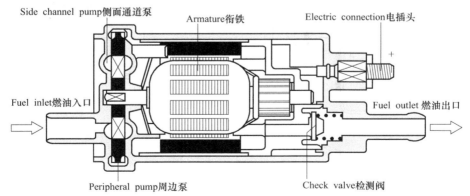

Fig2.63 Bosch fuel pump for delivery at pressures below 1 bar 博世低压（低于1巴）燃油供油泵

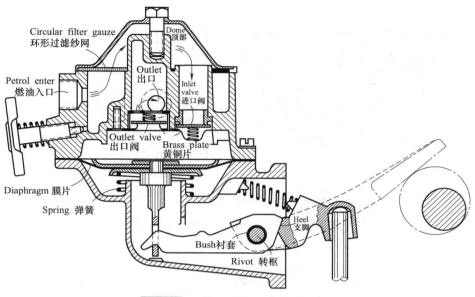

Fig2.64 AC fuel pump 交流燃油泵

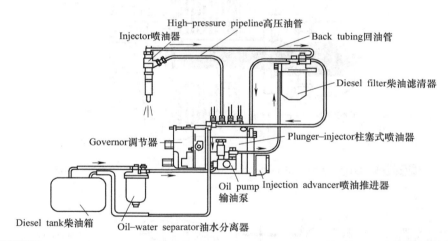

Fig2.65 Plunger-type fuel injection pump diesel system 柱塞式喷油泵柴油机燃油系统

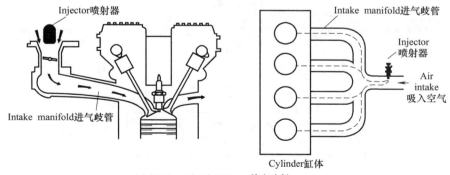

(a) Single-point injection 单点喷射

Fig2.66

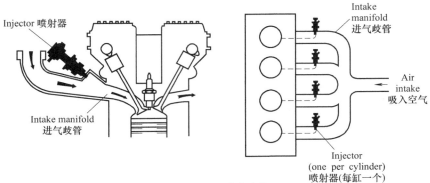

(b) Multi-point injection 多点喷射

Fig 2.66　Types of injection　喷射类型

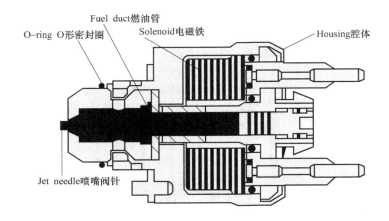

Fig 2.67　Single point CFI (central fuel injection) unit　单点中心喷油单元

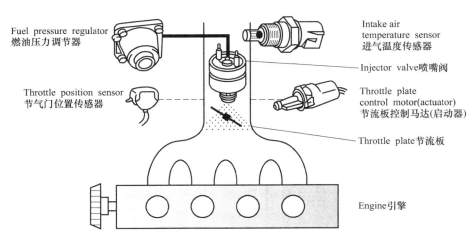

Fig 2.68　Single-point injection details　单点喷射详解

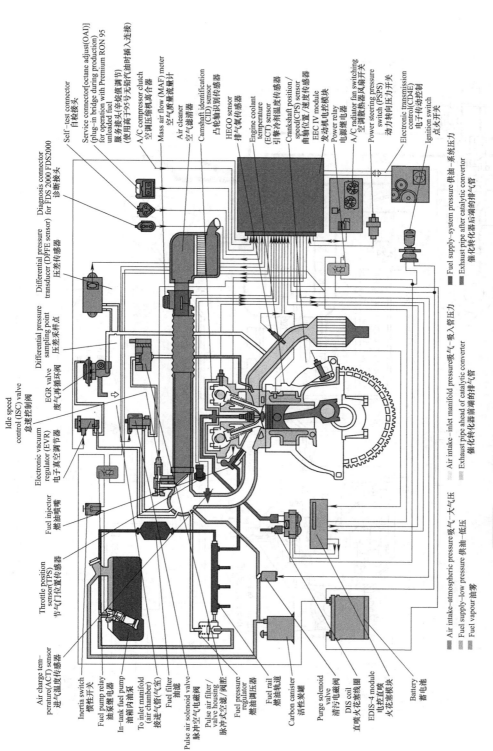

Fig2.69 Multi-point petrol injection system 多点燃油喷射系统

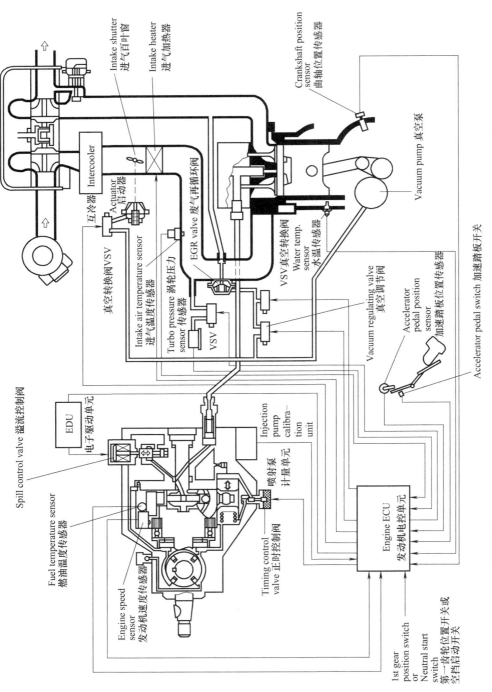

Fig2-70 Diesel engine system controlled by computer 计算机控制的柴油发动机系统

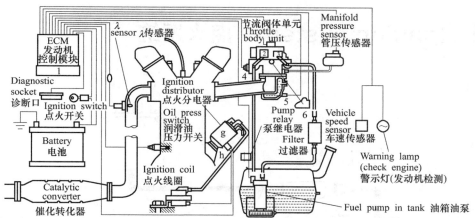

Fig2.71　The GM rochester multec single-point injection system　GM 罗切斯特复合技术单点燃油喷射系统

1—Plug-in calibration software EPROM　插入式校准软件只读存储器；2—Fuel pressure regulator　燃油压力调节器；
3—Injector　燃油喷射器；4—Idle air control valve　急速空气控制阀；5—Coolant temperature sensor　冷却剂温度传感器；
6—Throttle position sensor　节流阀位置传感器

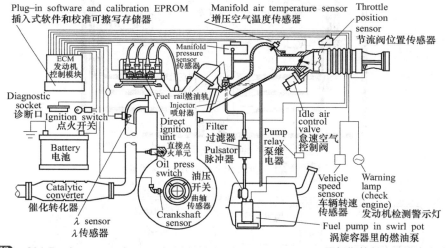

Fig2.72　GM Rochester multec multi-point injection system　GM 罗切斯特复合技术多点喷射系统

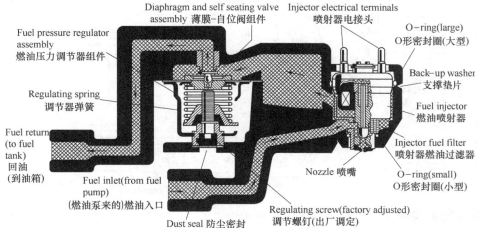

Fig2.73　The GM Rochester multec single-point injector (it is similar to that of the bosch mono-jetronic)
GM 罗切斯特复合技术单点燃油喷射器（与博世单点电喷类似）

2.4 Ignition system 点火系统

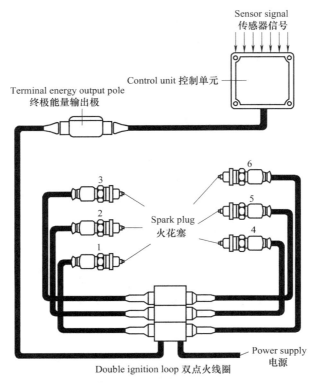

Fig2.74　Ignition system　点火系统

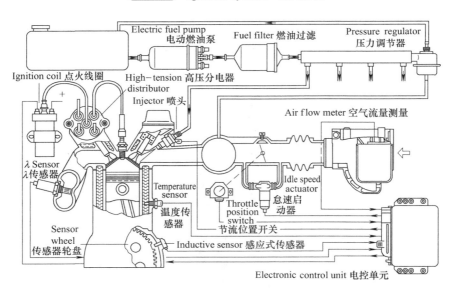

Fig2.75　Diagram issued by Bosch to represent their motronic system for a fourcylinder engine (which has a swinginggate-type air flow sensor)
博世四缸发动机的喷射/点火协同管理系统图解（发动机有摆动门式空气流传感器）

Chapter 2　Engine　发动机

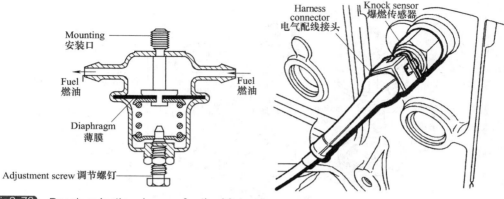

Fig2.76　Bosch pulsation damper for the Motronic system　博世发动机协同管理协同的脉冲阻尼器

Fig2.77　Knock sensor on the engine　发动机爆燃传感器

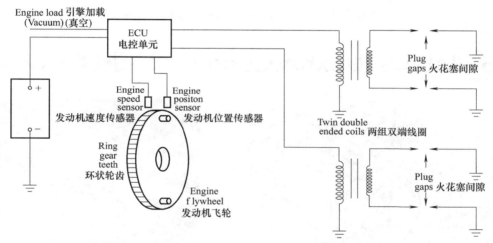

Fig2.78　Distributorless ignition system　无分配器的点火系统

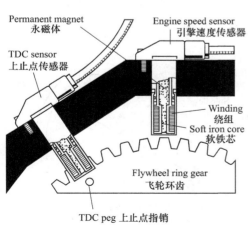

Fig2.79　Engine speed and crank position sensors　发动机转速和曲轴位置传感器

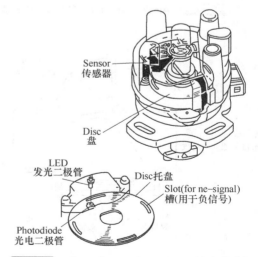

Fig2.80　Optoelectronic sensor　光电传感器

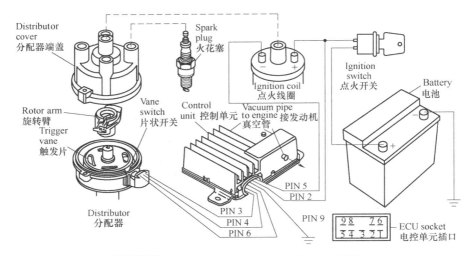

Fig2.81　Digital ignition system　数字点火系统

2.5 Intake & exhaust control　进/排气控制

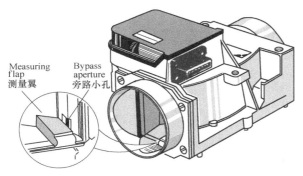

Fig2.82　Air flow sensor　空气流量传感器

Fig2.83　'Hot-wire' air flow sensor　'热线'空气流量传感器

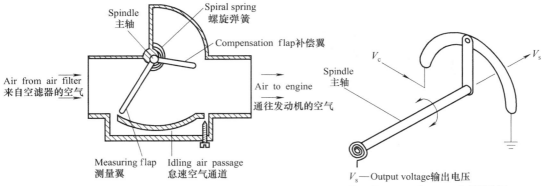

V_s—Output voltage 输出电压
V_c—Constant voltage supply 恒压电源
The voltage V_s represents air flow 电压代表空气流量

Fig2.84　Potential divider applied to an air flow sensor　应用于空气流量传感器的分电器

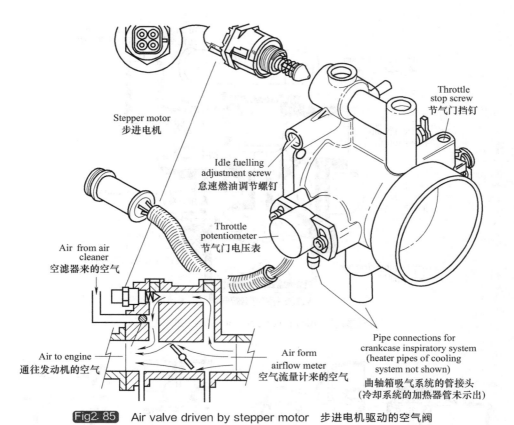

Fig2.85　Air valve driven by stepper motor　步进电机驱动的空气阀

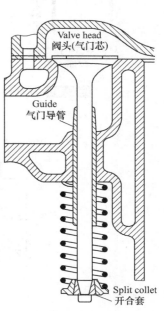

Fig2.86　Idle speed control valve driven by solenoid
电磁铁驱动的怠速控制阀

Fig2.87　Side-valve arrangement of poppet valve　侧面口提升阀（气门）的设计

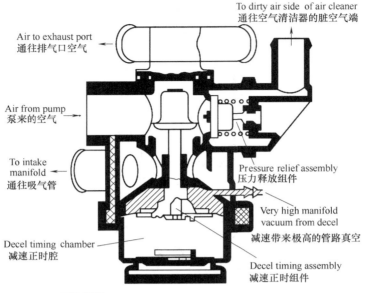

Fig2.88　Air intake control valve　进气控制阀

(a) Side-valve construction
侧阀结构

(b) Valve port direct access to the bore　阀口直通型

(c) Overhead valve(OHV) arrangement　顶置阀门

(d) Hemispherical head
半球头设计

Fig2.89　Four kinds of conventional layout for valves and combustion chamber
四种传统的气门与燃烧室布局设计

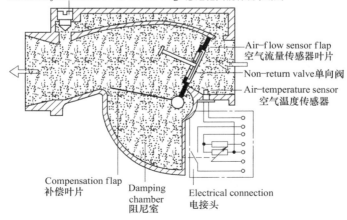

Fig2.90　Air-flow sensor　空气流量传感器

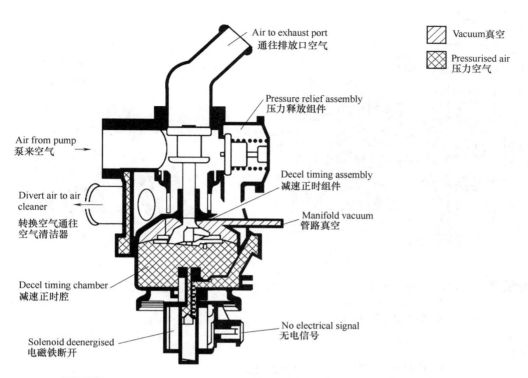

Fig2.91 The electrically actuated air-control valve, with solenoid energised
电磁铁断开状态的电启动空气控制阀

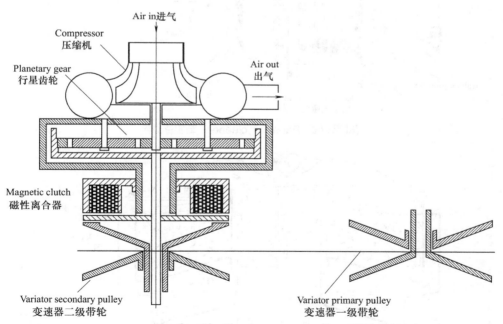

Fig2.92 Supercharger comprises (a centrifugal compressor driven by a variator with infinitely variable pulley-type transmission and a step-up planetary gear set)
超级增压器（包含一个带传动的无级变速器驱动的离心压缩机和一套行星齿轮装置）

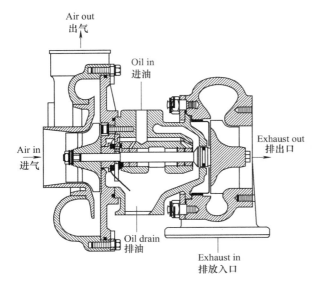

Fig2.93 KKK (künle, kausch and kopp) turbocharger with a single-entry turbine
KKK 单入口涡流增压器

Fig2.94 Cylinder (with three valves per cylinder, it is easy to accommodate two sparking plugs) 气缸（每个气缸有三个气门，易于两个火花塞工作）

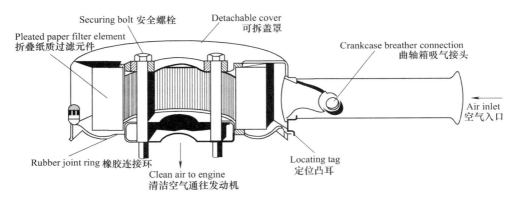

Fig2.95 Paper air cleaner 纸质空滤器

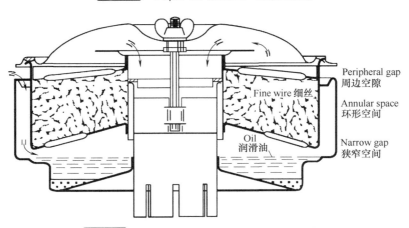

Fig2.96 AC oil bath cleaner AC 油池清洁器

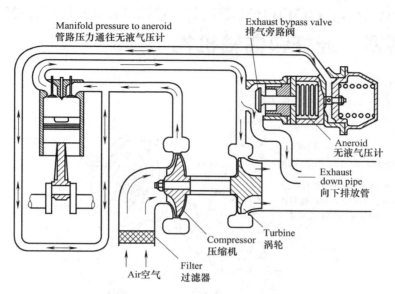

Fig2.97 Exhaust wastegate system 排放废气旁通系统

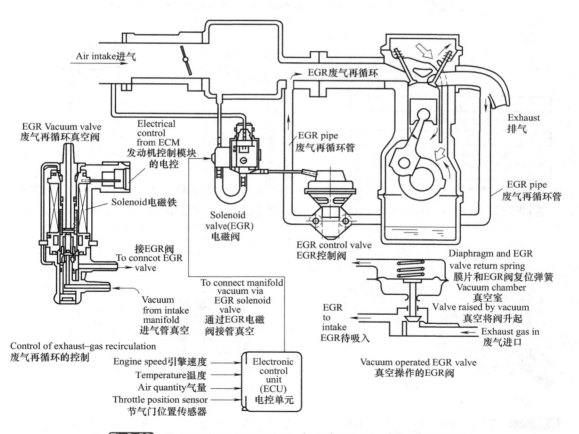

Fig2.98 Exhaust gas recirculation(EGR)system 废气再循环系统

2.6 Piston, connecting rod and crankshaft 活塞、连杆和曲轴机构

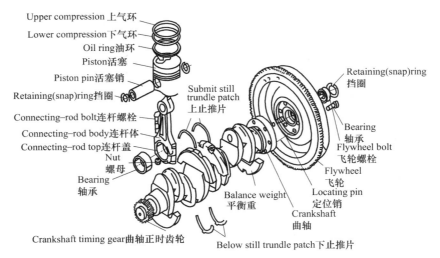

Fig2.99　Crankshaft and connecting rod framework　曲柄连杆机构

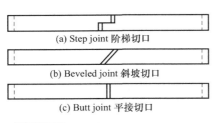

Fig2.100　Types of joints for rings 活塞环的切口形式

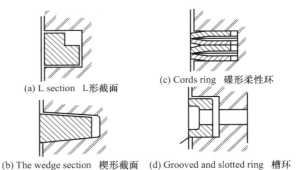

Fig2.101　Simple rectangular-section rings 矩形截面活塞环简图

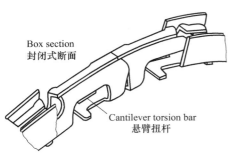

Fig2.102　Three-piece oil control rings 三组件活塞控油环

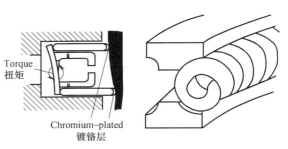

Fig2.103　A ring with a helical compression spring 内夹螺旋压缩弹簧的活塞环

Chapter 2　Engine　发动机

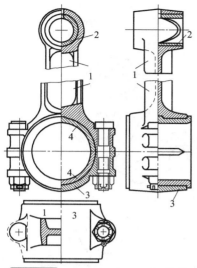

Fig2.104　Connecting rod　连杆
1—Steel forging　钢件锻压；
2—Small end bronze bush　小端铜套；
3—Big end bearing cap　大端轴承座；
4—Split big end bush of bronze lined with whitemetal
　　铜制里衬白色合金大端开合套

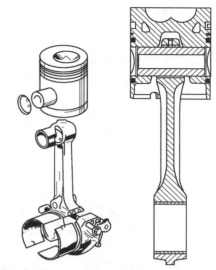

Fig2.105　Sturdy assembly for piston and connecting rod　活塞与连杆的紧固装配

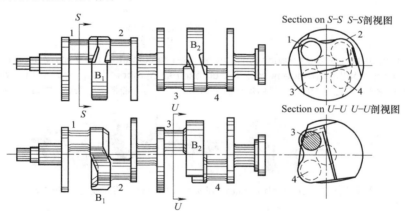

Fig2.106　Cast crankshaft for Ford V-eight　福特 V8 发动机的铸铁曲轴
1～4—Crankpin　曲柄销；B_1，B_2—Balance weight　平衡配重块

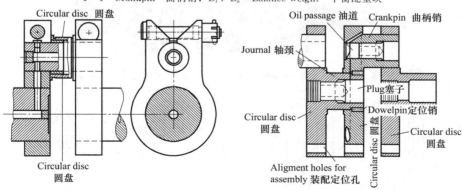

(a) Split crankweb　剖分式曲柄臂　　　(b) Circular disc crankweb　圆盘曲柄臂
Fig2.107　Built-up crankshaft　组合式曲轴

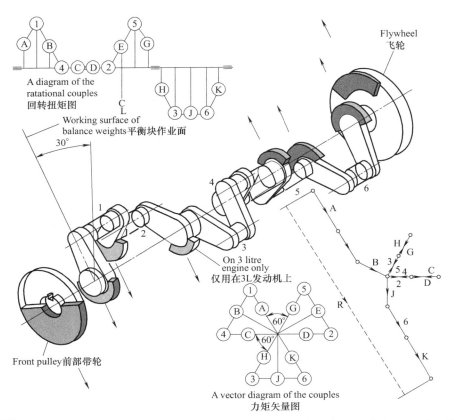

Fig2.108　Disposition of the balance weights on the crankshaft of the Ford V-six engine [With a diagrammatic layout of the arrangement of the crankpins (numbered 1 to 6) and the counterweights (lettered A to K)]　福特V6发动机曲轴平衡块的布局（1~6为曲柄销的布局，字母A~K为平衡块）

Fig2.109　Crankshaft with balanced throws　带平衡曲拐的曲轴

Fig2.110　Forged crankshaft with balanced webs　带平衡蹼的锻打曲轴

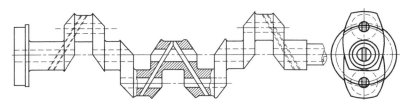

Fig2.111　Five-bearing shaft for CI (compression ignition) engine　压缩点火引擎的五支撑曲轴

2.7 Block group 机体组

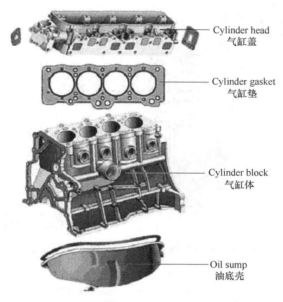

Fig2.112　Block group　机体组

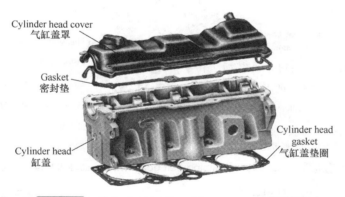

Fig2.113　Cylinder head and its cover　缸盖及盖罩

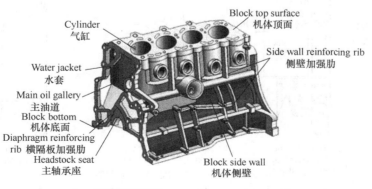

Fig2.114　Cylinder block　缸体

2.8 Valve train 配气机构

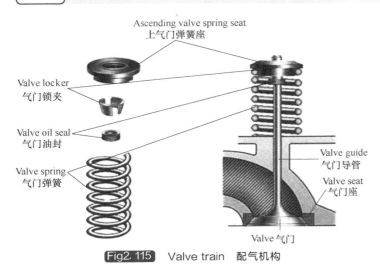

Fig2.115　Valve train　配气机构

Fig2.116　Chill casting camshaft 冷硬铸铁凸轮轴

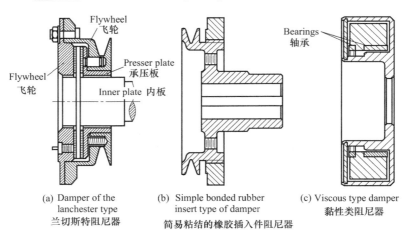

Fig2.117　Crankshaft timing belt gear wheel　曲轴正时齿形带轮

Fig2.118　Torsional vibration damper　扭转振动阻尼器

2.9 Starter 启动机

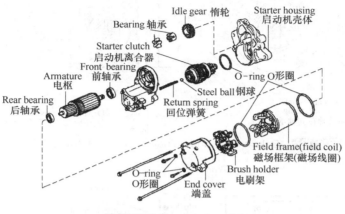

Fig2.119　Starter　启动机

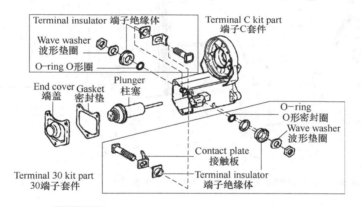

Fig2.120　Electromagnetic switch　电磁开关

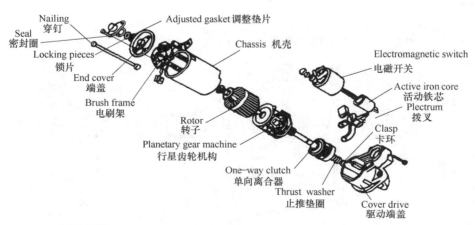

Fig2.121　Permanent magnet slowdown starter　永磁式减速启动机

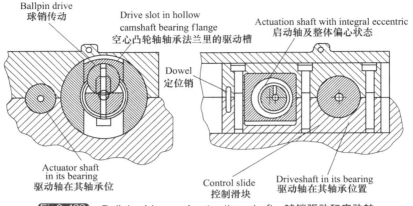

Fig2.122 Ballpin drive and actuation shaft 球销驱动和启动轴

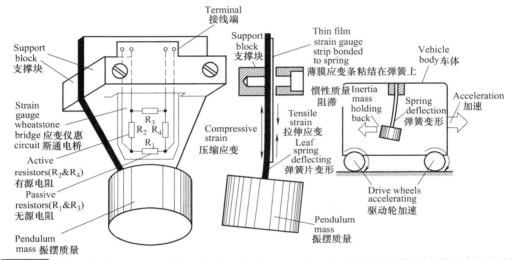

Fig2.123 Acceleration sensor (pendulum strain gauge type) 加速度传感器（振摆应变仪类型）

2.10 Lubrication system 润滑系统

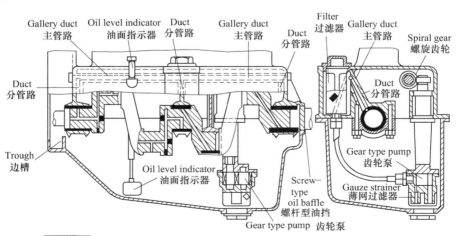

Fig2.124 An early pressure lubrication system 早期的压力润滑系统

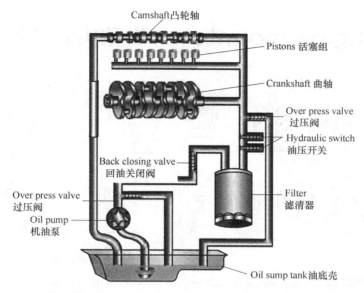

Fig2.125 Lubrication system composing 润滑系统组成

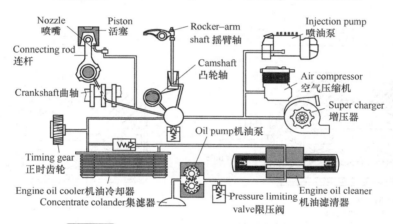

Fig2.126 Lubrication system oil route 润滑系统油路

2.11 Cooling system 冷却系统

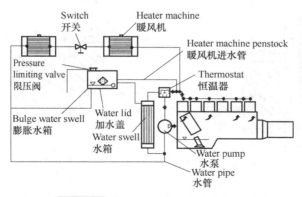

Fig2.127 Cooling system 冷却系统

2.12 Engine mounting 发动机安装垫

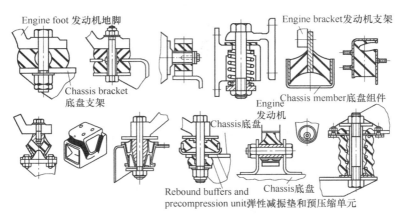

Fig2.128 Metalastik elastic engine mountings by Dunlop ploymer
邓禄普聚合物金属橡胶结合的弹性发动机安装垫

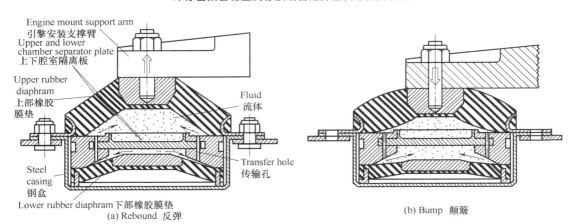

Fig2.129 Hydroelastic engine mounting 液压弹性引擎安装垫

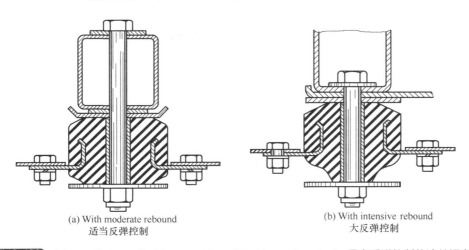

Fig2.130 Flanged sleeve bobin mounting with rebound coutrol 具有反弹控制的法兰短套筒安装垫

Chapter 2　Engine　发动机

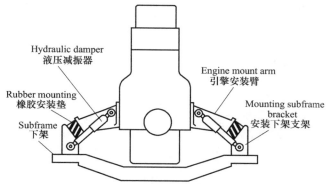

Fig2.131　Diagonally mounted hydraulic dampers suppress vertical and horizontal vibrations
对角安装的液压减振器抑制垂直和水平方向的振动

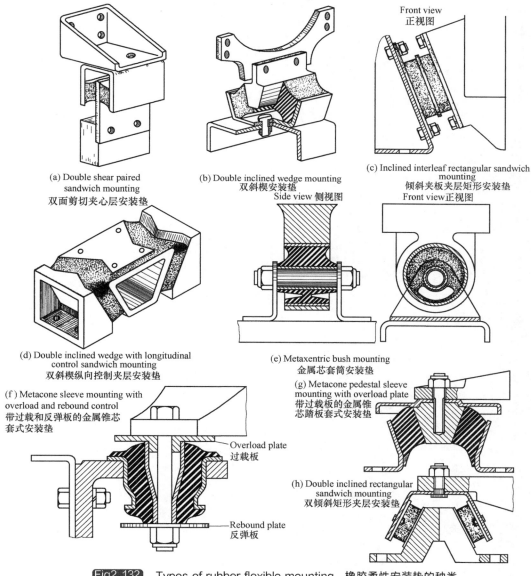

Fig2.132　Types of rubber flexible mounting　橡胶柔性安装垫的种类

Chapter 1
Perspective view
汽车外观

Chapter 2
Engine
发动机

Chapter 3
Body
车身

Chapter 4
Chassis
底盘

Chapter 5
Functional components
功能部件

Chapter 6
Special-purpose vehicles
特种车辆

Chapter 7
Electric vehicles
电动汽车

3.1 Types and structure of car bodies
车身类型与结构

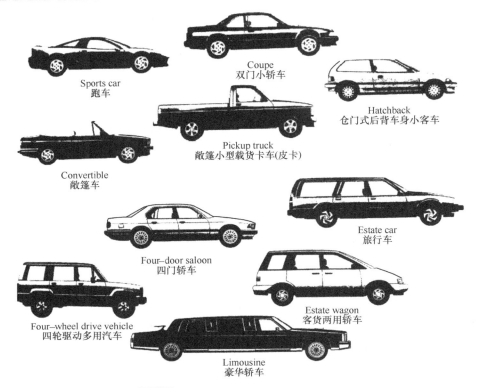

Fig3.1　Types of car bodies　车身类别

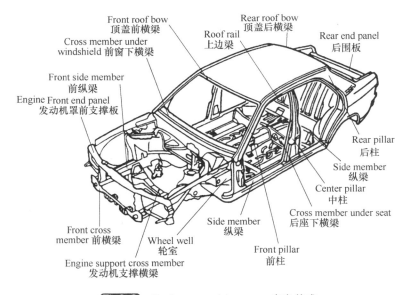

Fig3.2　Body assembly map　车身总成

Chapter 3　Body　车身

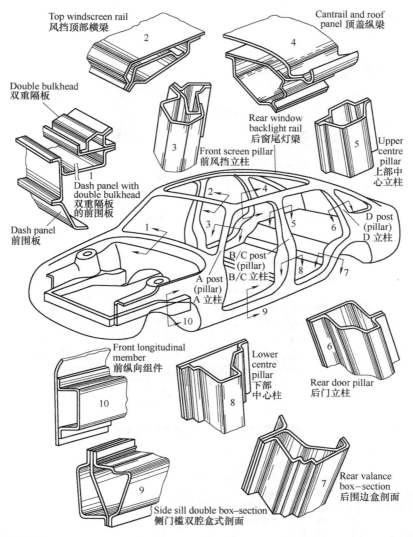

Fig3.3　Load bearing body box-section members　承载车身腔盒式组件剖面

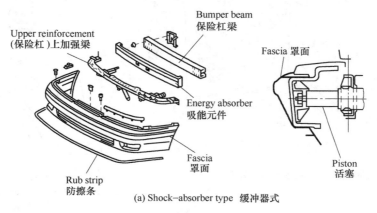

(a) Shock-absorber type　缓冲器式

Fig3.4

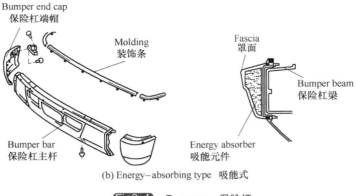

(b) Energy-absorbing type 吸能式

Fig3.4　Bumper 保险杠

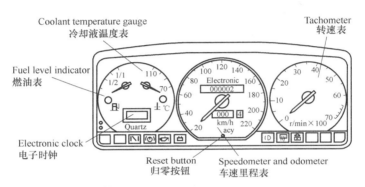

Fig3.5　Instrument cluster 仪表组合

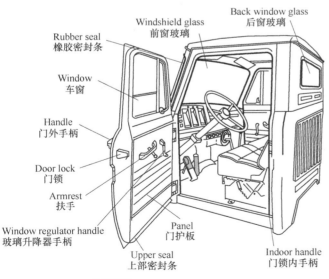

Fig3.6　Vehicle door 车门

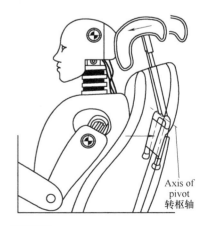

Fig3.7　Seat designed to prevent spinal damage due to whiplash 防止颈部扭伤造成脊椎损伤的座位设计

Chapter 3　Body　车身

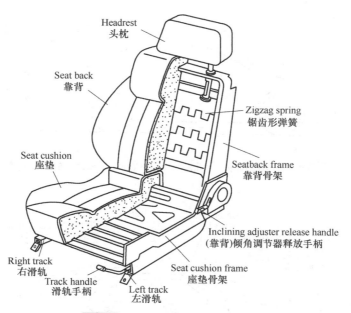

Fig3.8　Seat assembly　座椅总成

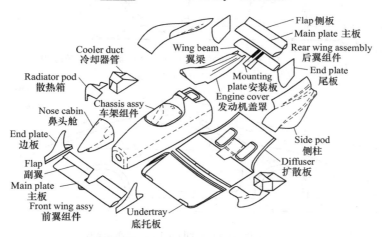

Fig3.9　Williams GP car　威廉 GP 车

3.2 Vehicle body aerodynamics
车身空气动力学

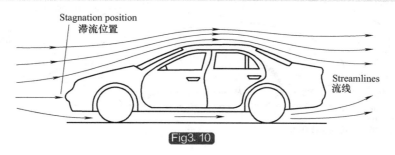

Fig3.10

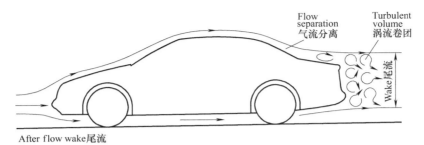

Fig3.10　Streamline air flow around car　汽车周边的流线气流

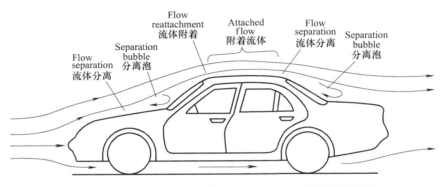

(a) Notch front and rear windscreens　前后挡风玻璃的凹口

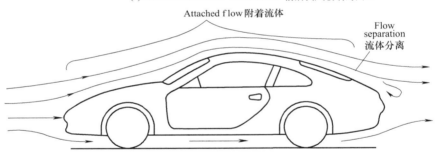

(b) Very streamlined shape　极度流线型

Fig3.11　Flow separation and reattachment　流体的分离与附着

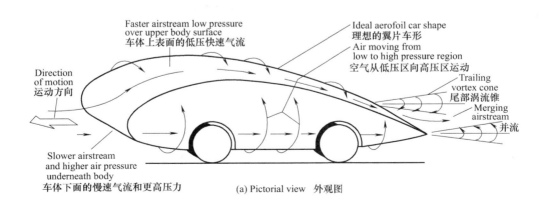

(a) Pictorial view　外观图

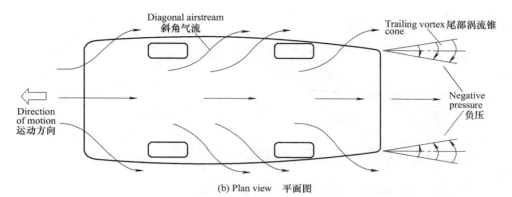

(b) Plan view 平面图

Fig3.12　Establishment of trailing vortices　尾部涡流的形成

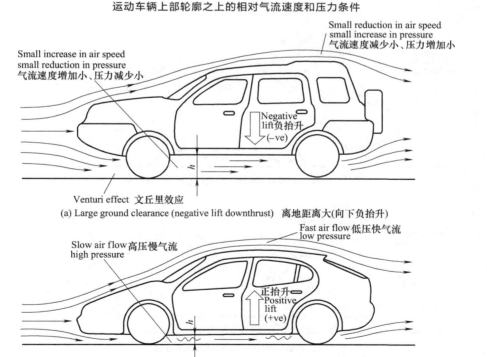

Fig3.13　Relative air speed and pressure condition over the upper profile of a moving car
运动车辆上部轮廓之上的相对气流速度和压力条件

(a) Large ground clearance (negative lift downthrust)　离地距离大(向下负抬升)

(b) Small ground clearance (positive lift upthrust)　离地距离小(向上正抬升)

Fig3.14　Effect of underfloor to ground clearance on the surrounding air speed, pressure and aerodynamic lift　下底面离地距离对周边空气速度、压力和空气动力抬升的影响

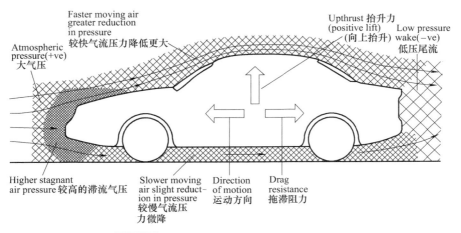

Fig3.15　Aerodynamic lift　空气动力抬升力

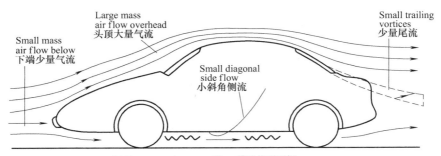

(a) Downturned nose profile　前端构形下倾

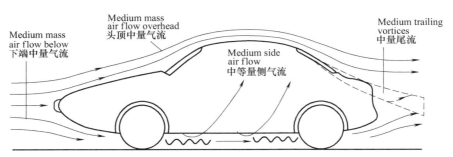

(b) Central nose profile　前端构形居中

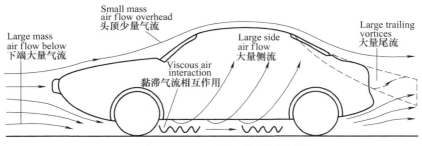

(c) Upturned nose profile　前端构形上倾

Fig3.16　A greatly exaggerated air mass distribution around a car body for various nose profiles
不同前端构形的绕车体的放大气流分布

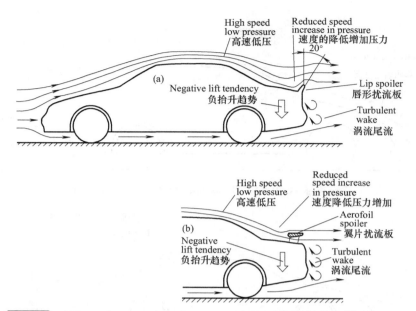

Fig3.17 Effect of rear end spoiler on both lift 后端扰流板对两种抬升的影响

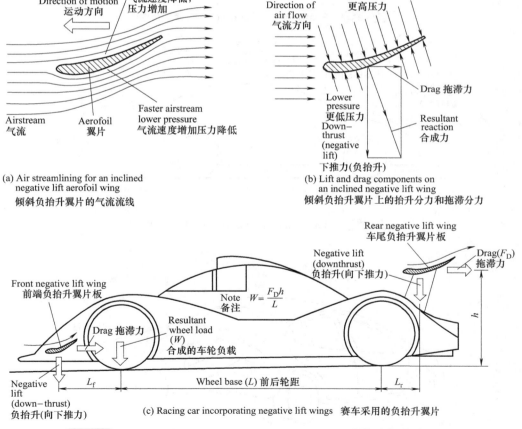

Fig3.18 Negative lift aerofoil wing considerations 负抬升翼片设计要点

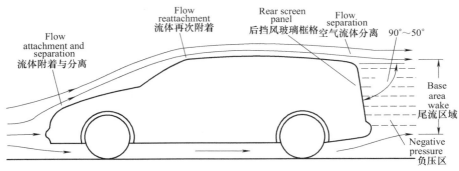

Fig3.19 Squareback configuration 方形后背盖构形

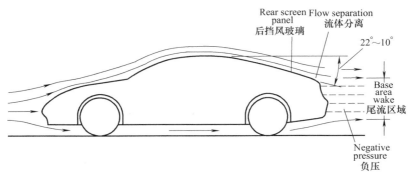

Fig3.20 Fastback configuration 快速后背构形

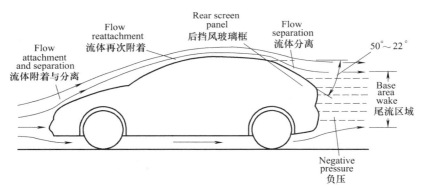

Fig3.21 Hatchback configuration 天窗背式构形

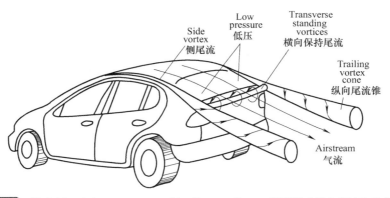

Fig3.22 Hatchback transverse and trailing vortices 天窗背式横向尾流和纵向尾流

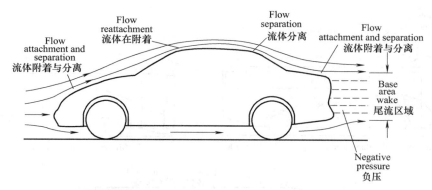

Fig3.23　Notchback configuration　凹口背部构形

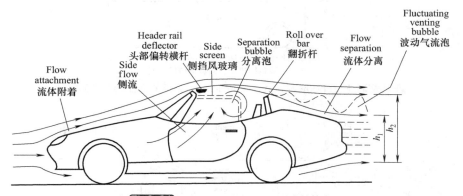

Fig3.24　Open cabriolet　开式敞篷车

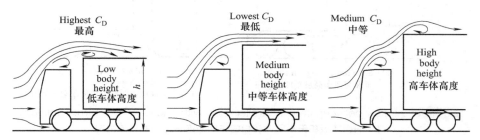

(a) Tractor cab with sharp windscreen / roof leading edge(flow separation over cab roof)
尖角挡风玻璃/顶部领边的卡车车厢(流体在车厢顶部分离)

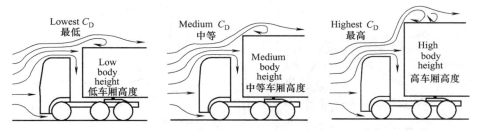

(b) Tractor cab with rounded windscreen / roof leading edge(attached air flow over cab roof)
圆角挡风玻璃/顶部领边的卡车车厢(流体在车厢顶部附着)

Fig3.25　Comparison of air flow condition with both sharp and rounded roof leading edge cab with various trailer body head　不同拖车车厢车头尖角和圆角顶部领边车厢气流条件的比较

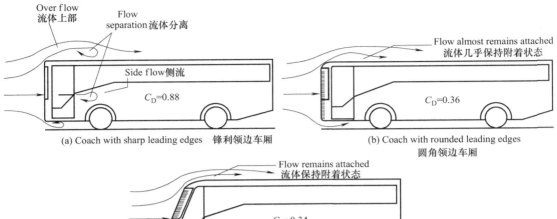

Fig3.26 Forebody coach streamlining 旅行车厢的流线型前部车体

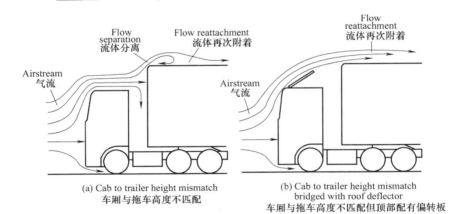

Fig3.27 Air flow between cab and trailer body with and without cab roof deflector 有车厢偏转板和无车厢偏转板的车厢与拖车之间的气流情况

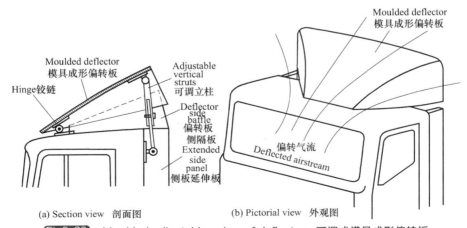

Fig3.28 Moulded adjustable cab roof deflector 可调式模具成形偏转板

Chapter 1
Perspective view
汽车外观

Chapter 2
Engine
发动机

Chapter 3
Body
车身

Chapter 4
Chassis
底盘

Chapter 5
Functional components
功能部件

Chapter 6
Special-purpose vehicles
特种车辆

Chapter 7
Electric vehicles
电动汽车

4.1 Overall structure 总体构成

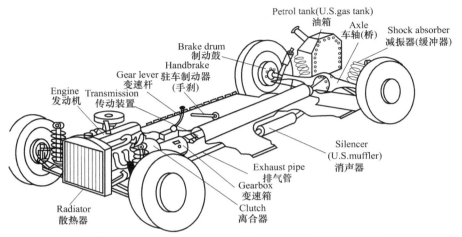

Fig4.1 Construct of automobile chassis 汽车底盘结构

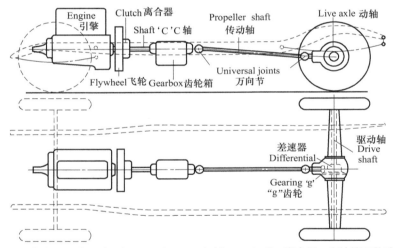

Fig4.2 Universal design for clutch, gearbox and driven shaft 离合器、齿轮箱和从动轴的通用设计

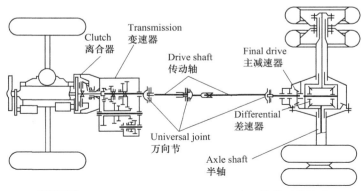

Fig4.3 Power train system assembly 传动系的组成

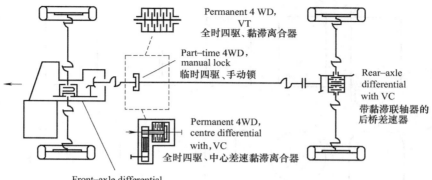

Fig4.4　Four-Wheel drive System　四轮驱动系统

4.2　Chassis　底盘

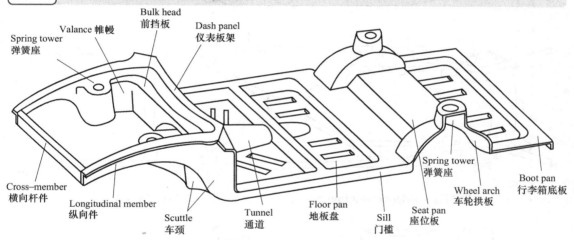

Fig4.5　Platform chassis (small central tunnel, sills, front valance, rear wheel arches and all round spring towers)　平台式底盘（小中心通道、门槛、前帷幔、后轮拱板和全部圆形弹簧座）

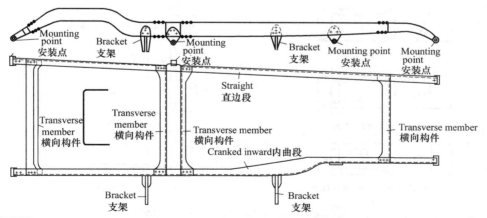

Fig4.6　Cross-section of both the longitudinal and transverse members　纵横构件的剖切面图

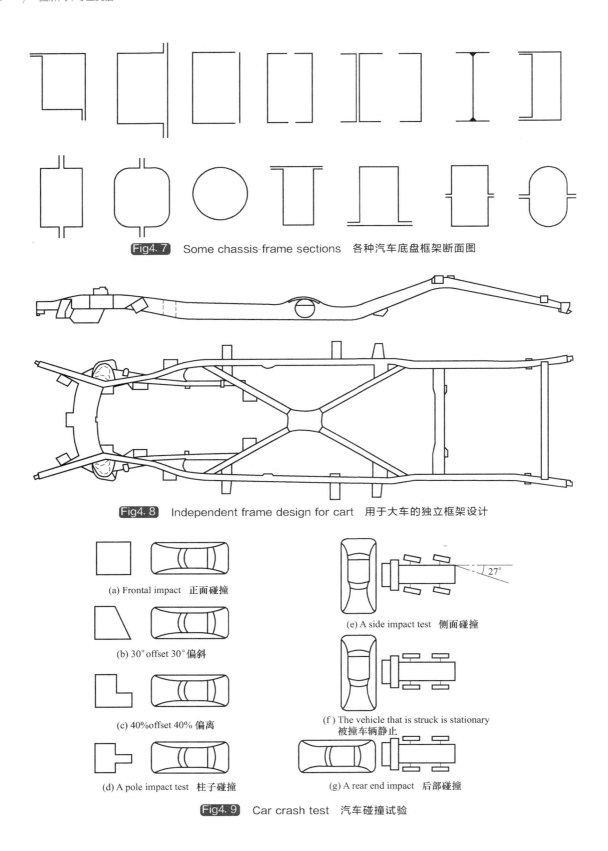

Fig4.7　Some chassis-frame sections　各种汽车底盘框架断面图

Fig4.8　Independent frame design for cart　用于大车的独立框架设计

(a) Frontal impact　正面碰撞

(b) 30° offset　30°偏斜

(c) 40%offset　40% 偏离

(d) A pole impact test　柱子碰撞

(e) A side impact test　侧面碰撞

(f) The vehicle that is struck is stationary　被撞车辆静止

(g) A rear end impact　后部碰撞

Fig4.9　Car crash test　汽车碰撞试验

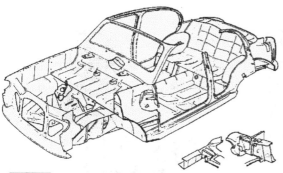

Fig4.10　Austin A30 (it was almost certainly the first car of truly chassisless construction to go into quantity production anywhere in the world)
奥斯丁 A30（几乎可以肯定是第一辆真正意义上的在世界各地投入批量生产的无底盘结构轿车）

Fig4.11　Chassis　汽车底盘

4.3　Axle　车桥（轴）

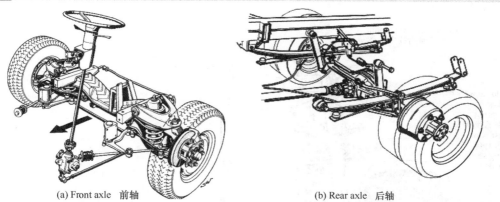

(a) Front axle　前轴　　　　(b) Rear axle　后轴

Fig4.12　Axles on the VW light commercial vehicle　大众轻型商用车轴

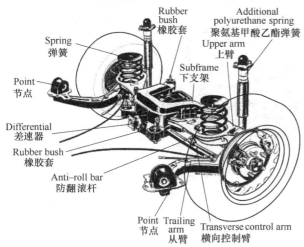

Fig4.13　Multi-link rear axle　多连杆后轴

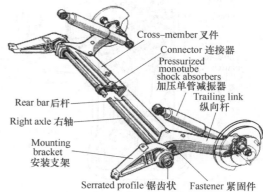

Fig4.14　Extremely compact four-bar twist beam axle　极其紧凑的四杆扭转梁轴

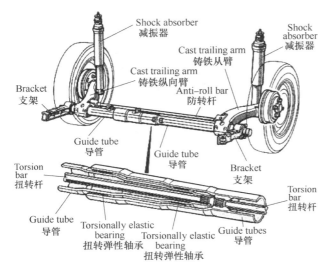

Fig4.15 Compact trailing arm rear axle 紧凑型纵向臂后轴

Fig4.16 McPherson front drive axle and suspension 麦弗逊前驱动轴和悬架

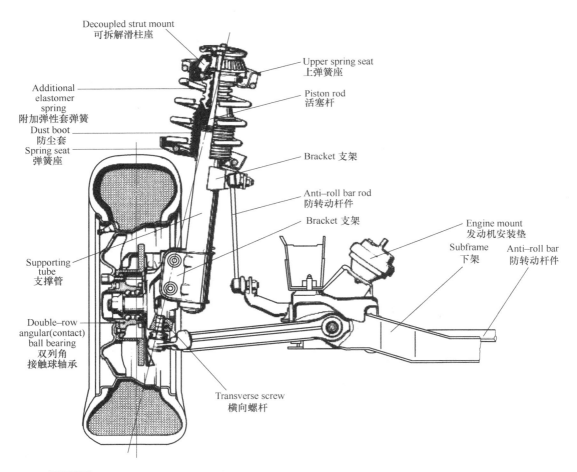

Fig4.17 Rear view of the left-hand side of the McPherson front axle 麦弗逊前轴左侧后视图

Chapter 4　Chassis　底盘

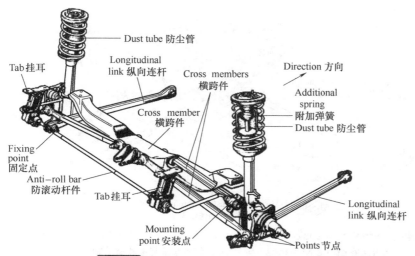

Fig4.18　McPherson strut rear axle　麦弗逊滑柱后轴

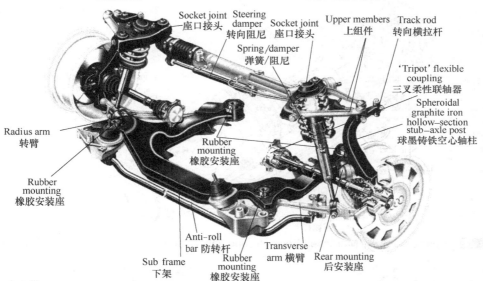

Fig4.19　Double wishbone front axle assembly of the Audi A4　奥迪 A4 的双叉形杆前轴组件

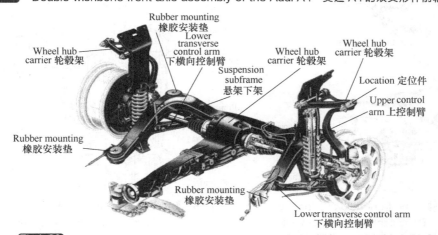

Fig4.20　Double wishbone rear axle on the Audi A4　奥迪 A4 双叉形杆后轴

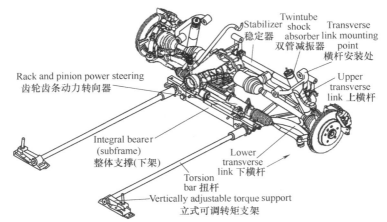

Fig4.21　Front suspension and drive axle of the Mercedes-Benz off-road vehicle of the M series　奔驰 M 系越野车前悬架和驱动轴

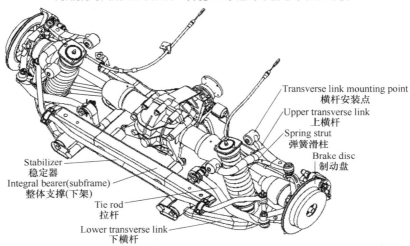

Fig4.22　Rear axle of the Mercedes-Benz off-road vehicle of the M series　奔驰 M 系越野车的后轴

Fig4.23　The front rigid axle on the Mercedes-Benz light commercial vehicle 梅赛德斯奔驰轻型商务车的刚性前轴

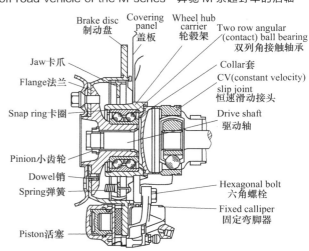

Fig4.24　Rear axle wheel hub carrier with wheel and brake　后轴轮毂架及制动器

Chapter 4　Chassis　底盘

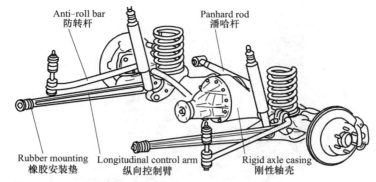

Fig4.25　The rear axle on the all-terrain general-purpose passenger car, Mitsubishi Pajero　三菱帕杰罗全地形通用客车的后轴

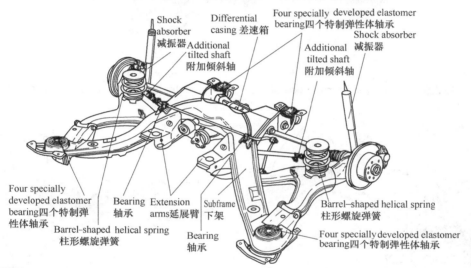

Fig4.26　Tilted-(Multiple) staft steering rear axle of the Opel Omega　欧宝欧米茄倾斜转向后轴

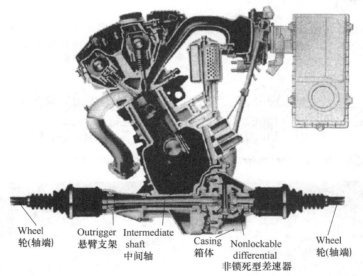

Fig4.27　Front cross-section view of the engine;and drive axle of a standard four-wheel drive vehicle(BMW assembly diagram)　发动机前部剖面图：标准四驱车辆驱动轴（宝马组件图）

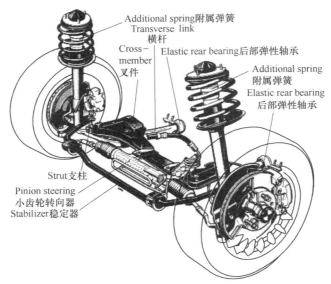

Fig4.28　Spring strut front axle of the BMW Roadster Z3　BMW Z3 的弹簧支柱前轴

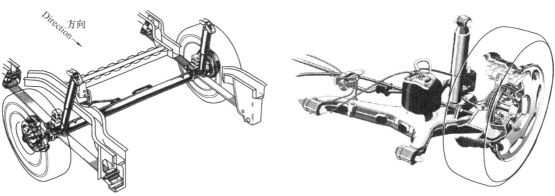

Fig4.29　The rear axle on a Ford Express delivery vehicle　福特快递车辆的后轴

Fig4.30　Flat, non-driven air-suspended semi-trailing-arm rear axle　平板型非驱动空气悬挂半转向臂后轴

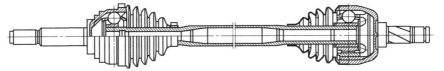

Fig4.31　Front-wheel output shaft of GKN Automotive　GKN 汽车的前轮输出轴

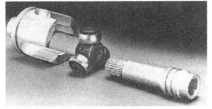

Fig4.32　Constant velocity sliding joints by GKN Automotive　GKN 汽车恒速滑动接头

Chapter 4　Chassis　底盘

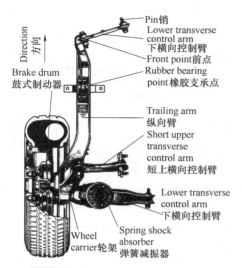

Fig4.33　Top view of the double wishbone rear axle on the Honda Civic
本田 Civic 双叉形杆后轴俯视图

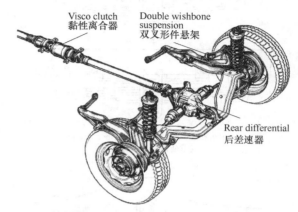

Fig4.34　Double wishbone rear axle of the Honda Civic Shuttle 4 WD
本田 Civic Shuttle 4 WD 双叉形件后轴

4.4　Suspension　悬架

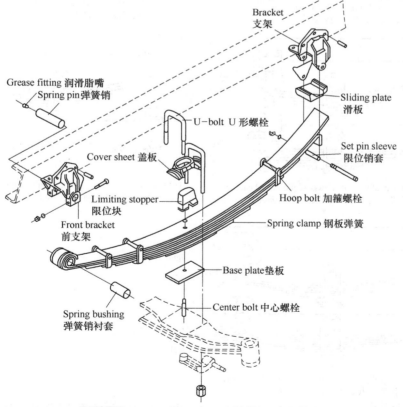

Fig4.35　Rigid axle suspension　刚性轴悬架

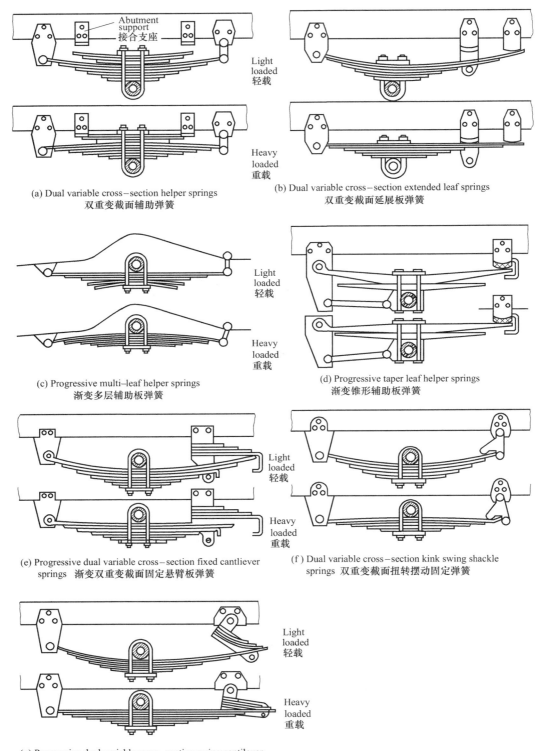

Fig4.36 Variable cross-section leaf spring suspension 变截面板弹簧悬挂

Chapter 4　Chassis　底盘

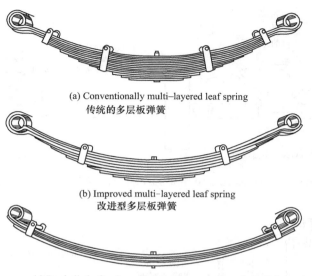

(a) Conventionally multi-layered leaf spring
传统的多层板弹簧

(b) Improved multi-layered leaf spring
改进型多层板弹簧

(c) Parabolic leaf spring with pressed layer-ends and plastic layers in between
冲压卷边层夹带塑料层的抛物线板弹簧

Fig4.37　Three different commercial vehicle rear leaf springs
三种不同的商用车辆后轴板弹簧

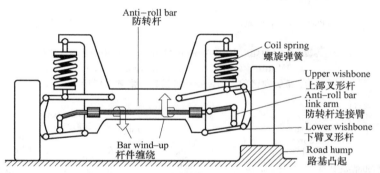

Fig4.38　Transverse double wishbone coil spring independent suspension with anti-roll bar
带防转杆的双横向叉形杆螺旋弹簧独立悬挂装置

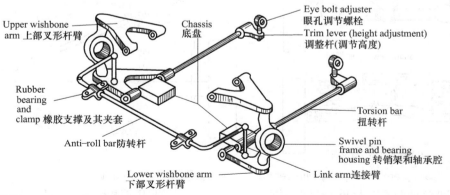

Fig4.39　Transverse double wishbone torsion bar independent suspension with anti-roll bar
带防转杆的双横向叉形杆扭转杆独立悬挂装置

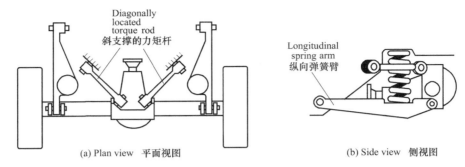

Fig4.40　Four-link coil spring live axle rear suspension　四连接螺旋弹簧活动轴后悬挂

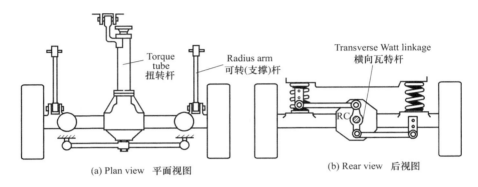

Fig4.41　Torque tube with trailing arm and transverse Watt linkage live axle rear suspension
带纵向臂和横向瓦特杆的扭转杆活轴后悬挂

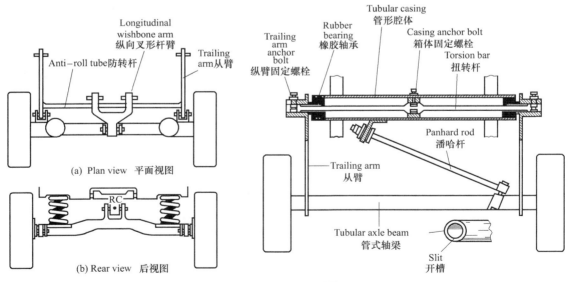

Fig4.42　Trailing arm coil spring with central longitudinal wishbone and anti-roll tube dead axle suspension　中心纵向叉形杆的纵臂螺旋弹簧和防转管固定轴悬架

Fig4.43　Trailing arm and torsion bar spring with dead axle rear suspension
纵臂和固定轴扭转杆弹簧后悬架

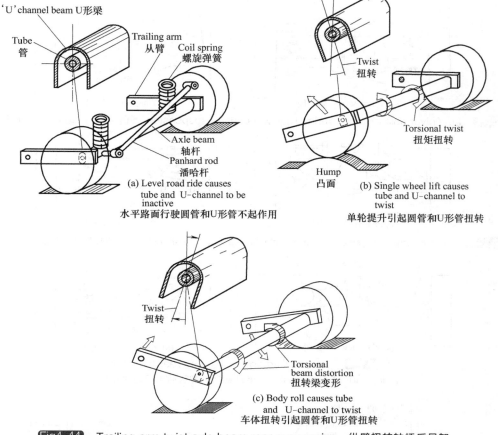

Fig4.44 Trailing arm twist axle beam rear suspension 纵臂扭转轴桥后悬架

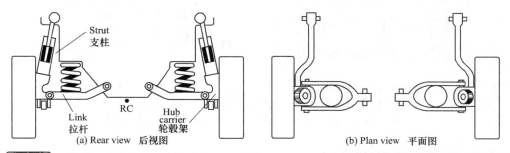

Fig4.45 Strut and link non-drive independent rear suspension 支柱及拉杆非传动独立后悬架

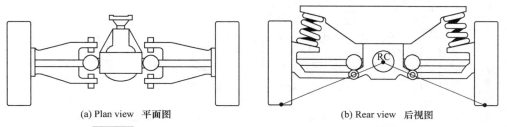

Fig4.46 Transverse swing arm coil spring rear wheel drive independent suspension 横向摆动臂螺旋弹簧后轮驱动独立悬架

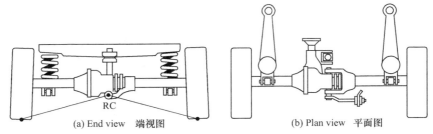

Fig4.47　Low pivot split axle coil spring rear wheel drive suspension　低转枢半轴螺旋弹簧后轮驱动悬架

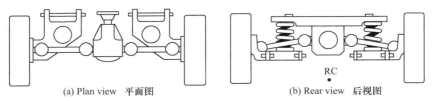

Fig4.48　Trailing arm coil spring rear wheel drive independent suspension　纵臂螺旋弹簧后轮驱动独立悬架

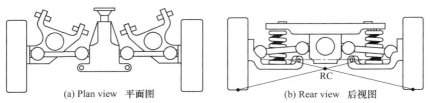

Fig4.49　Semi-trailing arm coil spring rear wheel drive independent suspension　半纵臂螺旋弹簧后轮驱动独立悬架

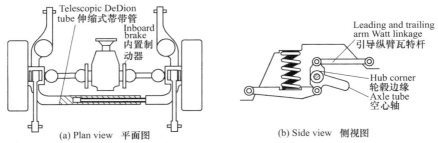

Fig4.50　DeDion axle with leading and trailing arm Watt linkage rear suspension　带引导纵臂瓦特杆的蒂带轴后悬架

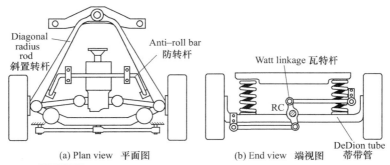

Fig4.51　DeDion tube with diagonal radius arms and Watt transverse linkage rear suspension　斜置转臂蒂带管和横向瓦特杆后悬架

Chapter 4　Chassis　底盘

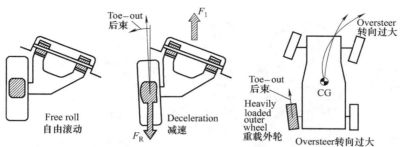
(a) Conventional semi-trailing arm suspension 传统的半纵臂悬挂

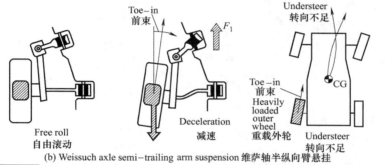
(b) Weissuch axle semi-trailing arm suspension 维萨轴半纵向臂悬挂

Fig4.52　Semi-trailing suspension compliance steer　半纵向悬挂协调转向装置

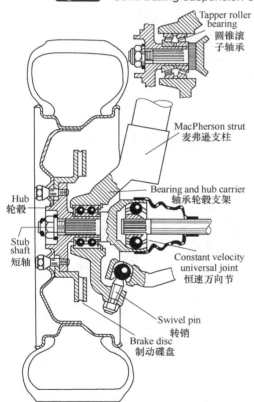

Fig4.53　Front wheel drive MacPherson strut suspension with single double row ball or roller wheel bearing　双列球轴承或滚子轴承支撑车轮的前轮驱动麦弗逊支柱悬挂

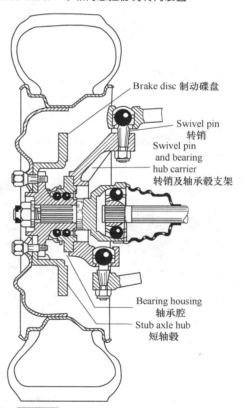

Fig4.54　Front wheel drive transverse wishbone suspension with fully integrated double low wheel bearings　整体式双低轮轴承的前轮驱动横向叉形杆悬挂

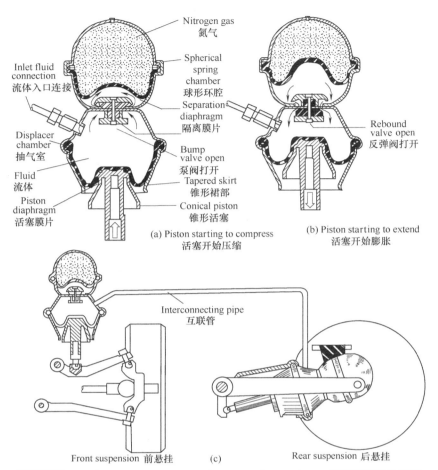

Fig4.55 Hydrogas interconnected suspension system 液气混联悬挂系统

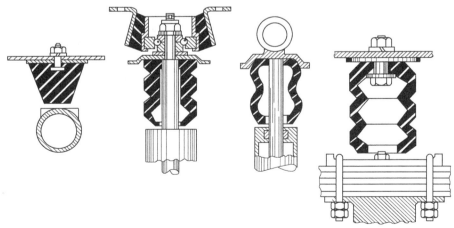

Fig4.56 Suspension bump stop limiter arrangements 悬架减振止停器的设计

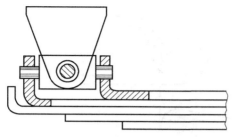

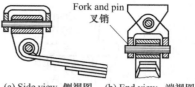

Fig4.58 Main spring to chassis pin and fork swivel anchorage
主弹簧接底盘叉销转动定位

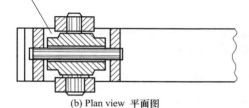

Fig4.57 Main spring to chassis hinged cross-pin anchorage
十字销铰链的底盘主弹簧

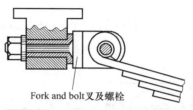

Fig4.59 Main spring to chassis bolt and fork swivel anchorage
主弹簧接底盘叉及螺栓转动定位

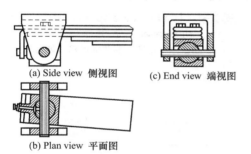

Fig4.60 Main spring to chassis pin and spherical swivel anchorage
主弹簧接底盘的销和球头转动定位

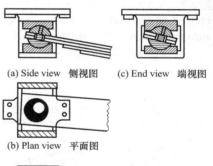

Fig4.61 Main spring to chassis spherical swivel anchorage
主弹簧接底盘球体转动定位

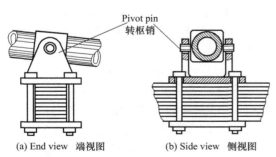

Fig4.62 Axle to spring pivot pin seat mounting
轴接弹簧转枢销座安装

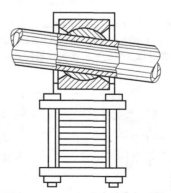

Fig4.63 Axle to spring spherical seat mounting 轴与弹簧的球座安装

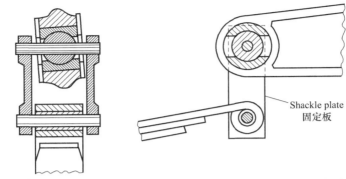

Fig4.64 Tandem axle balance beam to shackle plate spherical joint
串联轴平衡梁与固定板的球体连接

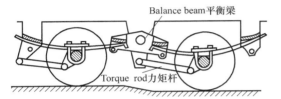

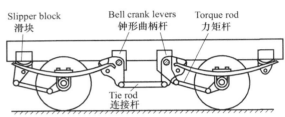

Fig4.65 Reactive balance beam with slipper contact blocks and torque arms tandem axle suspension 带打滑接触块和力矩臂串联轴悬挂的反馈平衡梁

Fig4.66 Tandem wide spread reactive bell crank lever taper leaf spring
串联宽分布反馈钟形曲柄锥形板弹簧

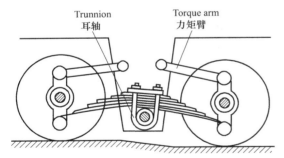

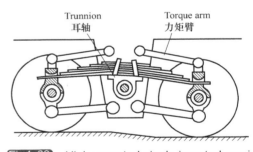

Fig4.67 Lower mounted single inverted semi-elliptic spring with upper torque rods 上部力矩杆在下部安装的单一倒置半椭圆弹簧

Fig4.68 High mounted single inverted semi-elliptic spring with lower torque rods
下部力矩杆在上部安装的单一倒置半椭圆弹簧

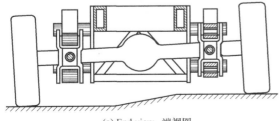

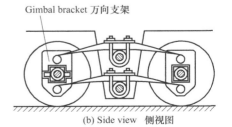

(a) End view 端视图 (b) Side view 侧视图

Fig4.69 Double inverted semi-elliptic spring 双倒置半椭圆弹簧

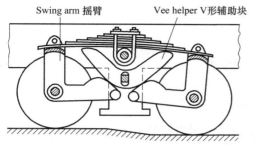

Fig4.70 Leading and trailing arms with inverted semi-elliptic spring 带倒置半椭圆弹簧的领臂和从臂

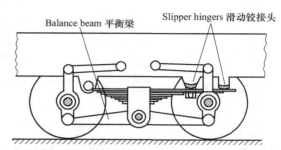

Fig4.71 Hendrickson long equalization balance beam with single semi-elliptic spring 带单一半椭圆弹簧的亨德里克斯长平衡梁

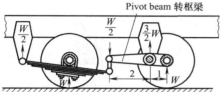

(a) Pivot beam with single semi-elliptic spring 带单一半椭圆弹簧的转枢梁

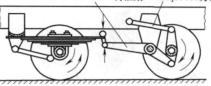

(b) Pivot beam with single semi-elliptic spring and torque rod 带单一半椭圆弹簧和力矩杆的转枢梁

Fig4.72 Pivot beam 转枢梁

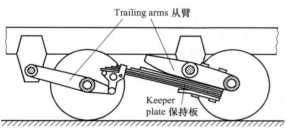

Fig4.73 Trailing arm with progressive quarter-elliptic spring 带渐变四分之一椭圆弹簧的从臂

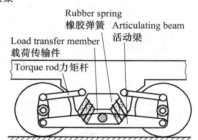

Fig4.74 Rubber spring mounted on balance beam with leading and trailing torque arms 带引导臂和纵向力矩臂的安装在平衡梁上的橡胶弹簧

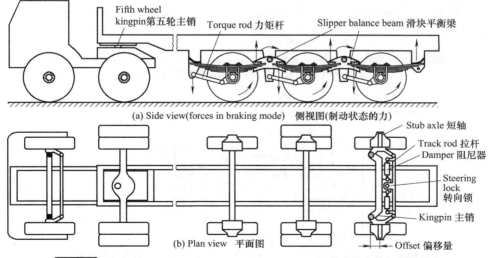

(a) Side view(forces in braking mode) 侧视图(制动状态的力)

(b) Plan view 平面图

Fig4.75 Tri-axle semi-trailer with self-steer axle 带自转向轴三轴半纵臂

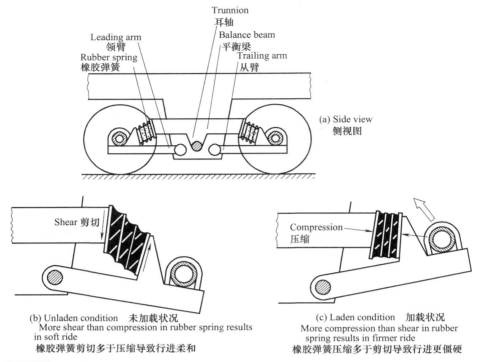

Fig4.76 Rubber spring mounted leading and trailing arms interlinked by rocking beam 摇臂互联的安装在领臂和从臂上的橡胶弹簧

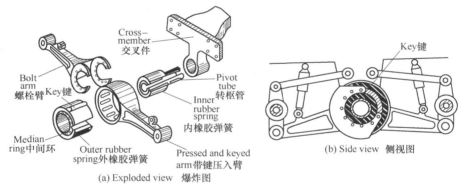

Fig4.77 Willets (velvet) leading and trailing arm torsional rubber spring suspension 威力领臂和从臂扭转橡胶弹簧悬挂

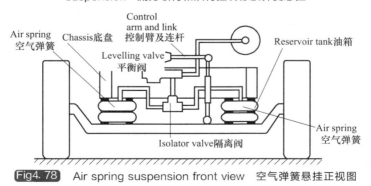

Fig4.78 Air spring suspension front view 空气弹簧悬挂正视图

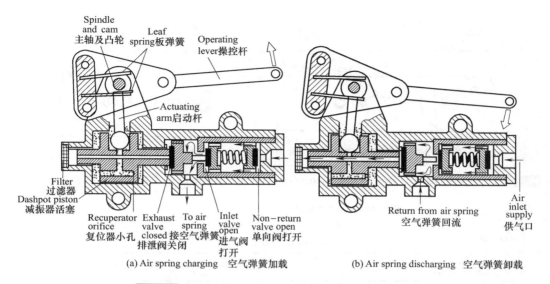

Fig4.79　Levelling air control valve　空气平衡控制阀

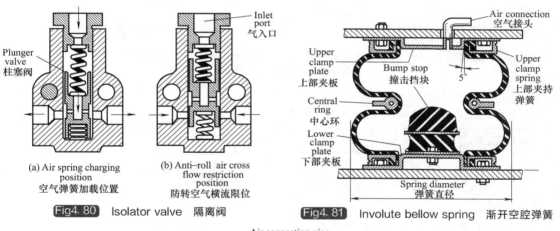

Fig4.80　Isolator valve　隔离阀

Fig4.81　Involute bellow spring　渐开空腔弹簧

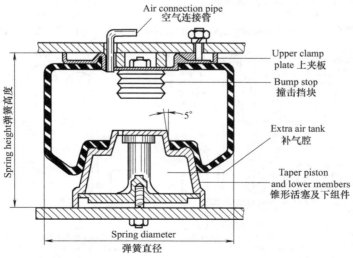

Fig4.82　Rolling diaphragm spring　可翻转膜片弹簧

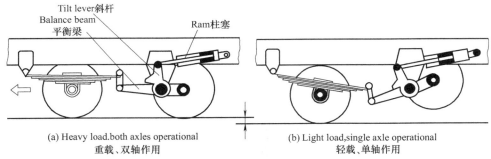

Fig4.83 Hydraulically operated lift axle suspension with direct acting ram 柱塞直接作用的液动抬升轴悬挂

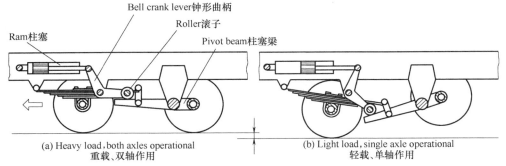

Fig4.84 Hydraulically operated lift axle suspension with bell-crank lever and ram 钟形曲柄和柱塞的液动抬升轴悬挂

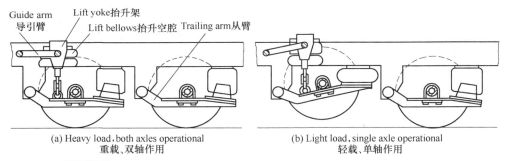

Fig4.85 Pneumatically operated lift axle suspension 气动抬升轴悬挂

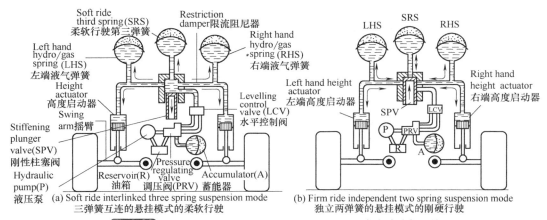

Fig4.86 Semi-active hydro/gas suspension 半主动液气悬挂

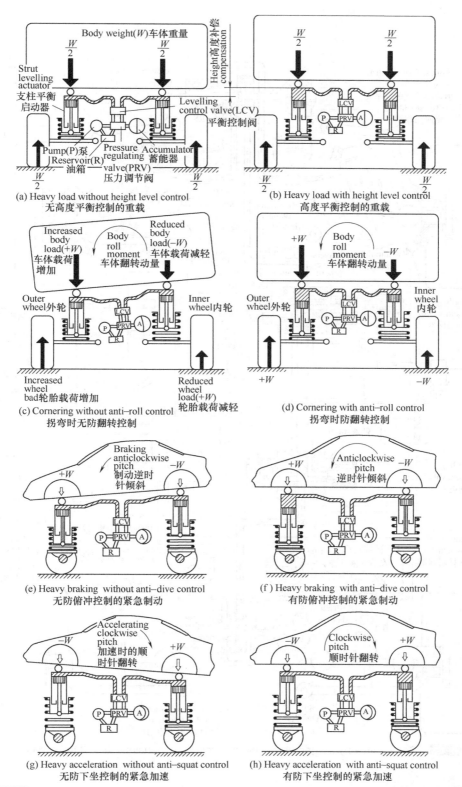

Fig4.87 Active self-levelling hydraulic/coil spring suspension 主动自平衡液压/螺旋弹簧悬架

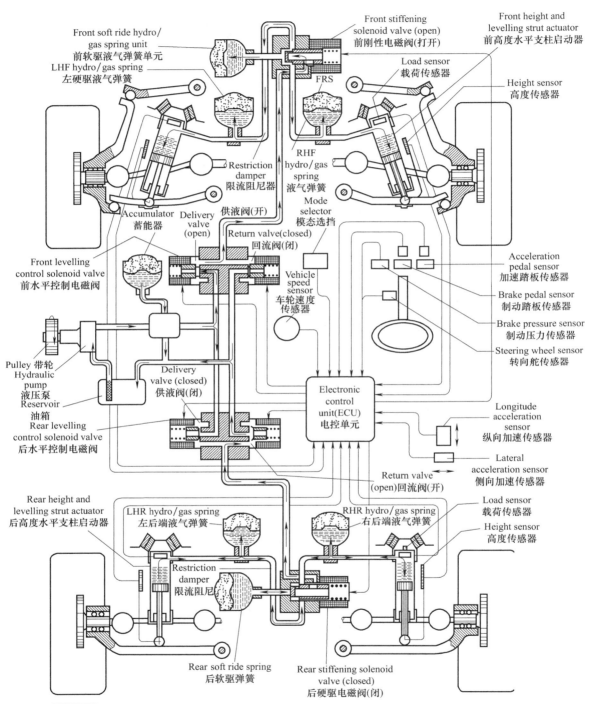

Fig4.88　Semi-active hydro/gas electronic controlled suspension　半主动电子控制液气悬挂

Chapter 4　Chassis　底盘

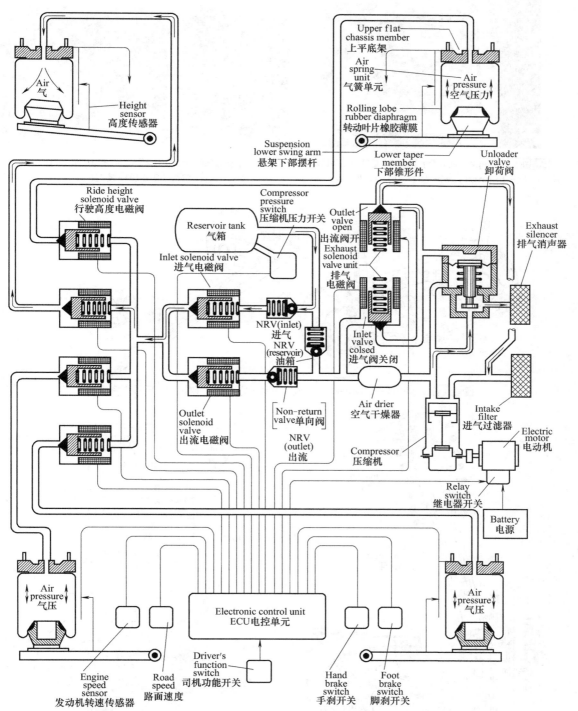

Fig4.89　Electronic controlled pneumatic (air) suspension　电子控制气压悬挂

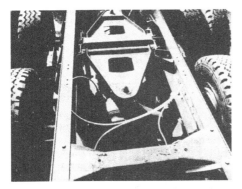

Fig4.90　Suspension for Dodge GR 1600 tipper
（16 tonnes）道奇 GR1600 的悬挂装置

Fig4.91　Foden 20-tonne suspension
佛登 20 吨悬挂装置

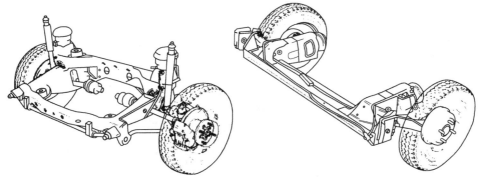

Fig4.92　Modified hydragas suspension system　改进型液气悬挂系统

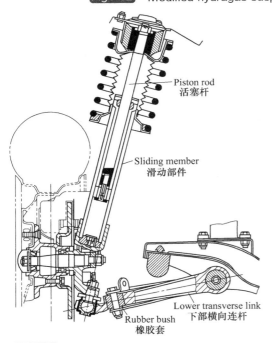

Fig4.93　MacPherson strut type suspension
麦弗逊滑柱型悬挂

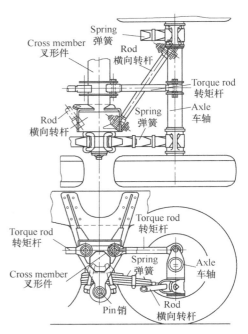

Fig4.94　The general arrangement of the suspension　悬架的通用设计

Chapter 4　Chassis　底盘

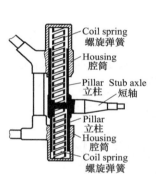

Fig4.95　Girling suspension　格林悬架

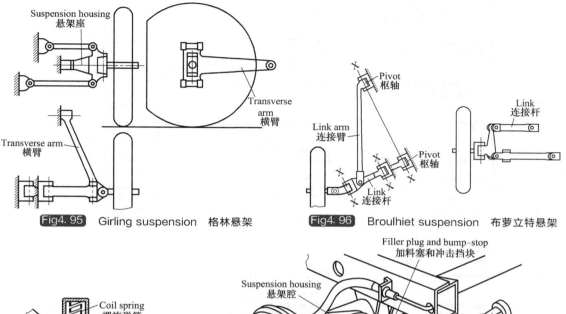

Fig4.96　Broulhiet suspension　布萝立特悬架

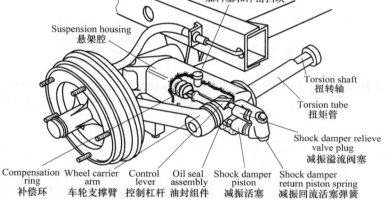

Fig4.97　Slider, or pillar, type
滑块（柱）式悬架

Fig4.98　Vauxhall front suspension (sectioned view)
氟斯霍前悬架（剖开图）

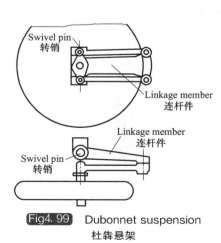

Fig4.99　Dubonnet suspension
杜犇悬架

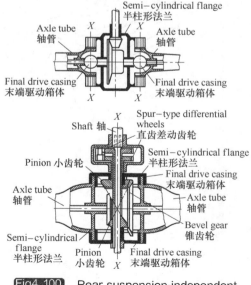

Fig4.100　Rear suspension-independent
后独立悬架

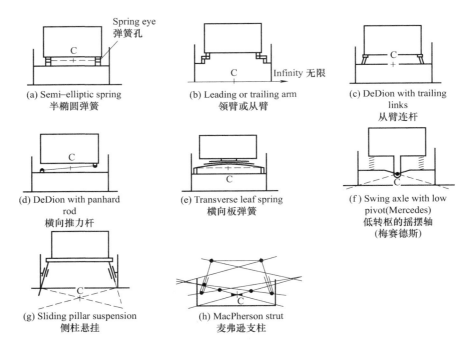

Fig4.101　Some typical linkage systems and their roll centres (with the suspension in its static position)
典型的连杆系统及其翻转中心（悬挂处于其静止位置）

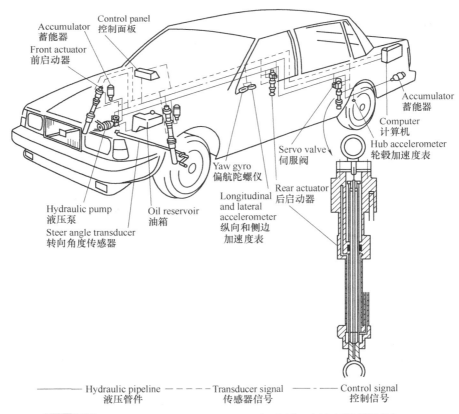

Fig4.102　Volvo computer suspension (CCS)　沃尔沃计算机悬架

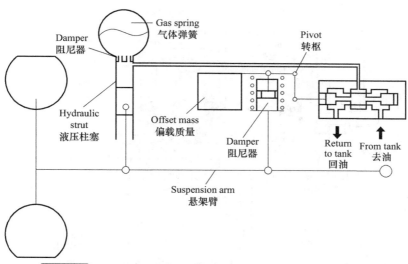

Fig4.103　A single AP suspension module　简易 AP 悬架模块

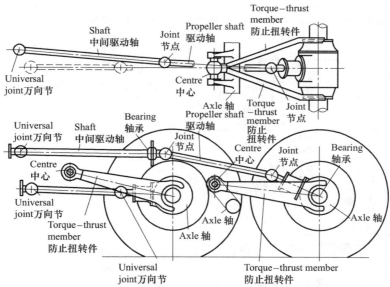

Fig4.104　The general arrangement of the rear bogie transmission system　后转向架传动系统的通用设计

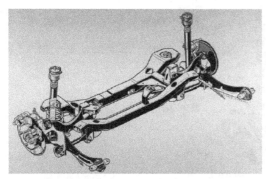

Fig4.105　Multi-link suspension of Ford WerkA Ge　福特 AG 的多杆悬架

Fig4.106　Twist-beam suspension of the VW Golf　大众高尔夫扭转梁悬架

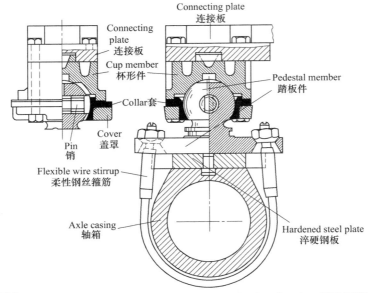

Fig4.107　The axles are positioned sideways by Panhard rods　潘哈杆侧面定位轴

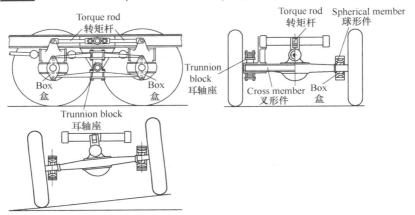

Fig4.108　WD (War Department) type suspension　战车型悬架

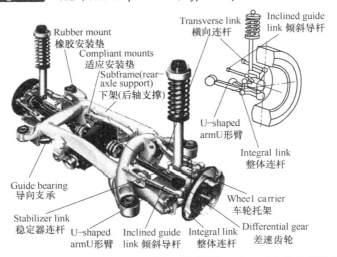

Fig4.109　Multi-link rear suspension of the BMW 5 series　BMW5系列的多杆后悬架

4.5 Shock absorber 减振装置

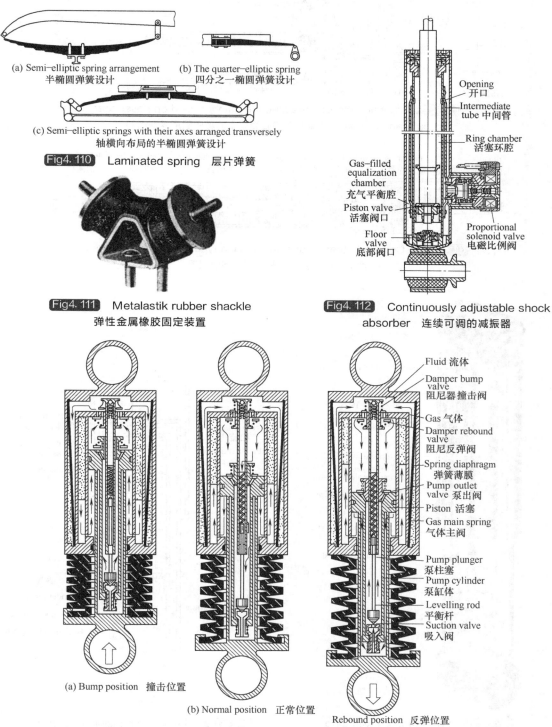

Fig4.110 Laminated spring 层片弹簧
(a) Semi-elliptic spring arrangement 半椭圆弹簧设计
(b) The quarter-elliptic spring 四分之一椭圆弹簧设计
(c) Semi-elliptic springs with their axes arranged transversely 轴横向布局的半椭圆弹簧设计

Fig4.111 Metalastik rubber shackle 弹性金属橡胶固定装置

Fig4.112 Continuously adjustable shock absorber 连续可调的减振器
Opening 开口
Intermediate tube 中间管
Ring chamber 活塞环腔
Gas-filled equalization chamber 充气平衡腔
Piston valve 活塞阀口
Floor valve 底部阀口
Proportional solenoid valve 电磁比例阀

Fig4.113 Self-levelling hydropneumatic suspension 自平衡液气悬挂
(a) Bump position 撞击位置
(b) Normal position 正常位置
Rebound position 反弹位置

Fluid 流体
Damper bump valve 阻尼器撞击阀
Gas 气体
Damper rebound valve 阻尼反弹阀
Spring diaphragm 弹簧薄膜
Pump outlet valve 泵出阀
Piston 活塞
Gas main spring 气体主阀
Pump plunger 泵柱塞
Pump cylinder 泵缸体
Levelling rod 平衡杆
Suction valve 吸入阀

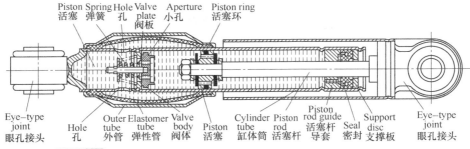

Fig4.114　Section through the steering damper used on passenger cars and light vans　乘用车和轻型车上的转向阻尼器剖面图

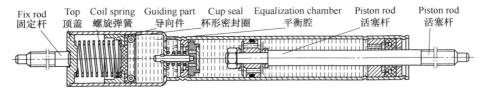

Fig4.115　Compact steering damper with pin-type joints on both sides　两端为销钉接头类紧凑型转向阻尼器

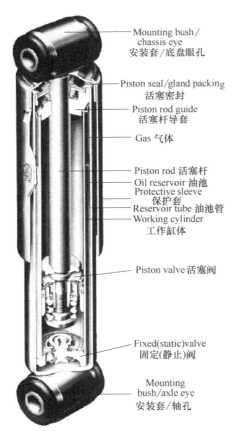

Fig4.116　Low-pressure twin-tube shock absorber　低压双管减振器

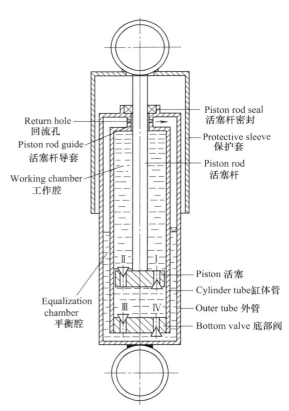

Fig4.117　Twin-tube principle to explain the function　双管减振器的作用原理

Chapter 4　Chassis　底盘

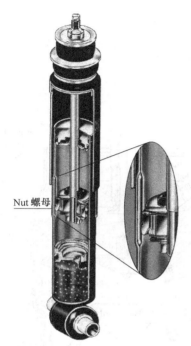

Fig4.118　Pressure-loaded single-tube shock absorber with bypass technology 压力加载的单筒减振器及旁路技术

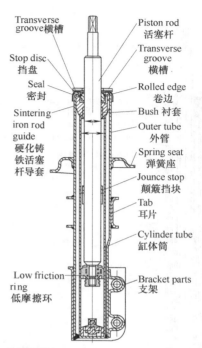

Fig4.119　MacPherson strut of the Fiat Panda 菲亚特熊猫的麦弗逊滑柱

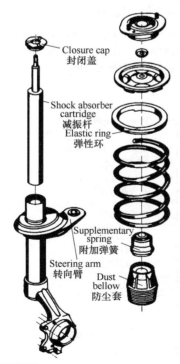

Fig4.120　Exposive view of damping suspension strut 阻尼悬架柱爆炸图

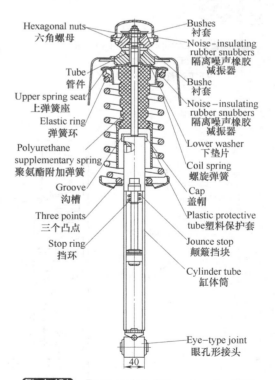

Fig4.121　Rear spring damper on the VW Golf 大众高尔夫后弹簧阻尼器

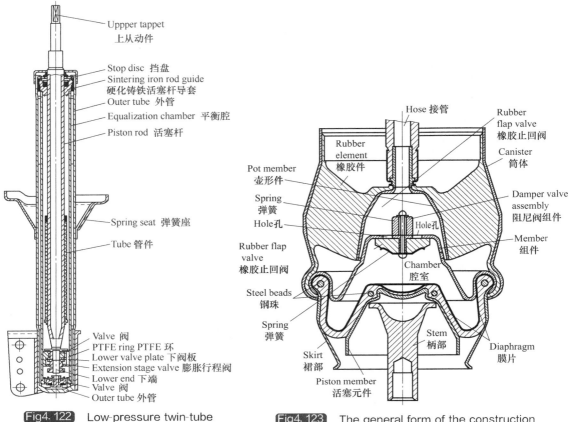

Fig4.122 Low-pressure twin-tube MacPherson strut 低压双管麦弗逊滑柱

Fig4.123 The general form of the construction of hydrolastic suspenion systems 液体弹性悬挂的通用构造

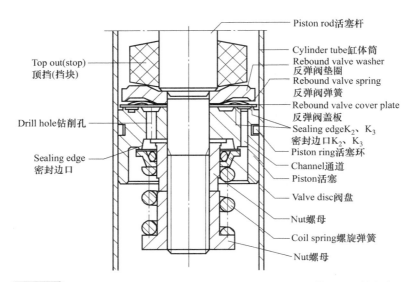

Fig4.124 Valve combination on twin-tube dampers 双管阻尼器的组合阀

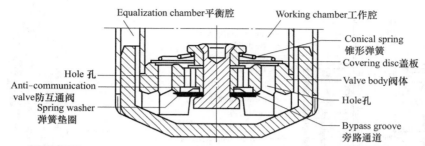

Fig4.125 Bottom valve of the twin-tube dampers 双管阻尼器底部阀

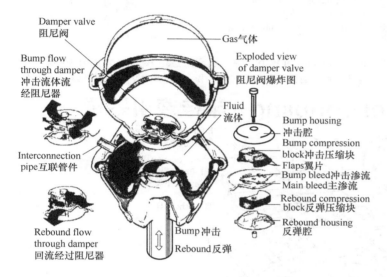

Fig4.126 Exploded view of Hydragas unit 液气单元爆炸图

Fig4.127 Air-spring-and-shock-absorber assembly of the front axle of the Mercedes Benz W220 series 梅赛德斯奔驰 W220 系列车前轴的气簧减振器组件

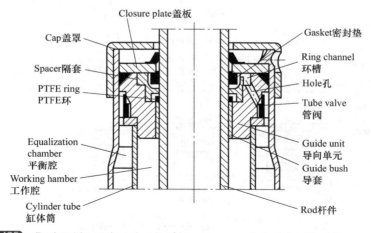

Fig4.128 Rod guide and seal unit of low-pressure twin-tube MacPherson strut 低压双管麦弗逊滑柱的活塞杆导套和密封单元

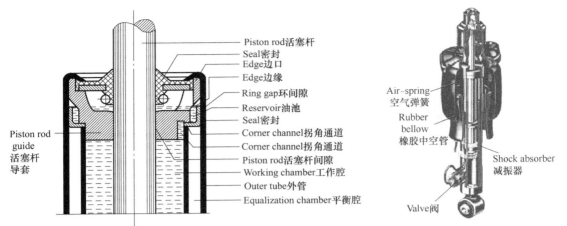

Fig4.129 Guide and seal set in series production of twin tube dampers 系列生产双管阻尼器的导向件和密封件装置

Fig4.130 Air-spring-and-shock-absorber assembly 空气弹性减振器组件

4.6 Fifth wheel coupling 半挂牵引装置

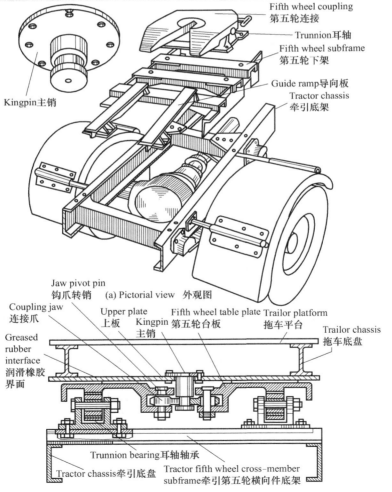

(a) Pictorial view 外观图

(b) Front section view of fifth wheel coupling assembly 第五轮组件前剖视图

Fig4.131 Fifth wheel coupling assembly 第五轮连接组件图

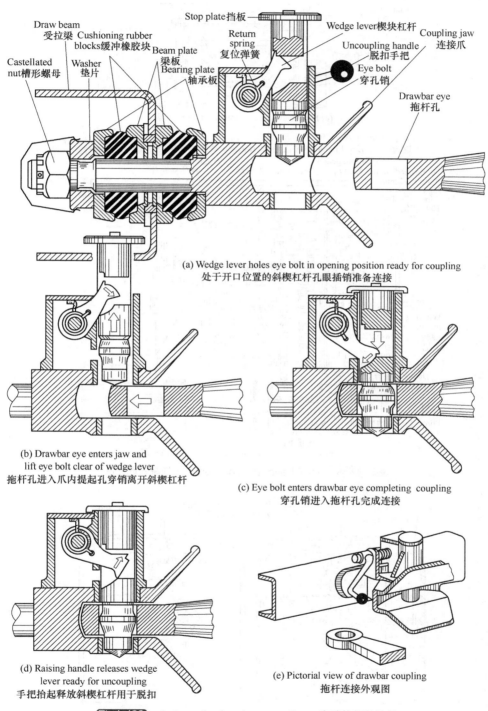

Fig4.132 Automatic drawbar coupling 自动拖杆的连接

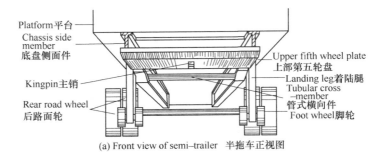

(a) Front view of semi-trailer 半拖车正视图

(b) Sectional view of landing gear 着地装置剖视图

Fig4.133 Semi-trailer landing gear 半拖车着地装置

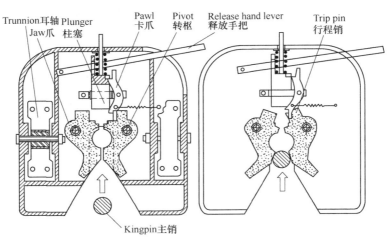

(a) Ready for coupling 准备结合

(b) Kingpin engaging jaws trips pawl to release plunger 主销进入爪里推动卡爪释放柱塞

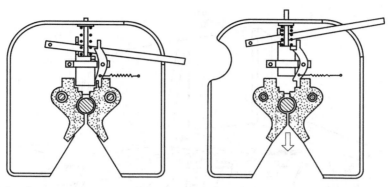

(c) Coupling to trailer with kingpin in position 主销到位后连接上拖车
(d) Plunger withdrawn jaws ready for uncoupling 柱塞回退爪准备脱离连接

Fig4.134　Fifth wheel coupling with twin jaws plunger and pawl　双爪柱塞和卡爪实现第五轮连接

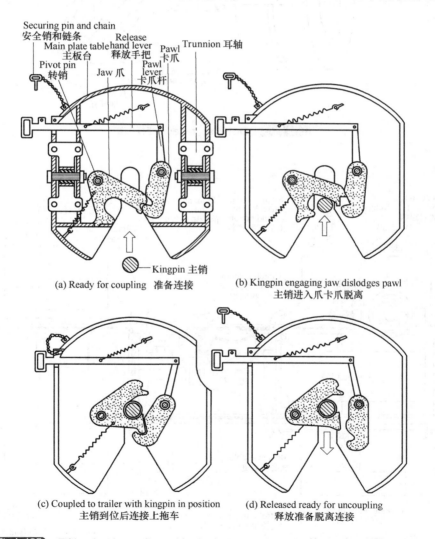

(a) Ready for coupling 准备连接
(b) Kingpin engaging jaw dislodges pawl 主销进入爪卡爪脱离
(c) Coupled to trailer with kingpin in position 主销到位后连接上拖车
(d) Released ready for uncoupling 释放准备脱离连接

Fig4.135　Fifth wheel coupling with single jaw and pawl　单爪和卡爪的第五轮连接

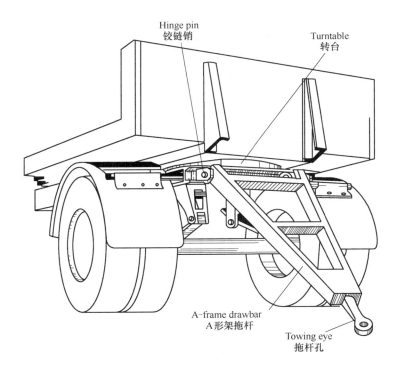

Fig4.136　Drawbar trailer　拖杆拖车

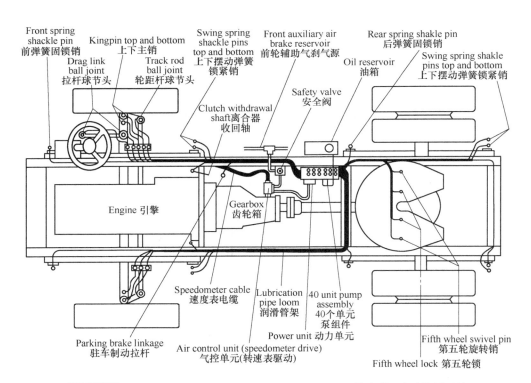

Fig4.137　Tractor unit automatic lubriction system　拖车单元自动润滑系统

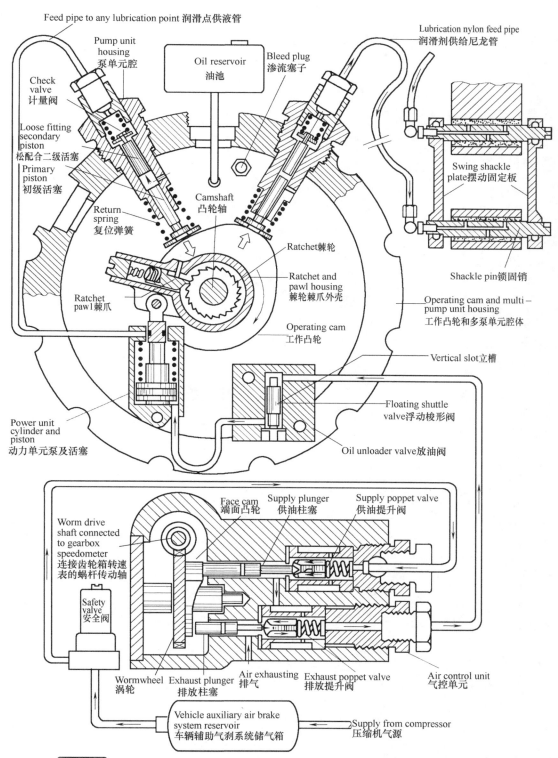

Fig4.138 Air dromic automatic chassis lubrication system 底盘气室自动润滑系统

Chapter 1
Perspective view
汽车外观

Chapter 2
Engine
发动机

Chapter 3
Body
车身

Chapter 4
Chassis
底盘

Chapter 5
Functional components
功能部件

Chapter 6
Special-purpose vehicles
特种车辆

Chapter 7
Electric vehicles
电动汽车

5.1 Refrigeration devices 制冷装置

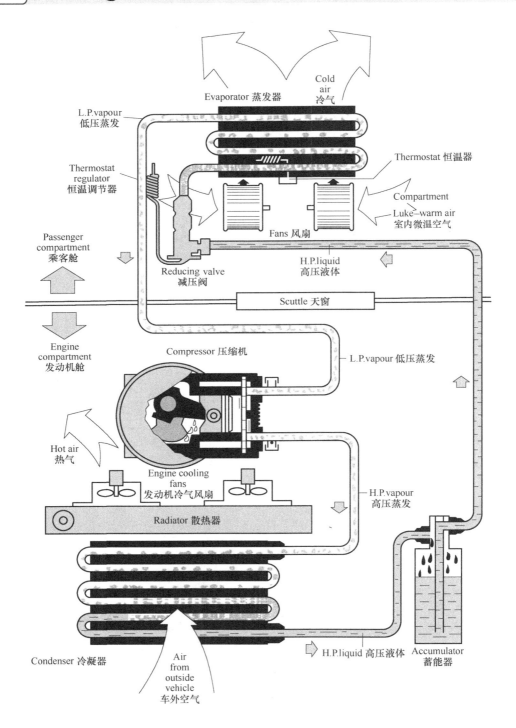

Fig5.1　The principles of air conditioning　空调原理

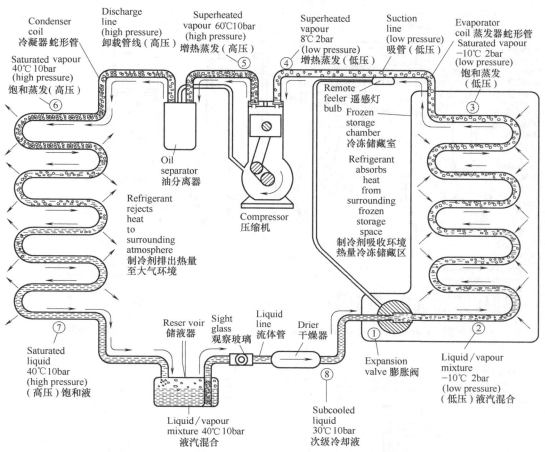

Fig5.2　Refrigeration vapour-compression cycle　制冷的蒸发压缩循环

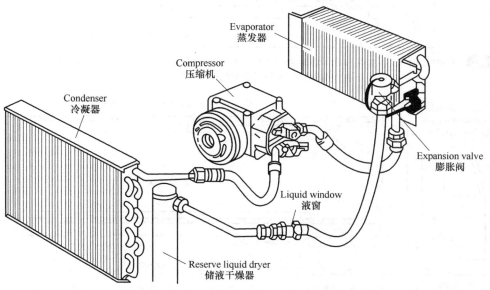

Fig5.3　Automotive air-conditioning refrigeration systems　汽车空调冷凝系统

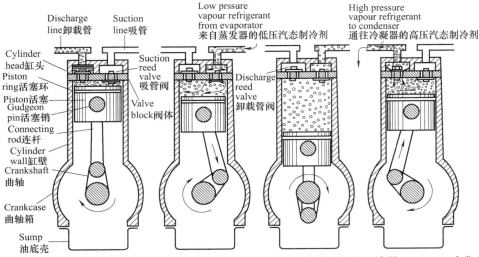

Fig5.4　Reciprocating compressor cycle of operation　往复式压缩机的工作循环

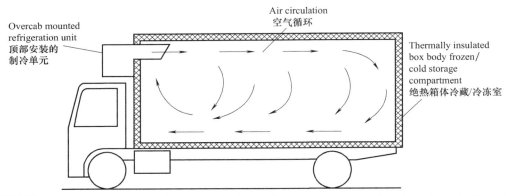

Fig5.5　Overcab mounted self-contained refrigeration system for small and medium rigid trucks
中小型刚性卡车顶部安装的自容式制冷系统

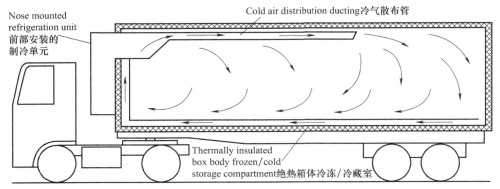

Fig5.6　Nose mounted self-contained refrigeration system for large articulated truck
大型活连接卡车前端安装的自容制冷系统

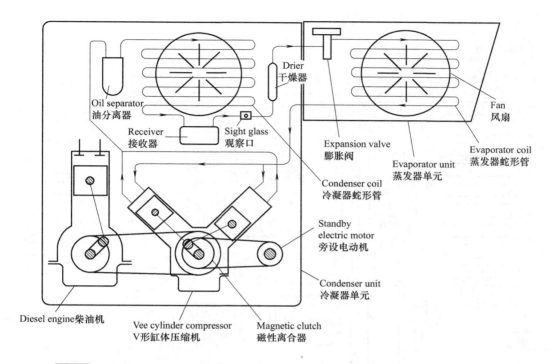

Fig5.7 Light to medium duty diesel engine and standby electric motor belt driven compressor refrigeration unit 轻型到中型柴油机及其旁设电动机皮带驱动的制冷单元

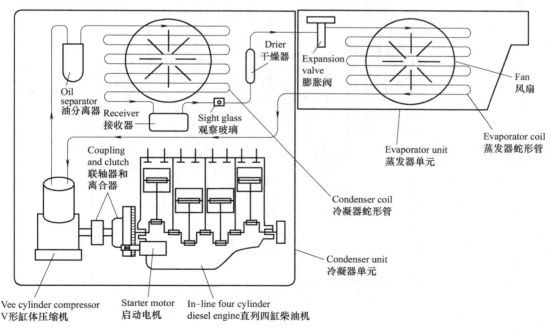

Fig5.8 Heavy duty diesel engine shaft driven compressor refrigeration unit 重载柴油机轴驱动压缩机制冷单元

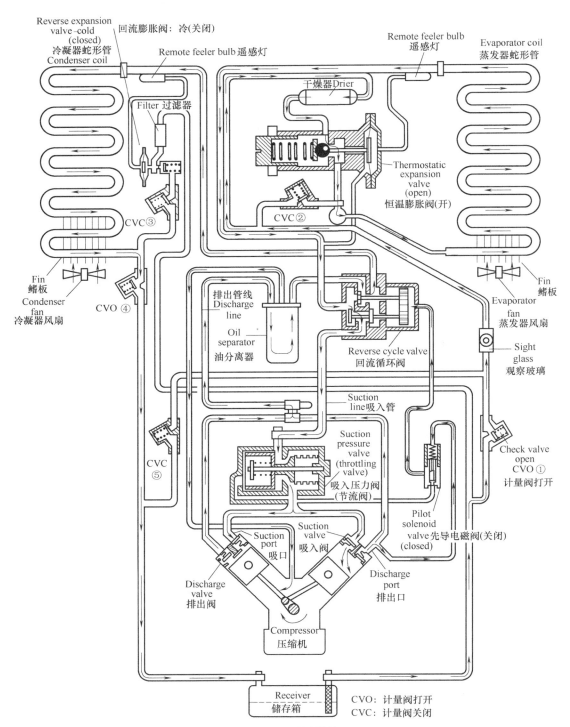

(a) Refrigeration cycle 制冷循环

Chapter 5　Functional components　功能部件　117

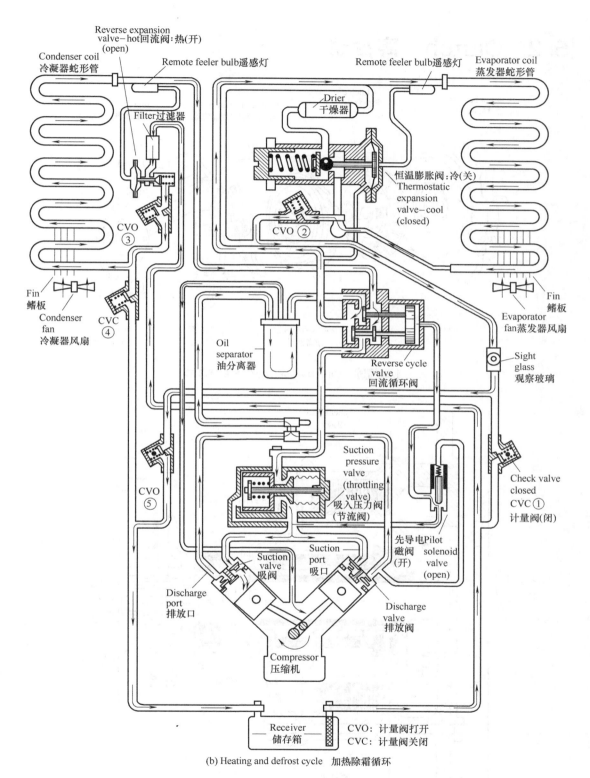

(b) Heating and defrost cycle　加热除霜循环

Fig5.9　Refrigeration system with reverse cycle defrosting　带回流循环除霜的冷却系统

5.2 Clutch 离合器

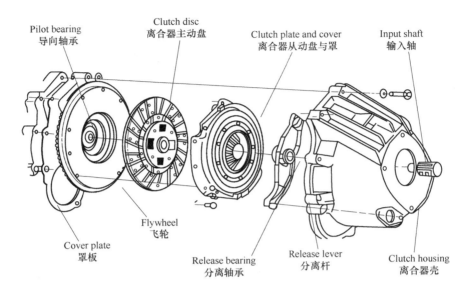

Fig5.10　Clutch Assembly　离合器总成

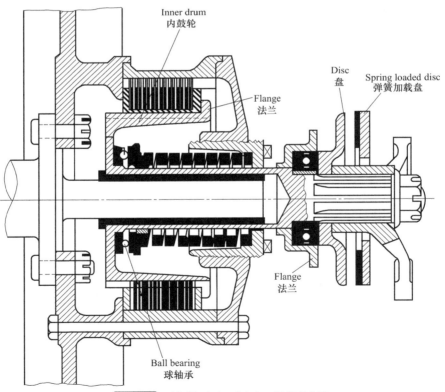

Fig5.11　Multi-plate clutch　多片离合器

Chapter 5　Functional components　功能部件

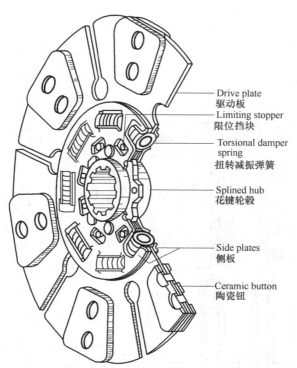

Fig5.12　Clutch driven plate with ceramic facings　陶瓷表面的离合器驱动板

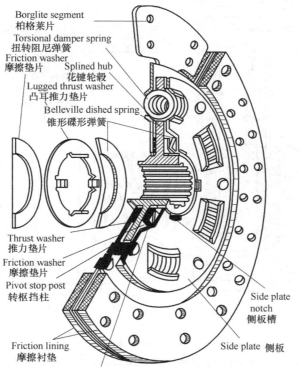

Fig5.13　Clutch driven centre plate　离合器驱动的中心盘

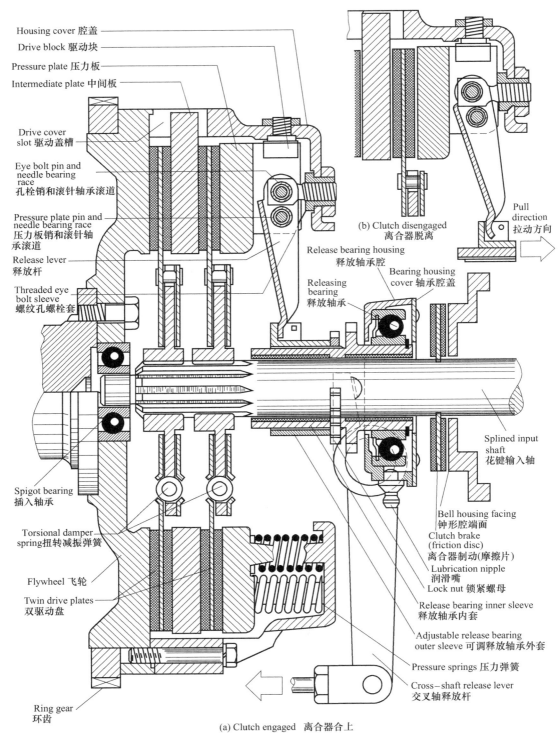

Fig5.14 Twin driven plate pull type clutch 双驱动板拉动型离合器

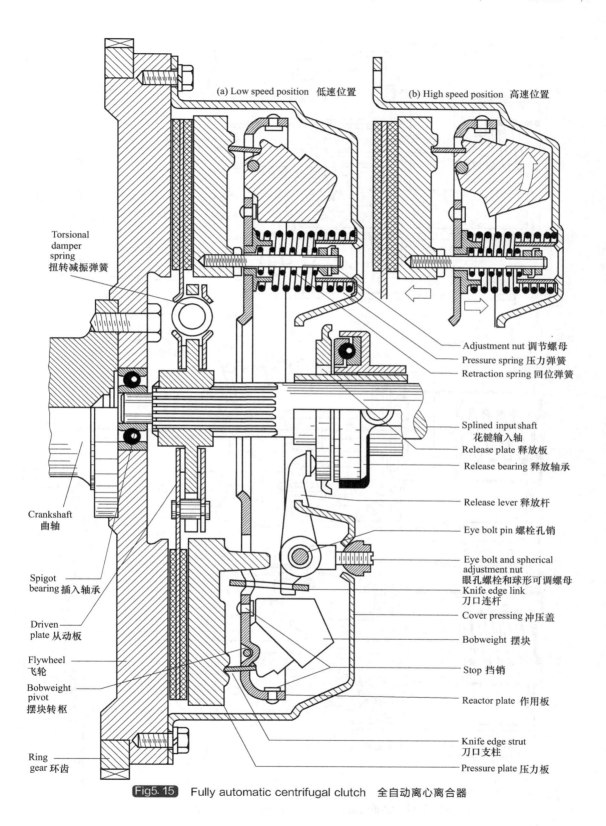

Fig5.15 Fully automatic centrifugal clutch 全自动离心离合器

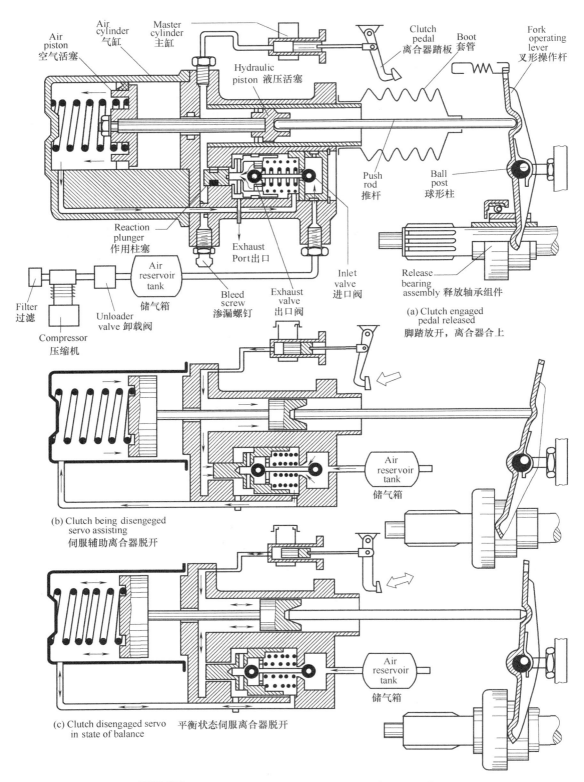

Fig5.16　Clutch air/hydraulic servo　离合器气/液伺服装置

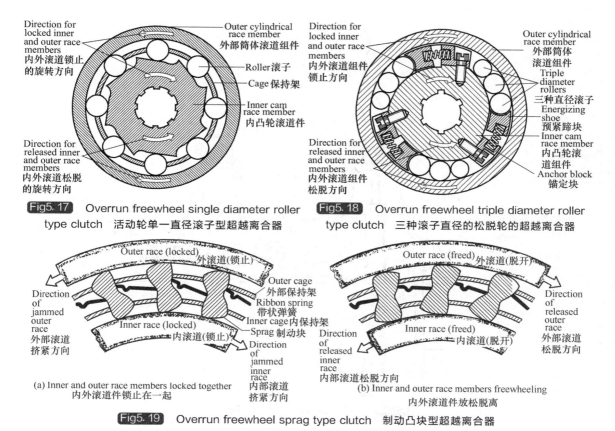

Fig5.17 Overrun freewheel single diameter roller type clutch 活动轮单一直径滚子型超越离合器

Fig5.18 Overrun freewheel triple diameter roller type clutch 三种滚子直径的松脱轮的超越离合器

(a) Inner and outer race members locked together 内外滚道件锁止在一起

(b) Inner and outer race members freewheeling 内外滚道件放松脱离

Fig5.19 Overrun freewheel sprag type clutch 制动凸块型超越离合器

5.3 Transmission 变速器

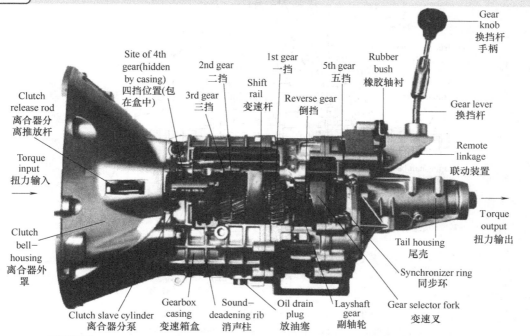

Fig5.20 Cutaway view of the 5-speed manual gearbox 五挡手动变速箱剖切图

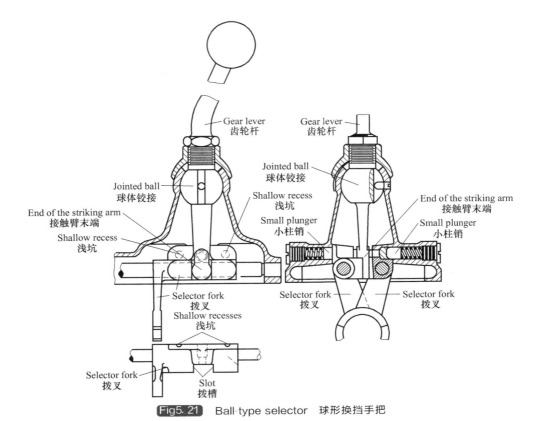

Fig5.21　Ball-type selector　球形换挡手把

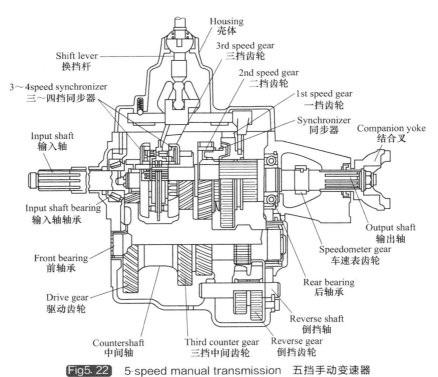

Fig5.22　5-speed manual transmission　五挡手动变速器

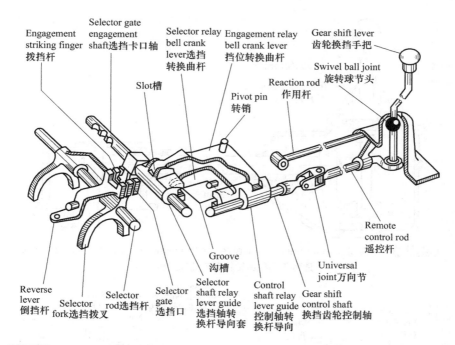

Fig5.23　Remote controlled bell crank level gear shift mechanism for a four speed transversely mounted gearbox　四速横置安装齿轮箱的遥控转销曲杆齿轮换挡机构

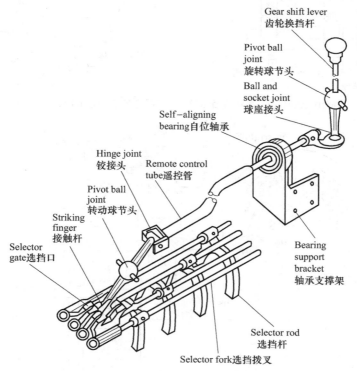

Fig5.24　Remote controlled sliding ball joint gear shift mechanism suitable for both five and six speed longitudinally mounted gearbox　适合于五速或六速纵向安装的齿轮箱遥控滑动球节头齿轮换挡机构

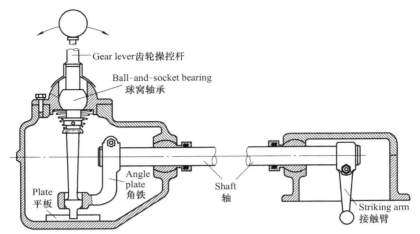

Fig5.25 Selector mechanism, suitable for the remote control of the gearbox
适合于远程齿轮箱操控的拨叉机构

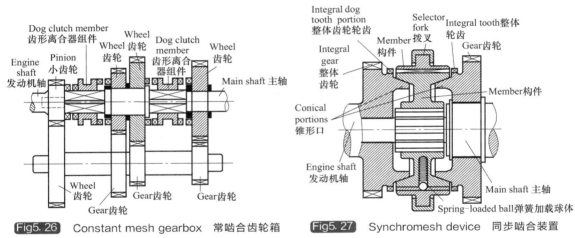

Fig5.26 Constant mesh gearbox 常啮合齿轮箱

Fig5.27 Synchromesh device 同步啮合装置

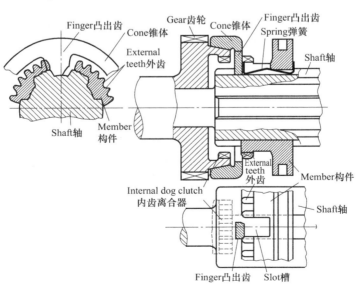

Fig5.28 Direct-drive engagement 直接驱动啮合

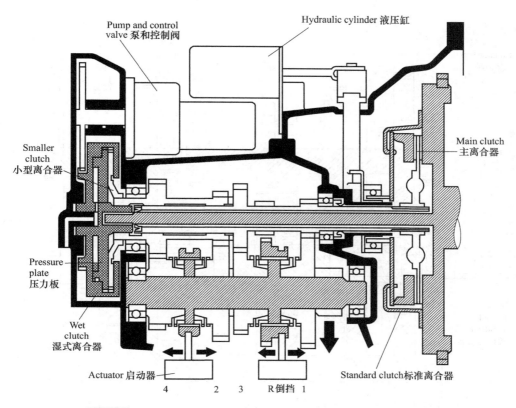

Fig5.29 Automatic gearbox with dual clutches (Changing gear without interrupting the power flow to the wheels)
双离合自动变速箱（齿轮改变时传输到车轮的力不会受到干扰）

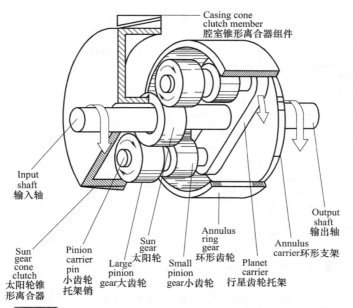

Fig5.30 Compound epicycle gear train 复合行星齿轮轮系

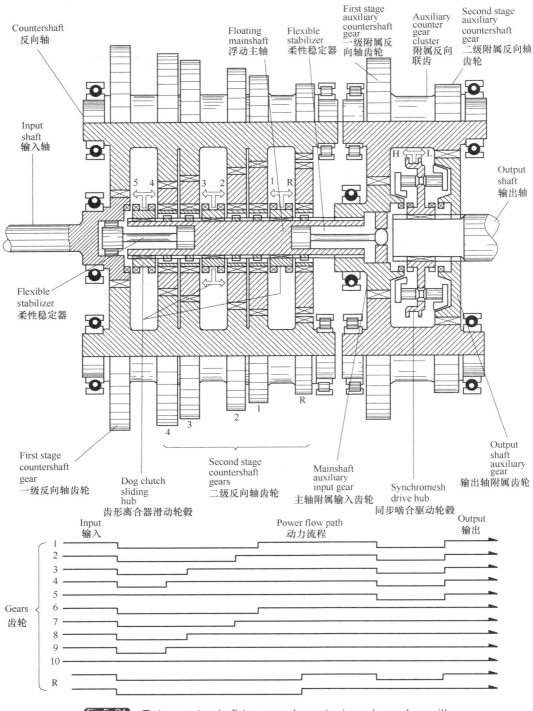

Fig5.31 Twin countershaft ten speed constant mesh gearbox with synchromesh two speed range change
同步啮合两速系列更换齿轮的双反向轴十速常啮合齿轮箱

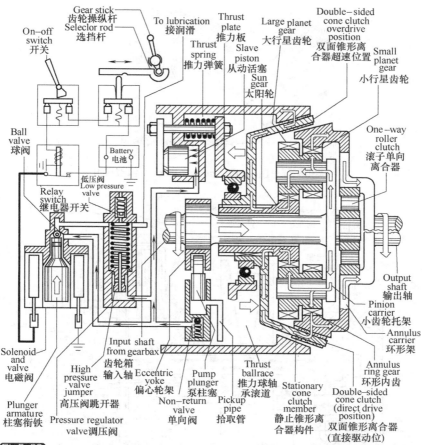

Fig5.32 Laycock double epicycle overdrive 直接驱动的双级行星齿轮超速装置

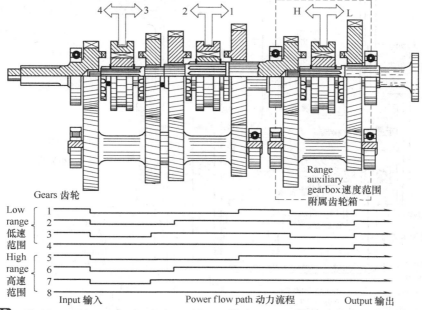

Fig5.33 Eight speed constant mesh gearbox with two speed rear mounted range change
具有两速后安装的系列更换齿轮的八速常啮合齿轮箱

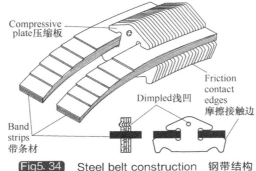

Fig5.34　Steel belt construction　钢带结构

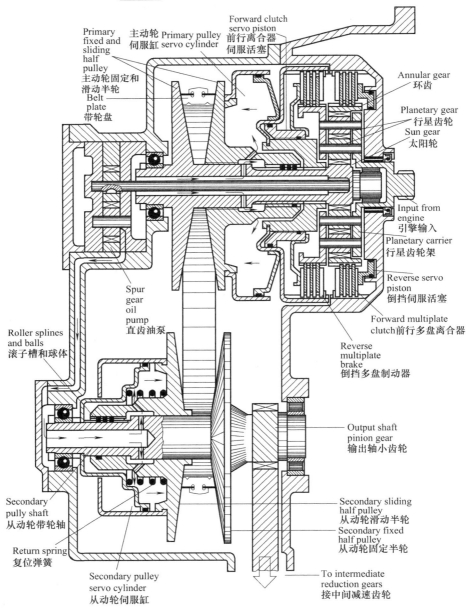

Fig5.35　Section view of a transverse continuously variable transmission (CVT)　横向无级变速机构剖视图

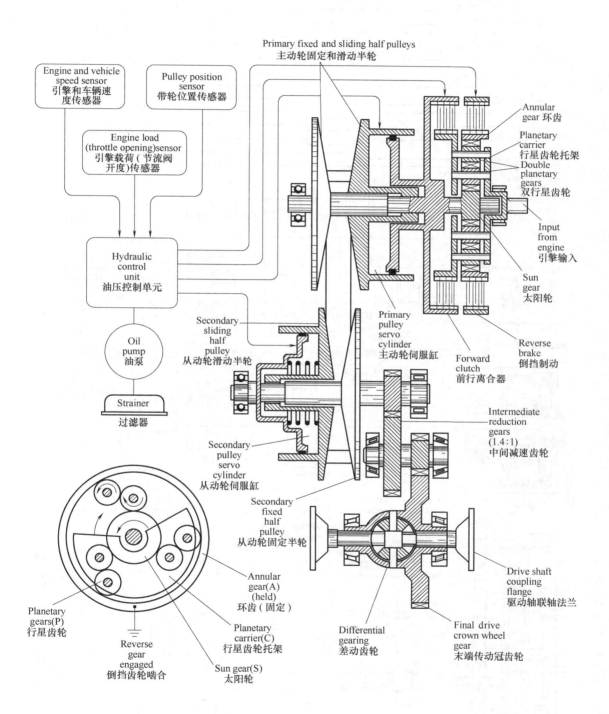

Fig5.36 Transaxle continuously variable belt and pulley transmission layout
横轴无级变速带及带轮传动设计

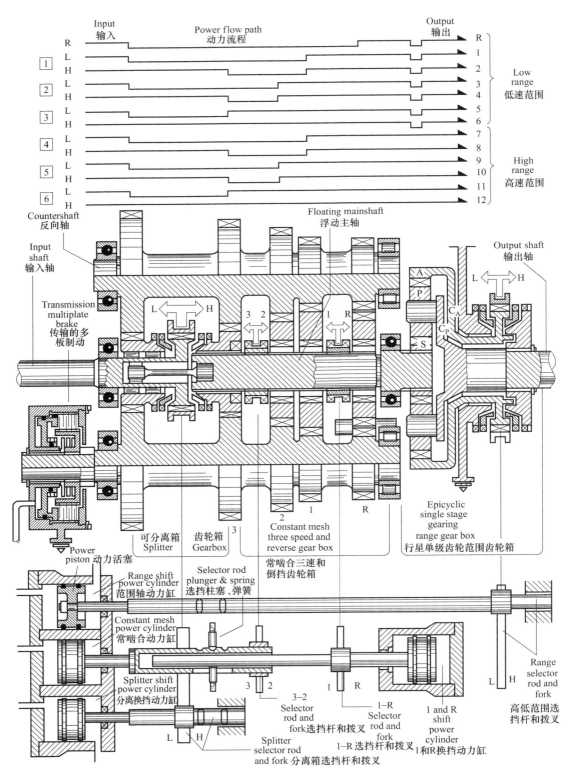

Fig5.37 Twin countershaft 12 speed constant mesh gearbox with synchromesh two speed splitter and rang change 双反向轴12速常啮合齿轮箱和同步双速分离箱及高低范围改变装置

Chapter 5 Functional components 功能部件

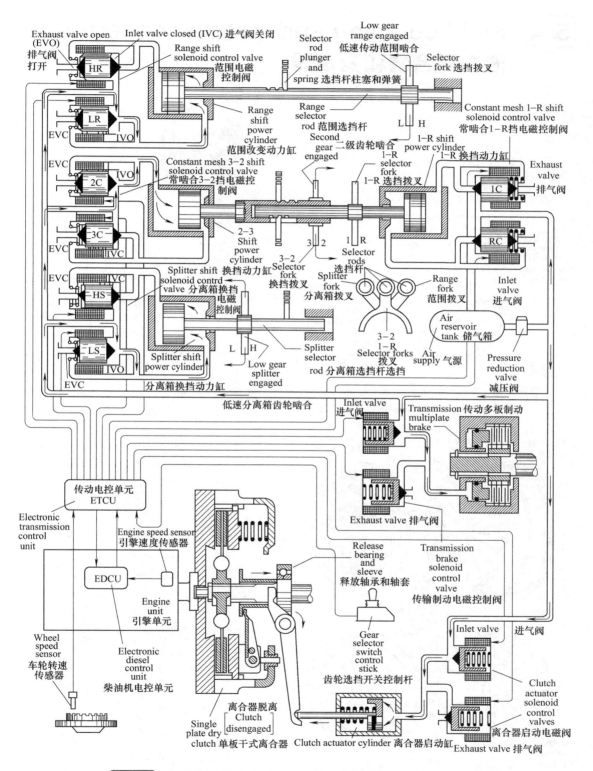

Fig5.38 A simplified electro/pneumatic gear shift and clutch control
简易电/气齿轮换挡和离合器控制

5.4 Fluid coupling and torque convertor 液力偶合器和变矩器

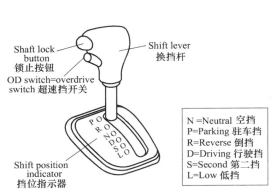

Fig5.39　Selector lever of automatic transmission　自动变速器换挡杆

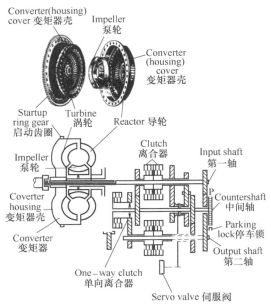

Fig5.40　Automatic transmission（AT）自动变速器

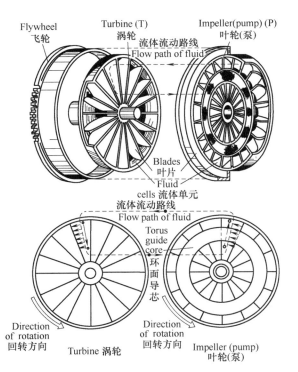

Fig5.41　Fluid couping action　液力耦合作用

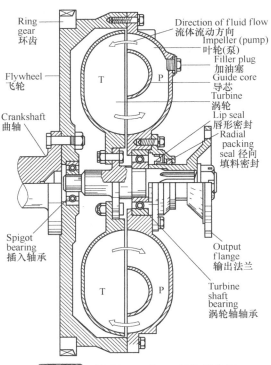

Fig5.42　Fluid coupling　液力偶合器

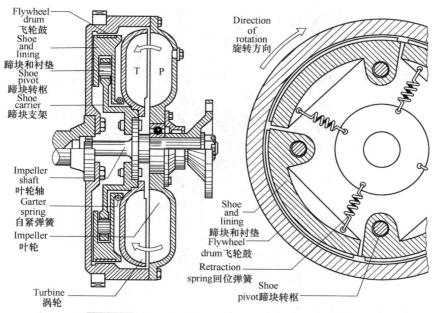

Fig5.43 Fluid friction coupling 流体摩擦偶合器

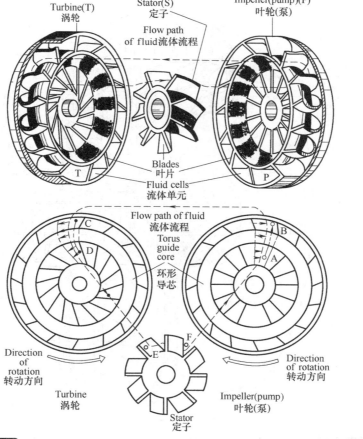

Fig5.44 Three element torque converter action 三元件液力变矩器作用

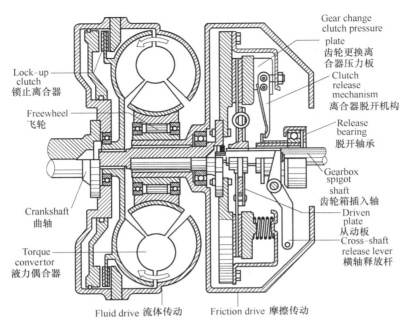

Fig5.45 Torque converter with lock-up and gear change function clutch
带锁止和换齿功能离合器的液力变矩器

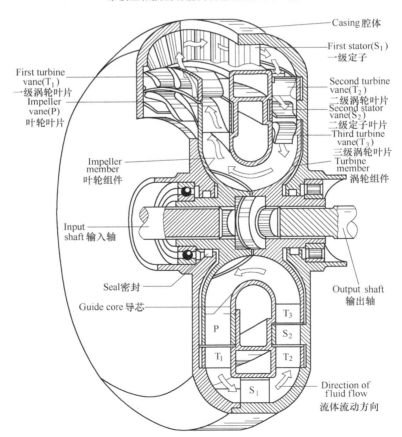

Fig5.46 Multistage (six element) torque converter 多级（六元件）液力变矩器

Chapter 5　Functional components　功能部件

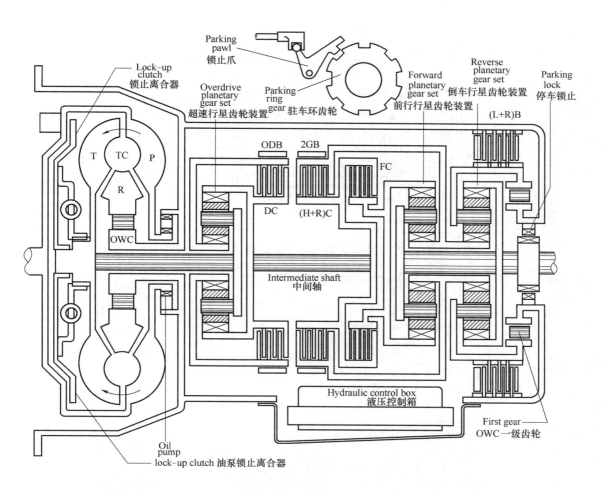

Fig5.47　Longitudinally mounted four speed automatic transmission layout
纵向安装的四速自动传动设计

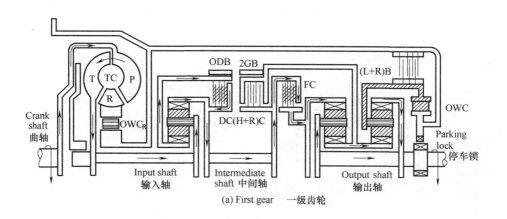

(a) First gear　一级齿轮

Fig5.48

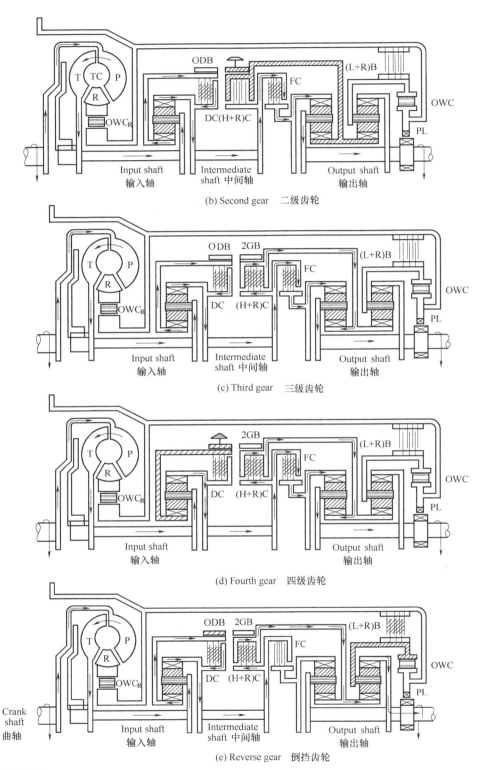

Fig5.48 Four speed and reverse automatic transmission for longitudinally mounted units
四速及倒挡纵向安装的自动传动系统

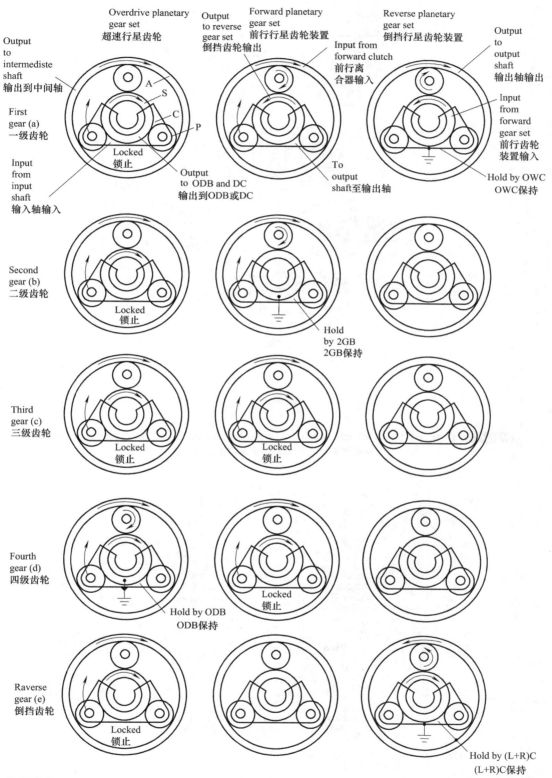

Fig5. 49 Four speed and reverse epicycle gear set directional motion 直接运动的四速和倒挡行星齿轮装置

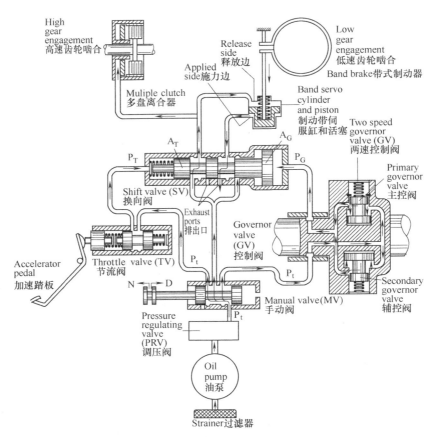

Fig5.50 Basic multiplate clutch and band brake transmission hydraulic control system
多盘离合器及带式制动液压传输控制系统

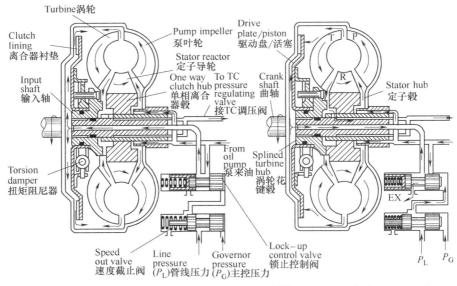

(a) Torque converter lock-up disengaged
液力变矩器锁止脱离

(b) Torque converter lock-up engaged
液力变矩器锁止

Fig5.51 Lock-up torque converter 锁止式液力变矩器

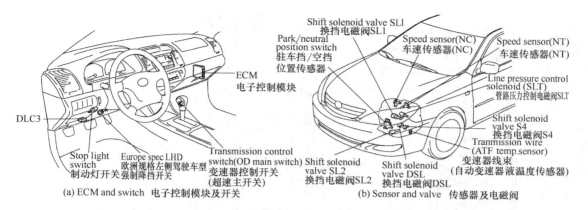

Fig5.52　Electronic controlled transmission (ECT, A/T) system　电子控制变速系统

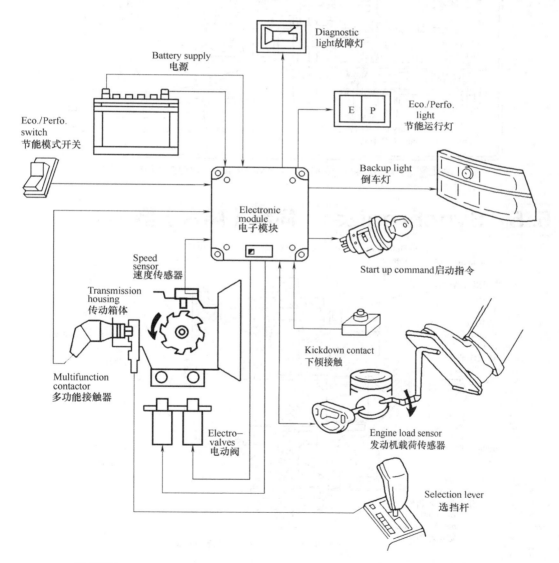

Fig5.53　Computer controlled transmission system　计算机控制的传动系统

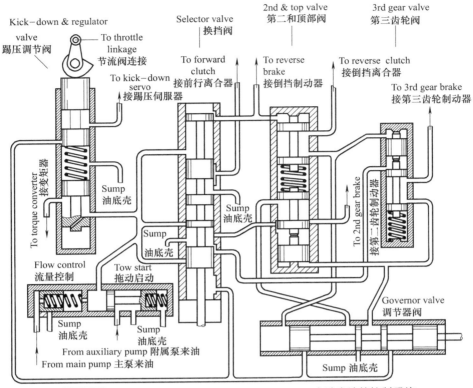

Fig5.54 Automatic gearbox control system 自动变速箱控制系统

5.5 Synchronizer 同步（离合）器

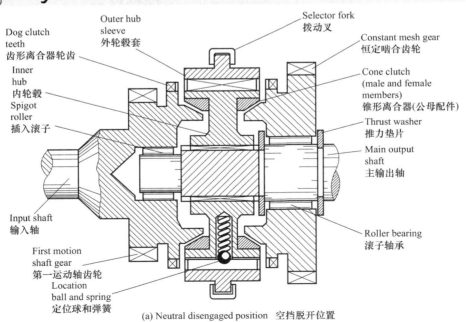

(a) Neutral disengaged position 空挡脱开位置

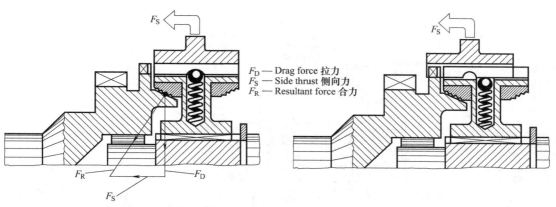

(b) Synchronization position 同步位置 (c) Engaged position 合上位置

Fig5.55　Non-positive constant load synchromesh unit　非增力恒载同步啮合单元

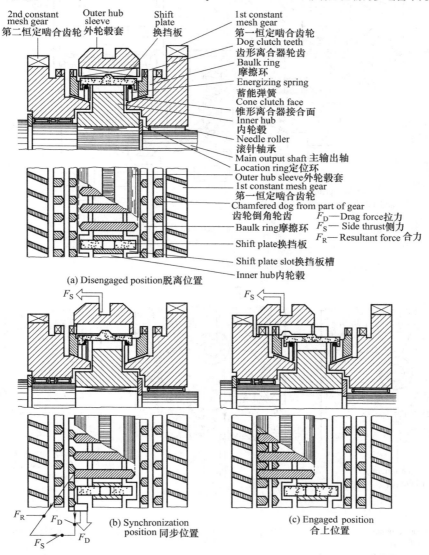

Fig5.56　Positive baulk ring synchromesh unit　增力摩擦环式同步离合器

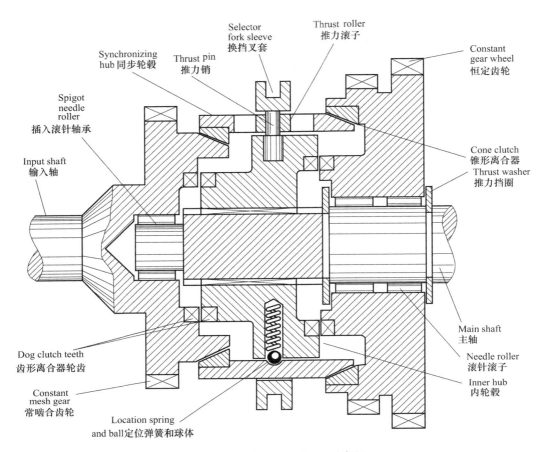

(a) Sectioned view 剖视图

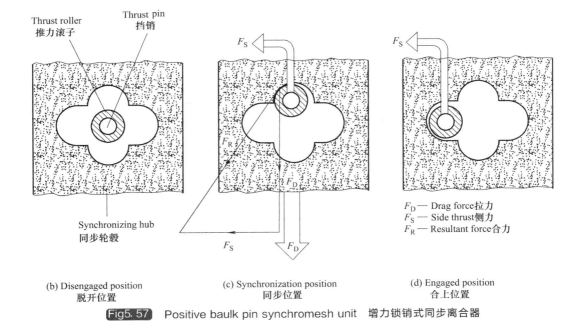

(b) Disengaged position
脱开位置

(c) Synchronization position
同步位置

(d) Engaged position
合上位置

F_D — Drag force 拉力
F_S — Side thrust 侧力
F_R — Resultant force 合力

Fig5.57　Positive baulk pin synchromesh unit　增力锁销式同步离合器

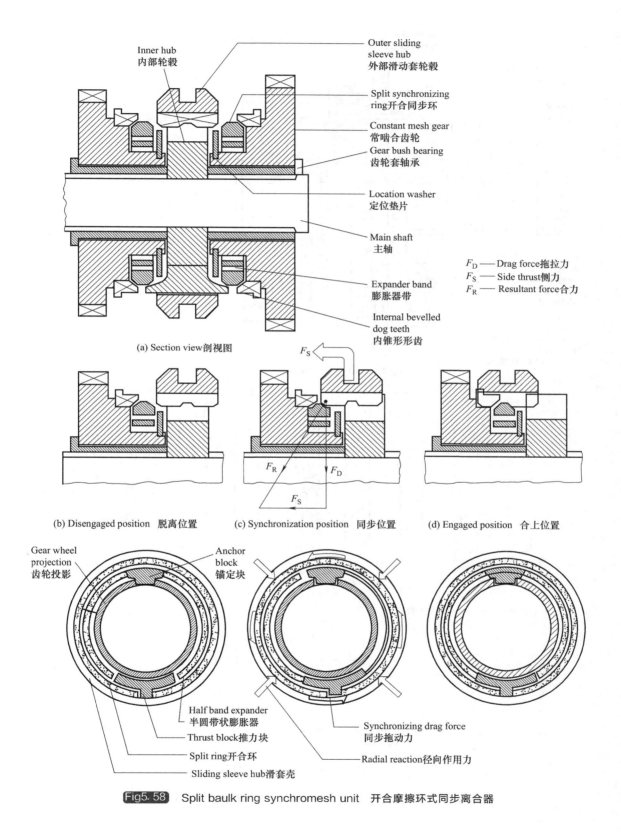

Fig5.58 Split baulk ring synchromesh unit 开合摩擦环式同步离合器

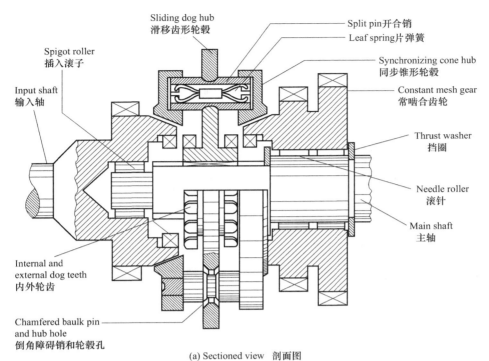

Fig5.59 Split baulk pin synchromesh unit 开合锁销式同步离合器

5.6 Differential 差速器

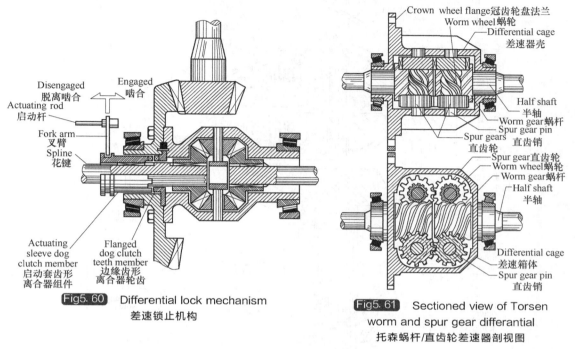

Fig5.60 Differential lock mechanism
差速锁止机构

Fig5.61 Sectioned view of Torsen worm and spur gear differantial
托森蜗杆/直齿轮差速器剖视图

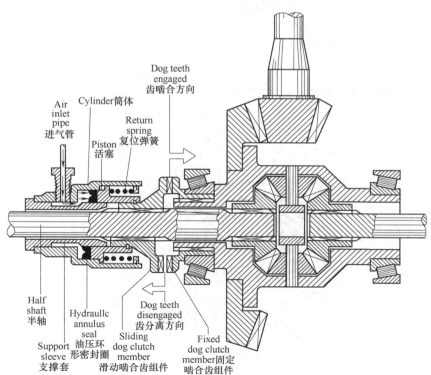

Fig5.62 Differantial lock mechanism with air control 气动控制的差速锁止机构

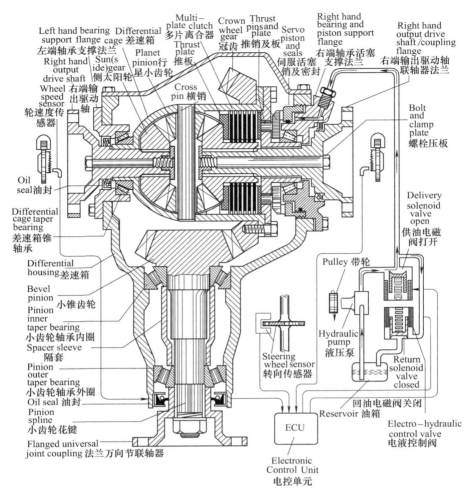

Fig5.63　Electro-hydraulic limited-slip (differential in locked position)　电液防滑（锁止位置差速器）

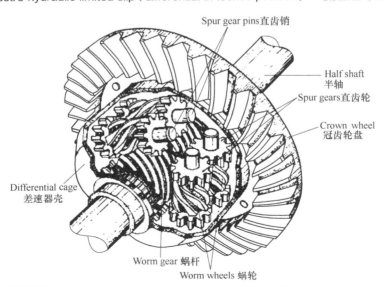

Fig5.64　Torsen worm and spur gear differantial　托森蜗杆/直齿差速器

Chapter 5　Functional components　功能部件

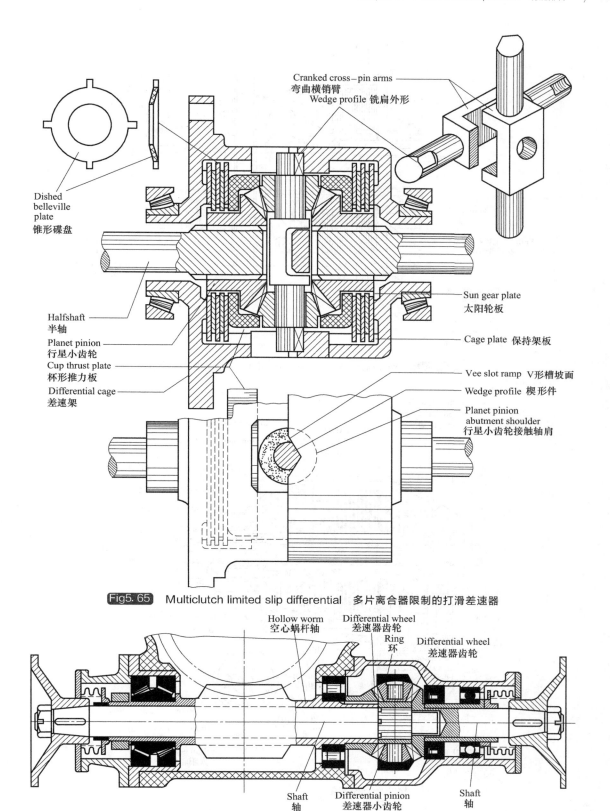

Fig5.65　Multiclutch limited slip differential　多片离合器限制的打滑差速器

Fig5.66　AEC third differential　AEC 第三差速器

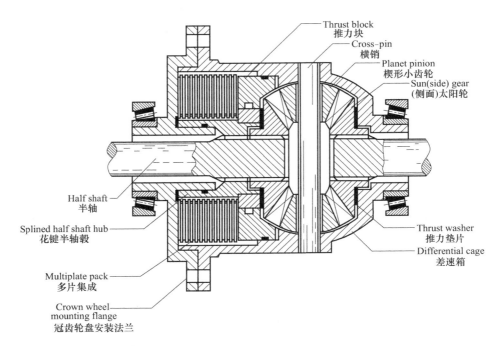

Fig5.67　Viscous coupling differential　黏液联轴器差速器

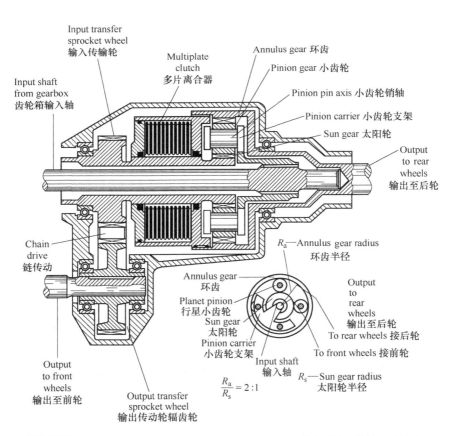

$\dfrac{R_a}{R_s} = 2:1$

Fig5.68　Third differential with viscous coupling　黏液联轴器的第三差速器

Chapter 5　Functional components　功能部件

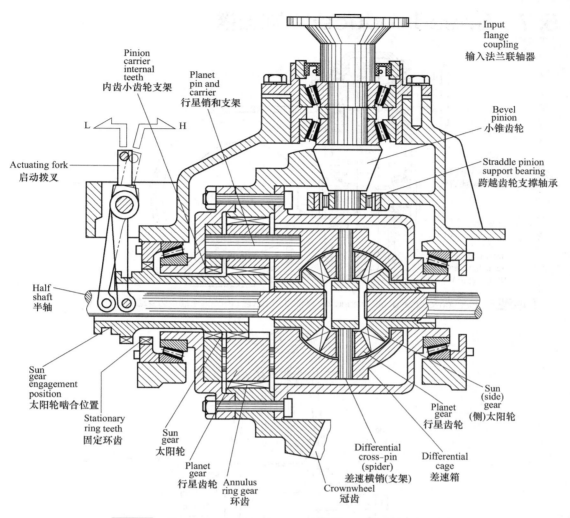

Fig5.69　Two speed epicyclic gear train axle　两速行星齿轮系轴

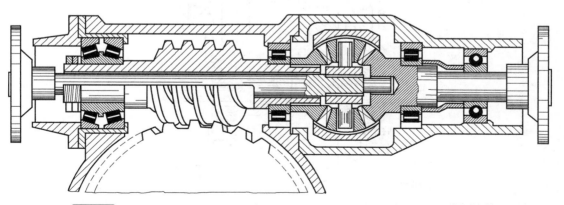

Fig5.70　Worm and worm wheel inter axle differential　蜗杆/蜗轮交互轴差速器

5.7 Speed reducer 减速器

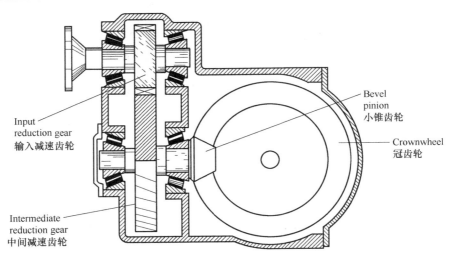

Fig5.71　Final drive spur double reduction ahead of bevel pinion　末端直齿驱动的小锥齿轮两级减速头

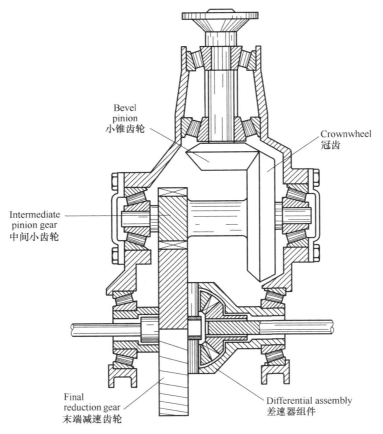

Fig5.72　Final drive spur double reduction between crownwheel and differantial
冠齿和差速器间的末端传动直齿双级减速器

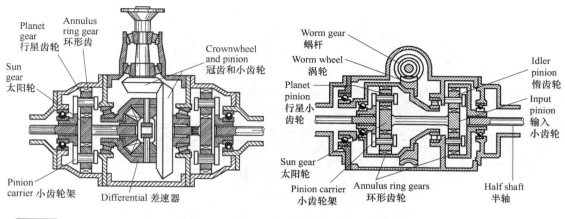

Fig5.73 Inboard epicyclic double reduction final drive axle 内置行星双级减速末端传动轴

Fig5.74 Inboard epicyclic double reduction axle 内置行星齿轮双级减速轴

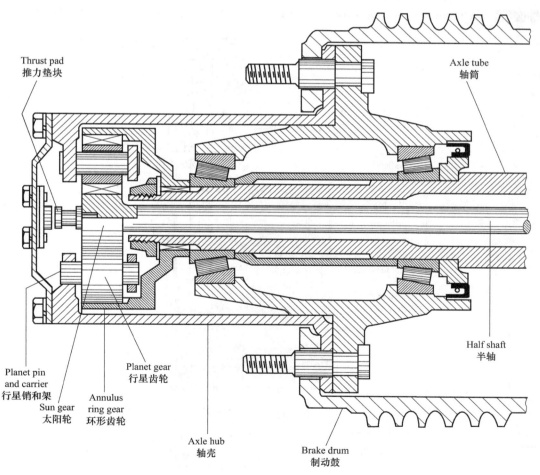

Fig5.75 Outboard epicyclic spur double reduction axle 外置行星直齿轮双级减速轴

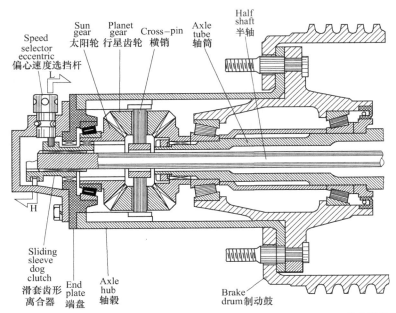

Fig5.76 Outboard epicyclic bevel gear two speed double reduction axle　外置行星锥齿轮两级速度双级减速轴

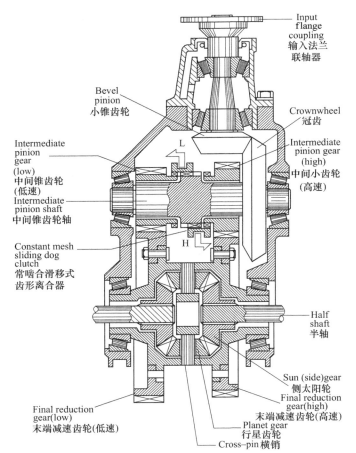

Fig5.77 Two speed double reduction helical gear axle　两速双级减速螺旋齿轮轴

Chapter 5 Functional components 功能部件

5.8 Drive shaft 传动轴

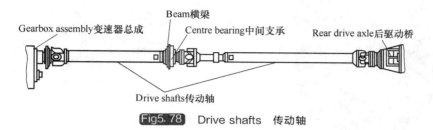

Fig5.78 Drive shafts 传动轴

5.9 Universal joint 万向节

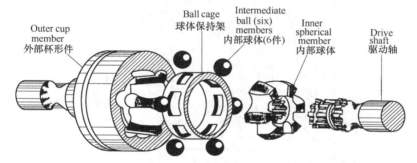

Fig5.79 Birfield joint exploded view 贝尔菲德万向节爆炸图

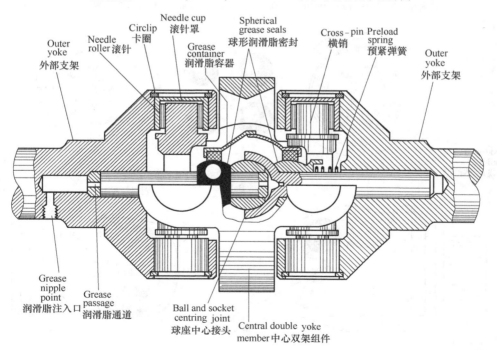

Fig5.80 Double Hooke's type constant velocity joint 双万向节恒速接头

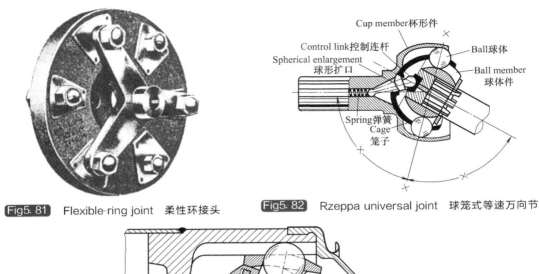

Fig5.81　Flexible-ring joint　柔性环接头

Fig5.82　Rzeppa universal joint　球笼式等速万向节

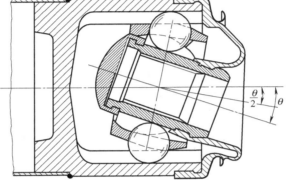

Fig5.83　Birfield constant-velocity universal joint　伯尔菲德等速万向节

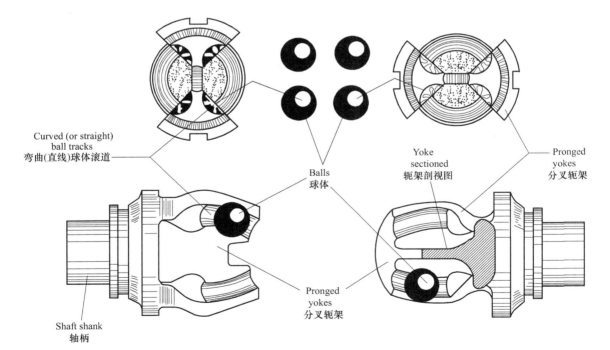

Fig5.84　Carl Weiss type joint　卡尔-维斯万向节

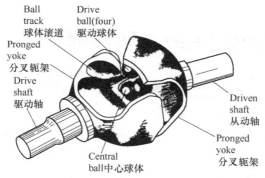

Fig5.85　Bendix Weiss constant velocity type joint　邦迪克斯-维斯恒速型万向节

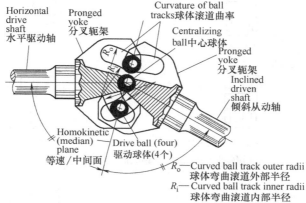

Fig5.86　Bendix Weiss constant velocity type joint　邦迪克斯-维斯恒速万向节

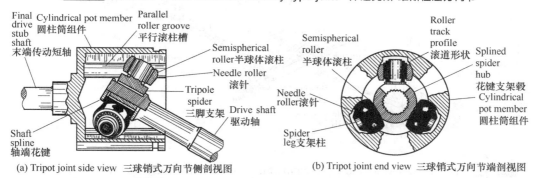

(a) Tripot joint side view　三球销式万向节侧剖视图

(b) Tripot joint end view　三球销式万向节端剖视图

Fig5.87　Tripot type universal joint　三球销式万向节

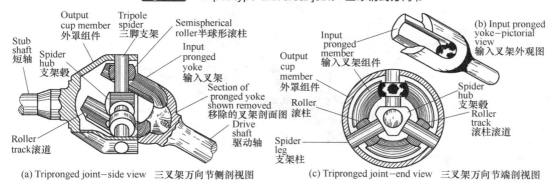

(a) Tripronged joint-side view　三叉架万向节侧剖视图

(b) Input pronged yoke-pictorial view　输入叉架外观图

(c) Tripronged joint-end view　三叉架万向节端剖视图

Fig5.88　Tripronged type universal joint　三叉架型万向节

5.10 Steering gear 转向器

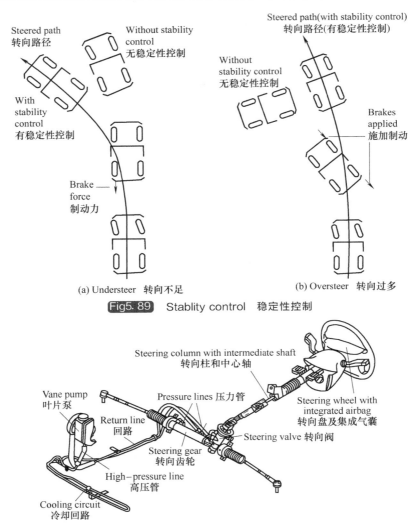

(a) Understeer 转向不足

(b) Oversteer 转向过多

Fig5.89 Stablity control 稳定性控制

Fig5.90 Hydraulic power steering system of the Opel Vectra 欧宝 Vectra 液压动力转向系统

Fig5.91 Electro-hydraulic power steering system of the Opel Astra 欧宝 Astra 的电液动力转向系统

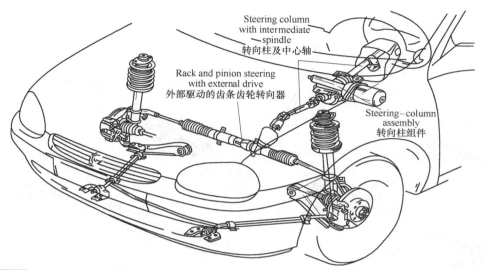

Fig5.92　Electric power steering system of the Opel Corsa (1997)　欧宝 Corsa 的电动转向系统

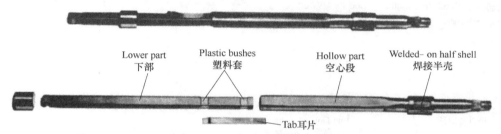

Fig5.93　Telescopic collapsible steering tubes　伸缩式可折叠转向管

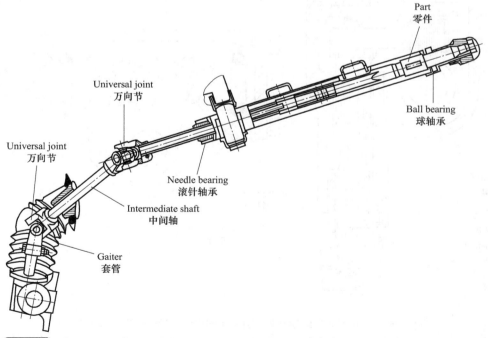

Fig5.94　Steering column of the VW Golf Ⅲ and Vento　大众 Golf Ⅲ and Vento 的转向柱

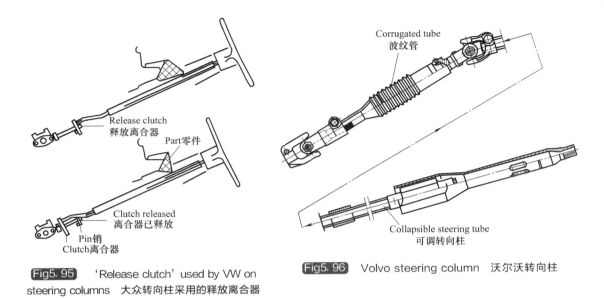

Fig5.95 'Release clutch' used by VW on steering columns 大众转向柱采用的释放离合器

Fig5.96 Volvo steering column 沃尔沃转向柱

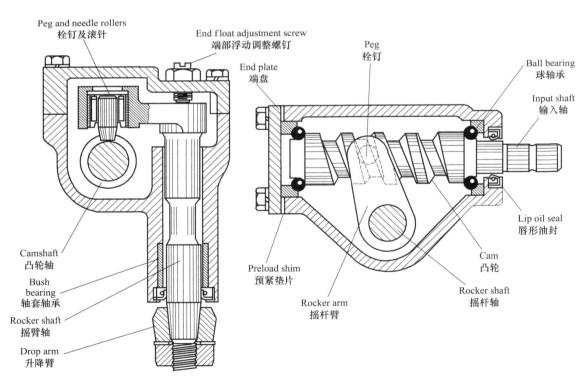

Fig5.97 Cam and peg steering type gearbox 凸轮与栓钉转向式齿轮箱

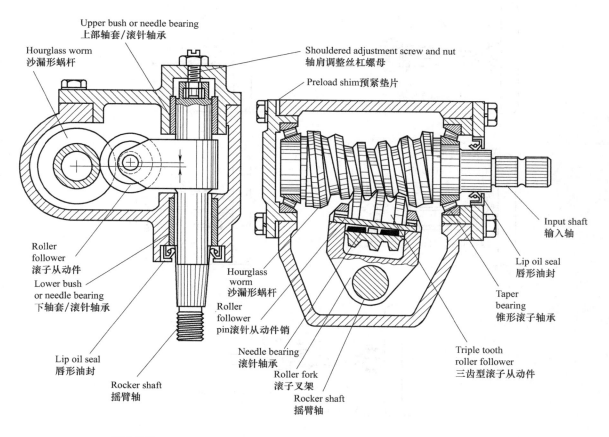

Fig5.98 Worm and roller type steering gearbox 蜗杆滚子类转向齿轮箱

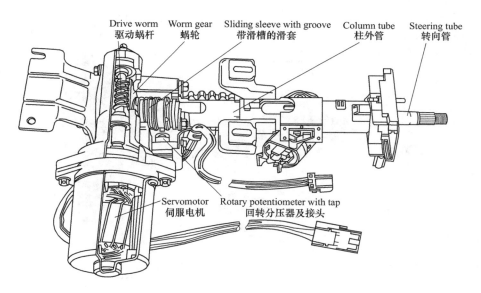

Fig5.99 Steering column with power-steering assembly of the Opel Corsa
欧宝 Corsa 动力转向柱总成

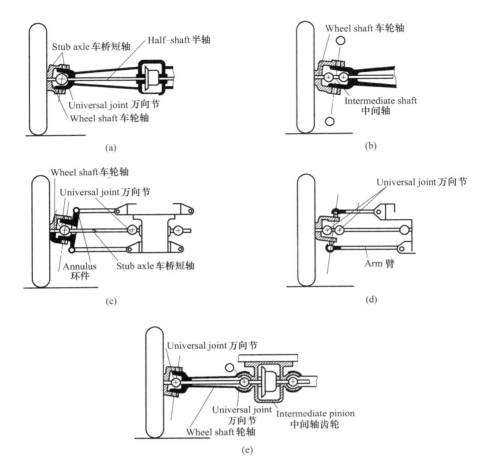

Fig5.100 Various methods of driving a steered wheel 驱动转向轮的不同方法

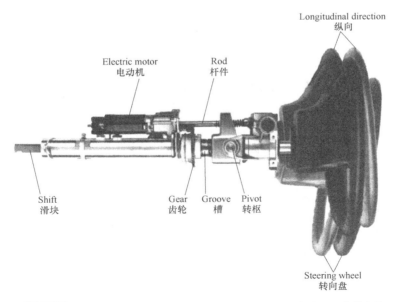

Fig5.101 Electrically adjustable steering column 电动可调节转向柱

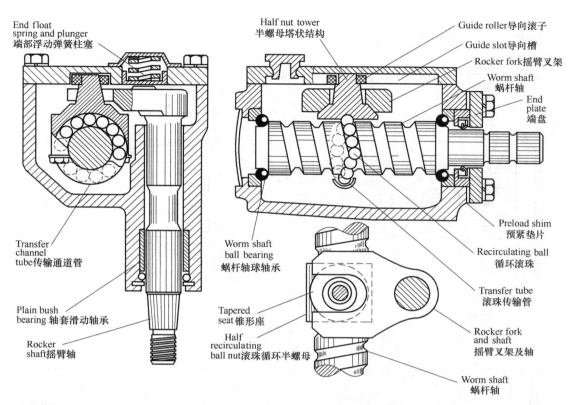

Fig5.102 Recirculating ball nut and rocker lever steering type gearbox 循环式滚珠螺母及摇杆转向齿轮箱

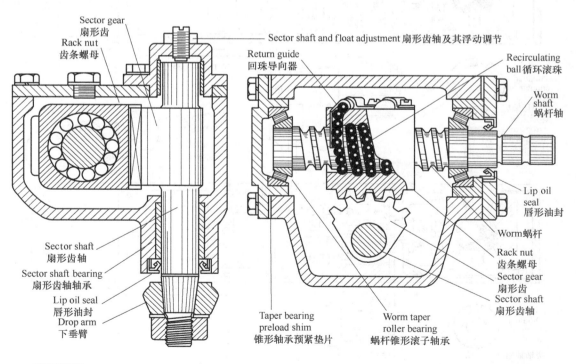

Fig5.103 Recirculating ball rack and sector steering gearbox 滚珠循环齿条/扇形齿转向齿轮箱

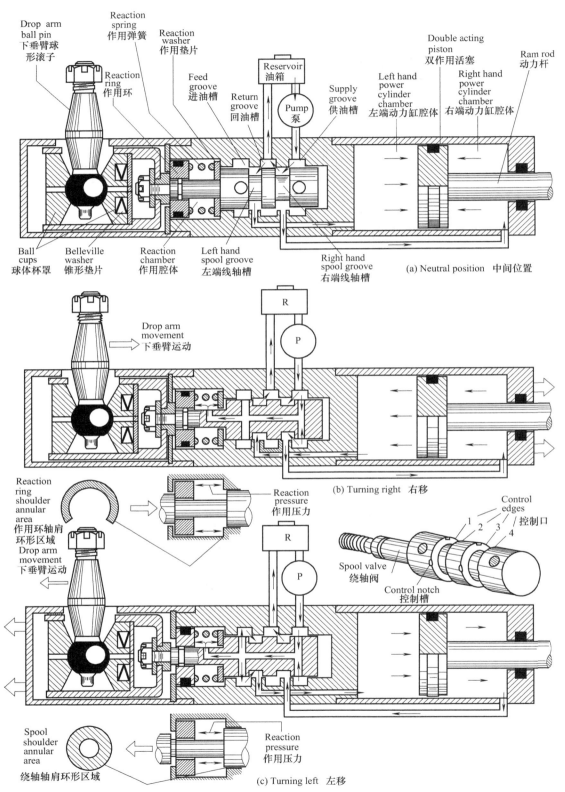

Fig5.104 External directly coupled power assisted steering 外部直联动力辅助转向装置

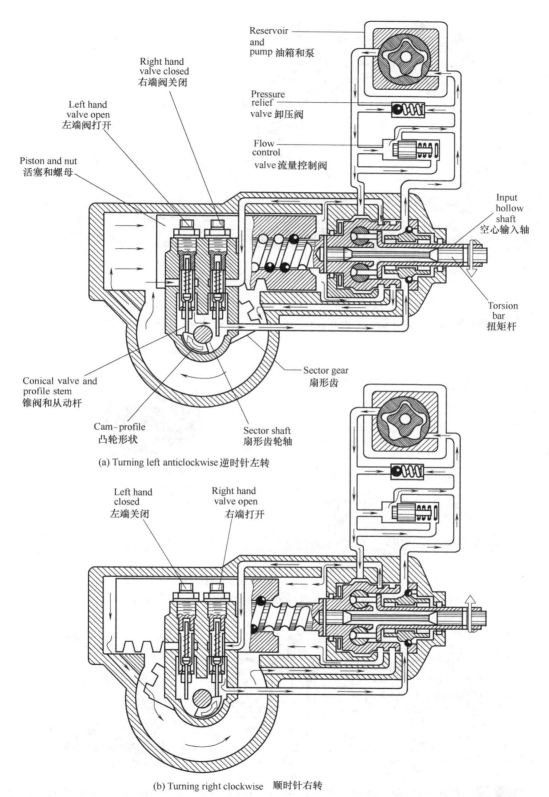

Fig5.105 Power assisted steering long stem conical valve lock limiter 动力辅助转向长柄锥形阀锁紧限位器

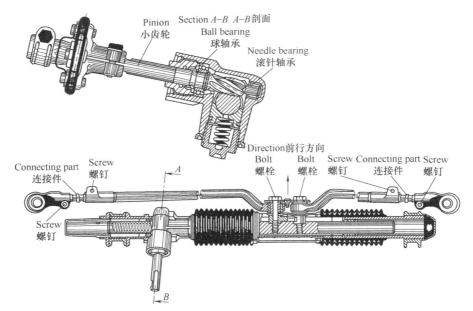

Fig5.106　Rack and pinion steering of the front-wheel drive　前驱车辆的齿条齿轮转向机构

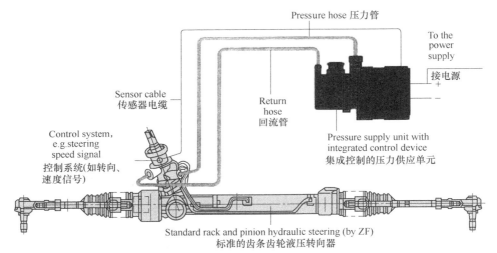

Fig5.107　Open-centre control system from ZF　ZF 开式中控系统

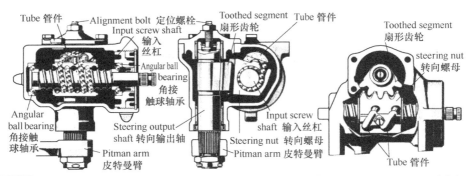

Fig5.108　Mercedes Benz recirculating ball steering suitable for passenger cars and light vans
适合于乘用车和轻型车的梅赛德斯滚珠循环转向器

Chapter 5　Functional components　功能部件

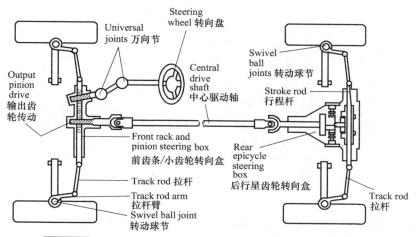

Fig5.109　Four wheel steering (4WS) system　四轮转向系统

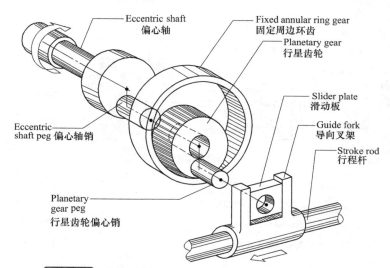

Fig5.110　Epicyclic rear steering box　行星齿轮后转向盒

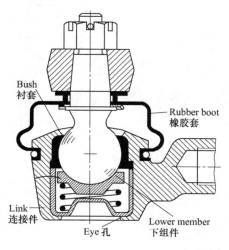

Fig5.111　Modern ball-and-socket joint construction　球座头结构

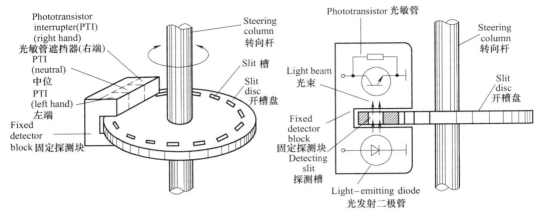

Fig5.112 Steering sensor (photo interrupter type) 转向传感器（光线遮挡式）

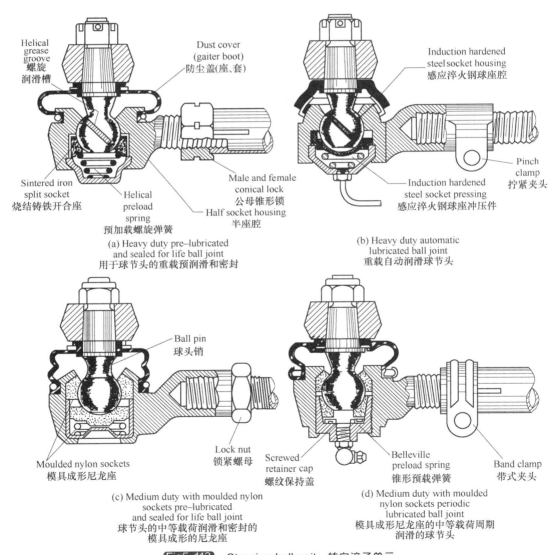

Fig5.113 Steering ball unit 转向滚子单元

Chapter 5　Functional components　功能部件　169

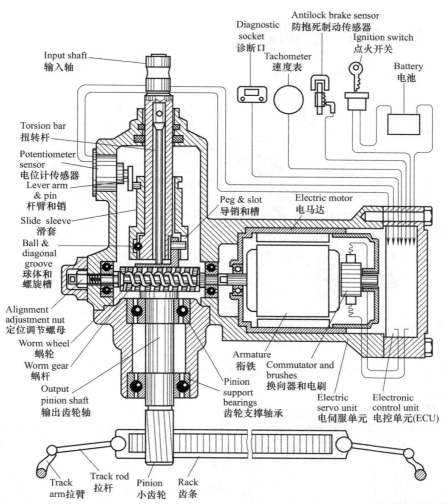

Fig5.114　Rack and pinion electric power assisted steering system　齿条/齿轮电动辅助转向系统

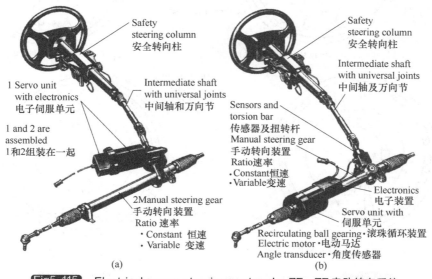

Fig5.115　Electrical power steering system by ZF　ZF电动转向系统

5.11 Brake 制动器

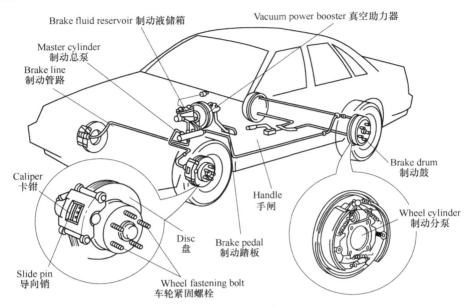

Fig5.116 Brake system components 制动系零件

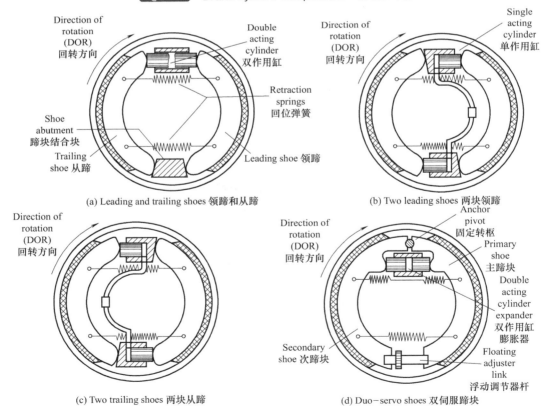

Fig5.117 Various brake shoe arrangements 多种制动蹄块的设计

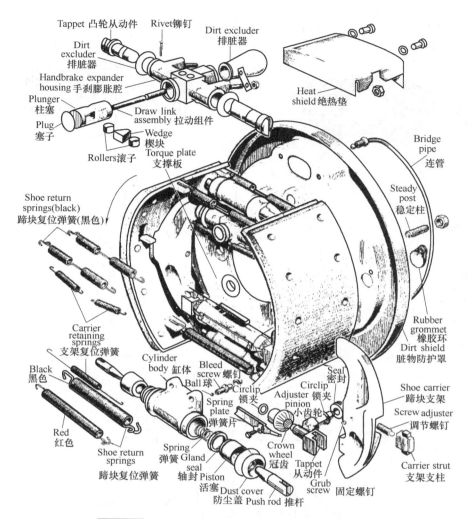

Fig5.118 Heavy-duty drum brake 重载鼓式制动器

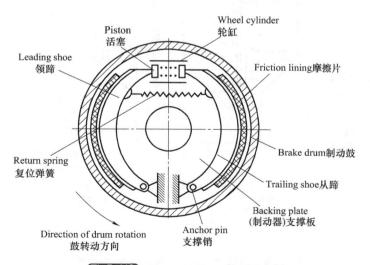

Fig5.119 Drum brake 鼓式制动器

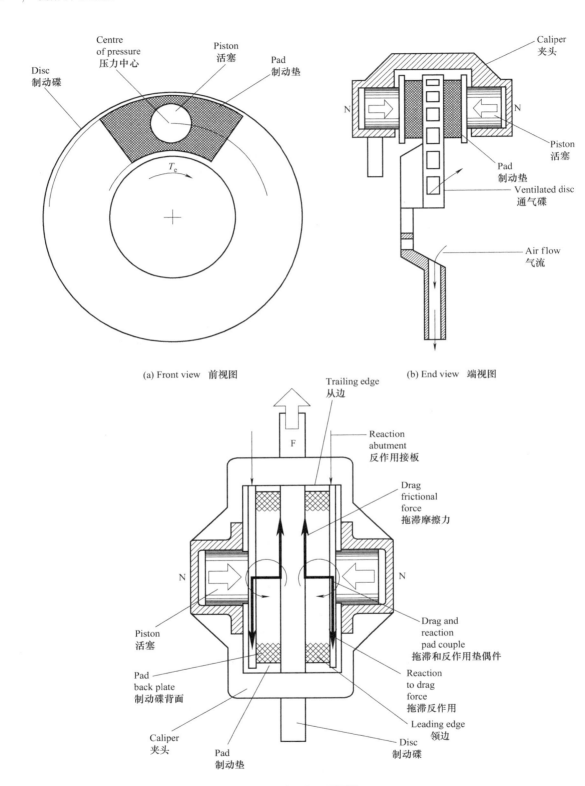

Fig5.120　Disc and pad layout　制动碟和制动垫

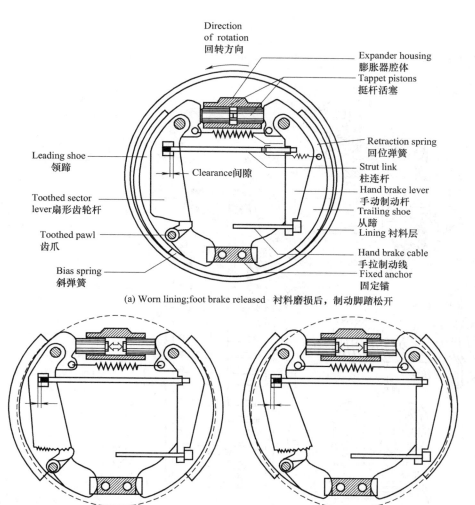

Fig5.121　Self-adjusting sector and pawl shoes with forward full hand brake
前行满手制动的自调节扇形块和爪型蹄块

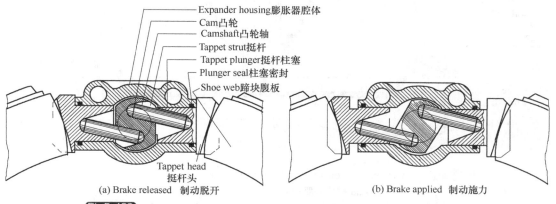

Fig5.122　Strut and cam brake shoe expander　支柱凸轮制动蹄膨胀器

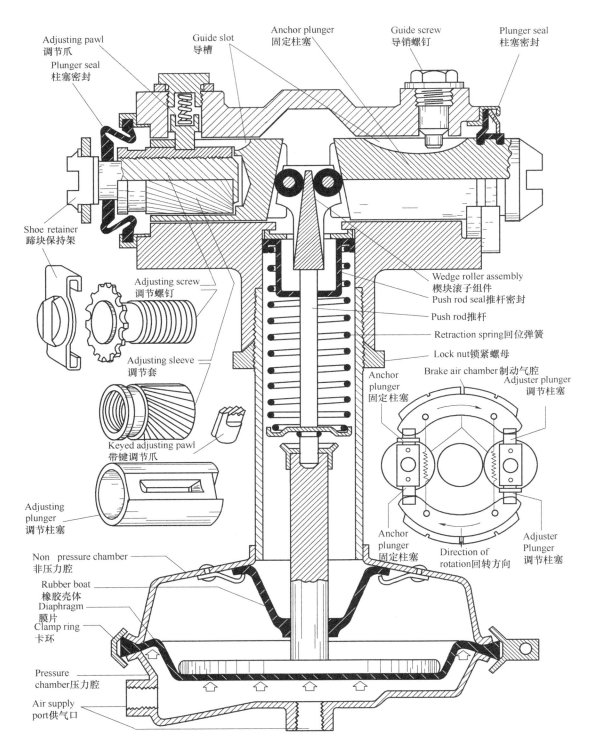

Fig5.123 Twin wedge foundation brake expander and automatic adjuster
双面楔块底座制动膨胀器及自动调节器

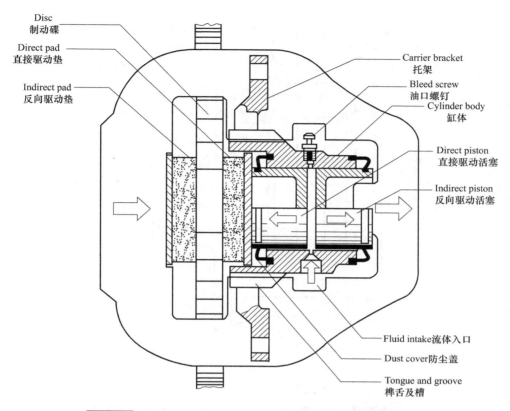

Fig5.124　Sliding yoke type brake caliper　轭架滑动型制动夹钳

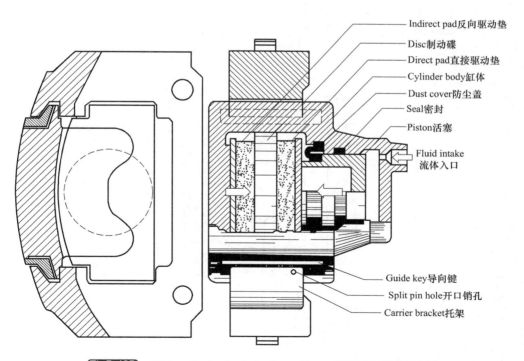

Fig5.125　Slide cylinder body brake caliper　缸体滑动型制动夹钳

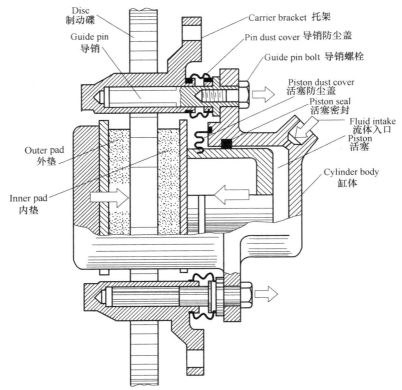

Fig5.126　Slide pin type brake caliper　滑柱型制动夹钳

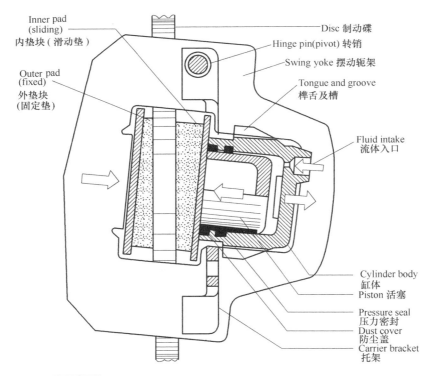

Fig5.127　Swing yoke type brake caliper　轭架摆动型制动夹钳

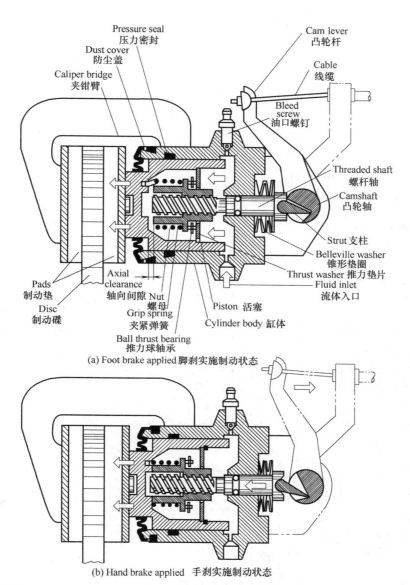

Fig5. 128 Combined foot and hand brake caliper with automatic screw adjustment
带自动调节螺钉的脚刹和手刹复合制动夹钳

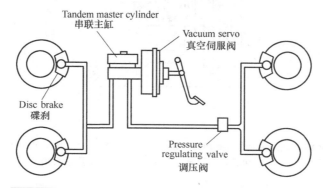

Fig5. 129 Front to rear brake line split 制动传动线路

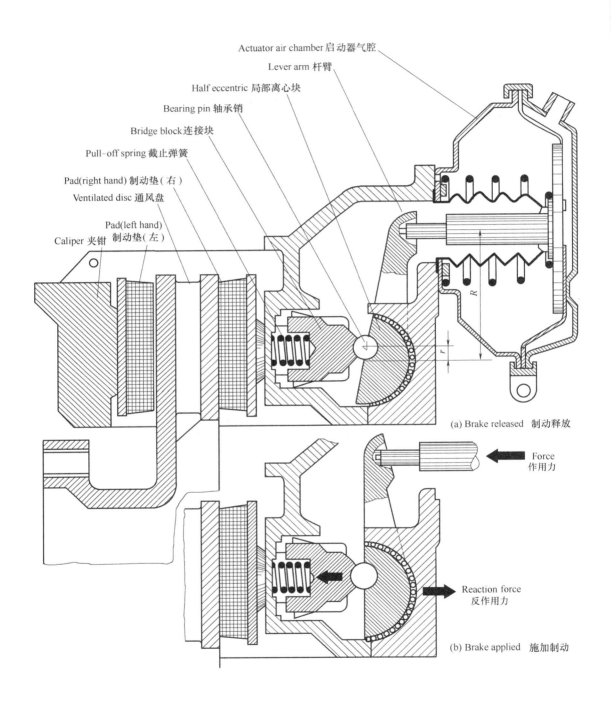

Fig5.130 Pneumatic operated disc brake-floating caliper with integral half eccentric lever arm
气动碟盘制动器：集成半离心杆臂的浮动夹钳

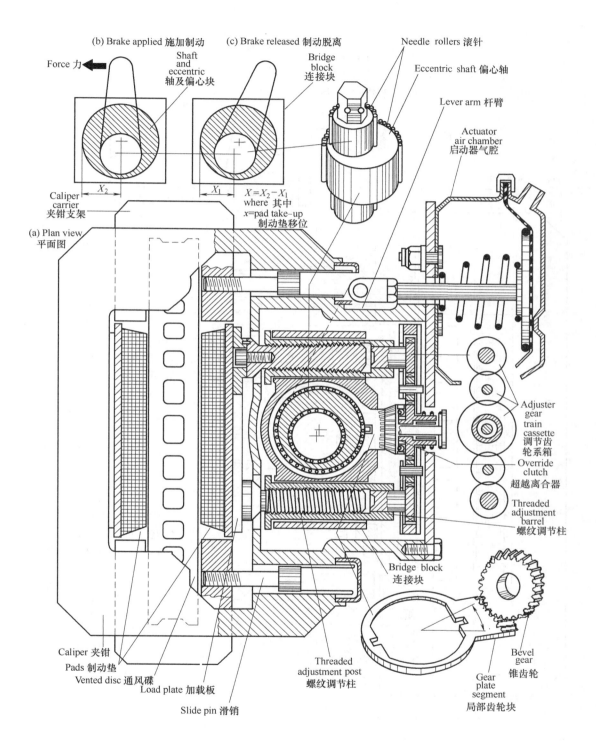

Fig5.131 Pneumatic operated disc brake-eccentric shaft and lever with gear driven automatic adjustment mechanism
气动操控的碟刹制动：带齿轮驱动的自动调节机构的偏心轴和杆

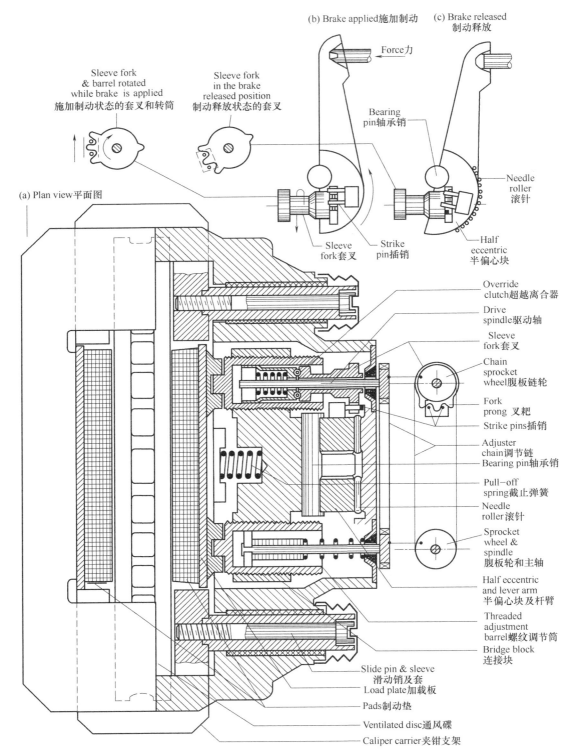

Fig5.132 Pneumatic operated disc brake-half eccentric shaft and lever with gear driven automatic adjustment mechanism
气动操控制动垫：带齿轮驱动的自动调节机构的半偏心轴和杆臂

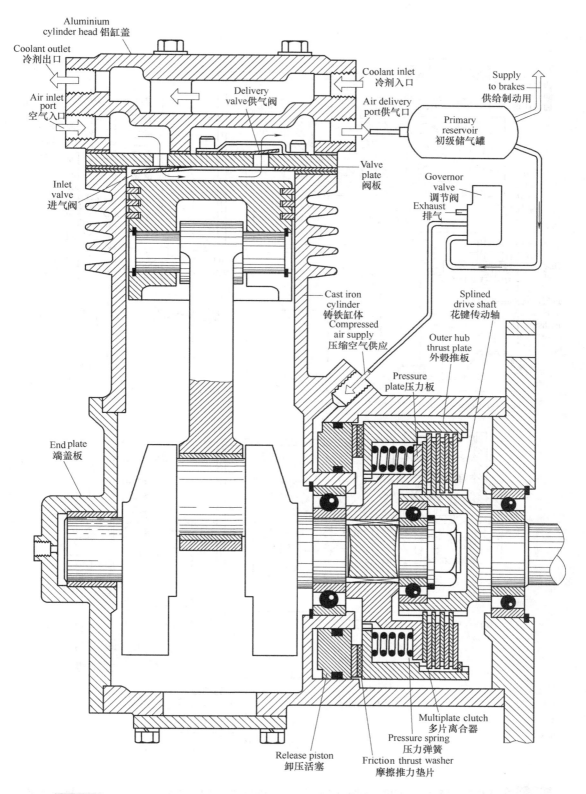

Fig5.133 Single cylinder air compressor with clutch drive 离合器驱动的单缸空气压缩机

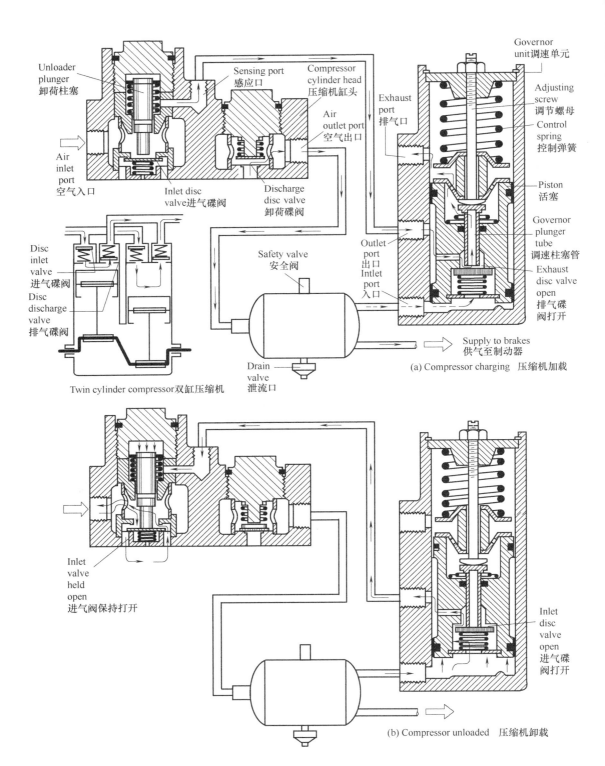

Fig5.134 Compressor mounted unloader with separate governor 安装独立调速及卸荷装置的压缩机

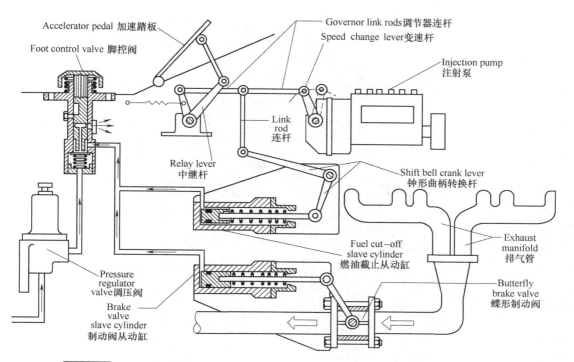

Fig5.135　Exhaust compression (brake) type retarder　排出压缩（制动）型缓速器

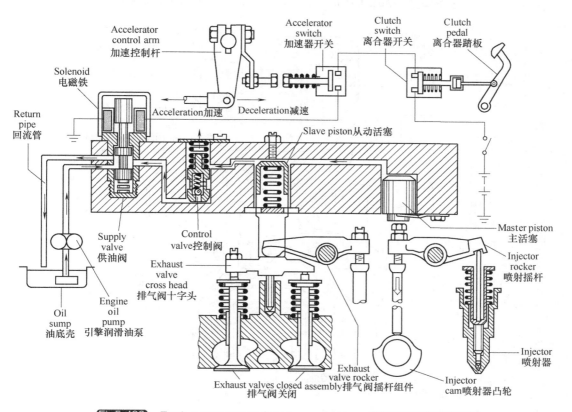

Fig5.136　Engine compressed air type retarder　引擎压缩空气型缓速器

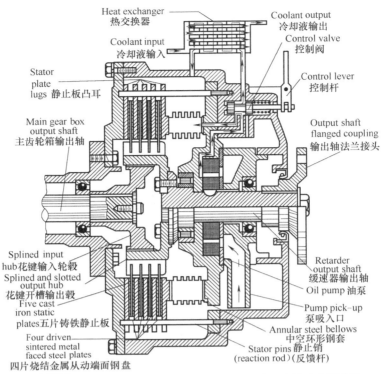

Fig5.137 Multiplate friction type retarder 多块摩擦片式缓速器

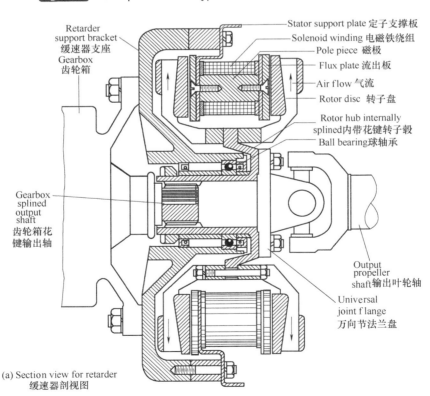

(a) Section view for retarder 缓速器剖视图

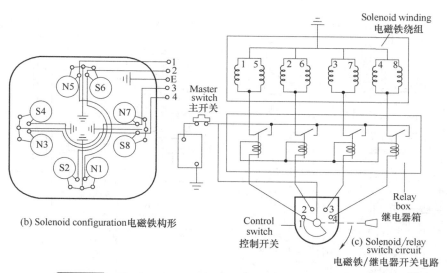

Fig5.138 Electric eddy current type retarder 电涡流类缓速器

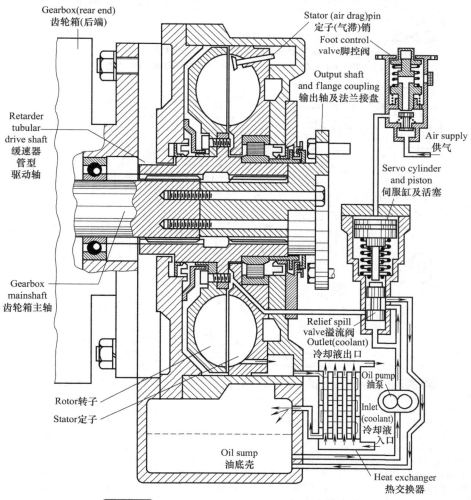

Fig5.139 Hydraulic type retarder 液压式缓速器

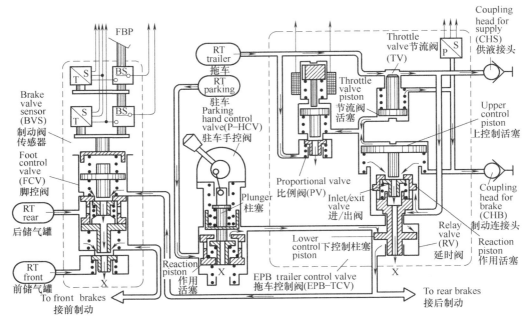

Fig5.140 Electronic pneumatic tractor unit brakes coupled to towed trailer 配挂到拖车的牵引车电/气单元制动
(trailer axles-foot brake released 拖车轴脚刹制动脱开)

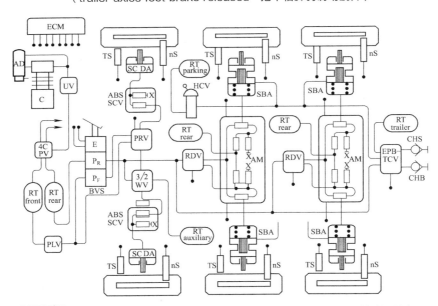

Fig5.141 Electronic-pneumatic brake component layout 电气制动组件布局

ECM—Electronic control module 电控模块；AD—Air dryer 空气干燥器；C—Compressor 压缩机；UV—Unloader valve 卸荷阀；4CPV—Four circuit protection valve 四回流保护；RT etc—Reservoir tank 储气罐；BVS—Brake value sensor 制动阀传感器；PRV—Proportional relay valve 比例延时阀；3/2-WV-AB—3/2-way valve for auxilary braking effect 三位二通阀辅助制动效果；ABS-SCV—ABS solenoid control valve ABS 电磁控制阀；SCDA—Single circuit diaphragm actuator 单回路膜片启动器；RDV—Redundancy valve 冗余阀；AM—Axle modulator 轴模块；SBA—Spring brake actuator 弹簧制动启动器；EPB-TCV—EPB trailer control valve EPB 拖车控制阀；P-HCV—Park hand control valve 驻车手控阀；CHS—Coupling head for supply 供气接头；CHB—Coupling head for brake 制动接头；TS—Travel sensor 里程传感器；nS—Speed sensor 速度传感器；P_F—Pneumatic control front 气控前制动；P_R—Pneumatic control rear 气控后制动；E—Electrical sensors & switches 传感开关；X—Air exit (exhaust) 排气

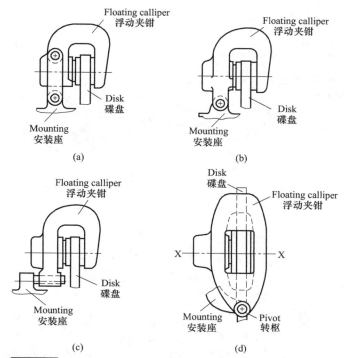

Fig5.142 Types of floating calliper disc brake arrangements
浮动夹头盘式制动器类型

5.12 Parking brake 驻车制动器

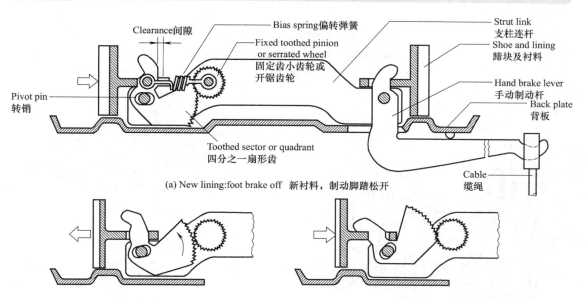

(a) New lining:foot brake off 新衬料，制动脚踏松开

(b) Half worn lining：foot brake on 半磨损、制动脚踏施力　　(c) Fully worn lining：foot brake off 全磨损、制动脚踏离开

Fig5.143 Self-adjusting sector and pinion brake shoes with cross-pull hand brake
横销手拉制动的自调节扇形齿和小齿轮制动蹄

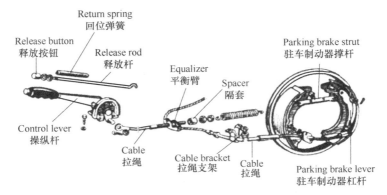

(a) Hand-operated parking brake 手动驻车制动器

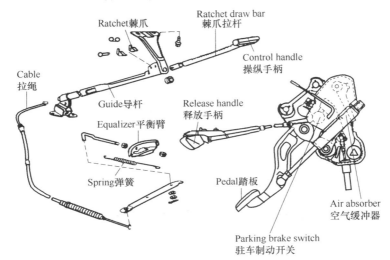

(b) Foot-operated parking brake 脚动驻车制动器

Fig5.144 Parking brake 驻车制动器

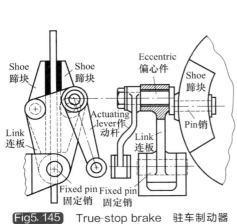

Fig5.145 True-stop brake 驻车制动器

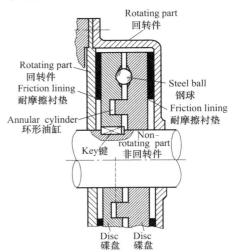

Fig5.146 Complete annular discs for the friction elements brake 全圆周盘摩擦元件制动器

5.13 Tyre 轮胎

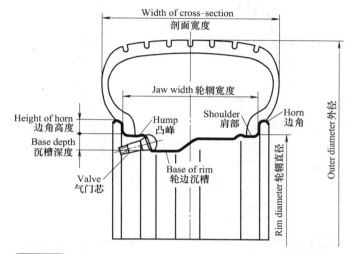

Fig5.147 Series 55 wide tyre designs 55系列宽度轮胎设计

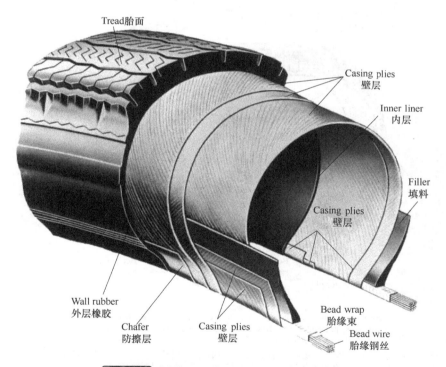

Fig5.148 45° crossply tyre 45°交叉股绳轮胎
(Relative flexure of the plies laid alternately at 45°to each other in crossply tyres tends to generate more heat than do those in the radial ply type(45°交叉股绳布局的轮胎相对易于弯曲会比子午线轮胎产生更多的热量))

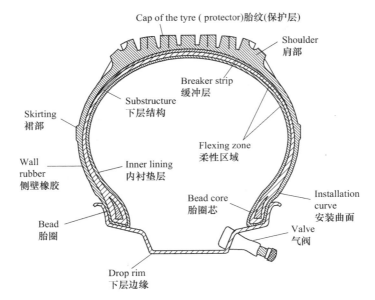

Fig5.149　Diagonal ply tubeless car tyre　斜交无内胎汽车轮胎

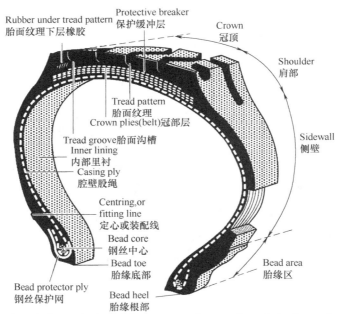

Beneath the treads of radial ply tyres are usually two or three steel or four or six textile cross braced bracing plies. These support the tread against centrifugal force, stabilise the contact patch and increase resistance to punctures
子午线轮胎胎面下层通常为两层或三层钢丝或四层或六层的交叉包覆的股绳，这有助于支撑胎面克服离心力、稳定接触区域和增加抵抗刺穿能力

Fig5.150　Radial ply tyre　子午线轮胎

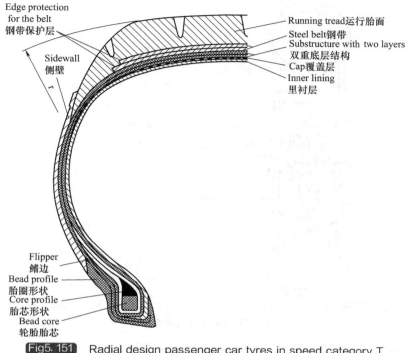

Fig5.151　Radial design passenger car tyres in speed category T
T类速度乘用车轮胎子午线设计

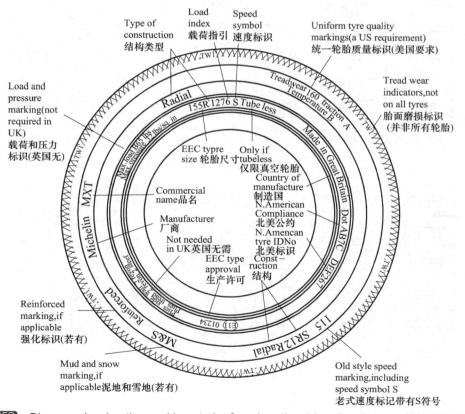

Fig5.152　Diagram showing the markings to be found on the sidewalls of tyres　轮胎侧面标识图解

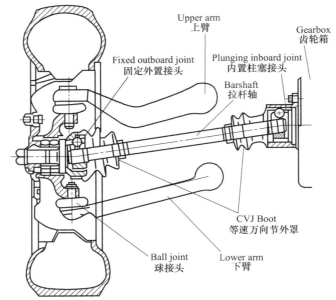

Fig5.153 Key elements to an independently suspended driven wheel
独立悬挂驱动车轮的关键要素

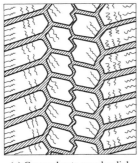

(a) Car moderate speed radial
轿车中等速度子午线胎面

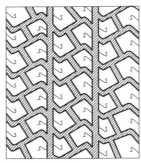

(b) Car high speed radial
轿车高速子午线胎面

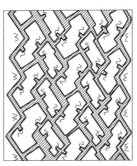

(c) Car very high speed radial
轿车极高速度子午线胎面

(d) Car wet weather radial
轿车雨天子午线胎面

(e) Car winter radial with moulded studholes
模具镶嵌柱孔的轿车冬季子午线胎面

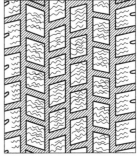

(f) Car winter radial
轿车冬季子午线胎面

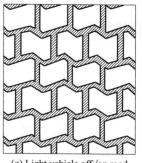
(g) Light vehicle off/on road winter tread
轻型车辆在路面或离开路面的冬季胎面

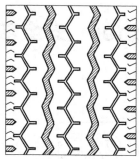
(h) Truck steer axle tread
卡车转向轴胎面

(i) Truck drive axle tread
卡车驱动轴胎面

Fig5.154 Tyre tread patterns 轮胎胎面图案

5.14 Distributor 分电器

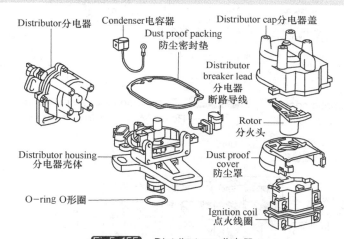

Fig5.155 Distributor 分电器

5.15 Alternator 发电机

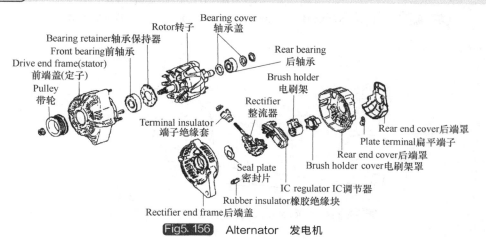

Fig5.156 Alternator 发电机

5.16 Belt tensioner 安全带张紧器

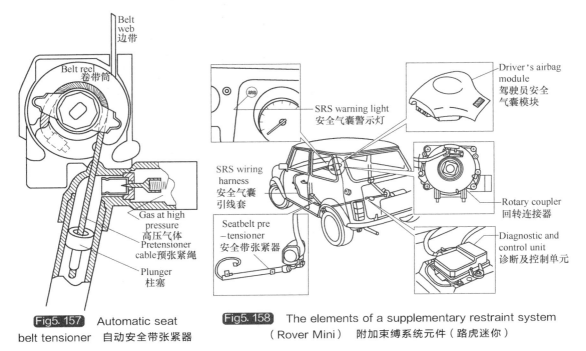

Fig5.157 Automatic seat belt tensioner 自动安全带张紧器

Fig5.158 The elements of a supplementary restraint system (Rover Mini) 附加束缚系统元件（路虎迷你）

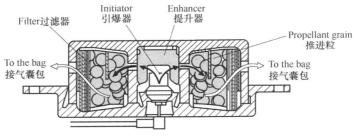

Fig5.159 A pyrotechnic device for inflating airbags 安全气囊膨胀用引爆装置

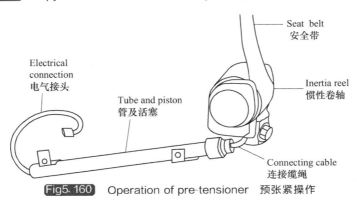

Fig5.160 Operation of pre-tensioner 预张紧操作

5.17 Instrument panel 汽车仪表盘

Table 5.1 Symbols 符号意义

Symbol	Name	Symbol	Name
	Fuel 燃油		Oil pressure warning light 机油压力警报灯
	Lighter 点烟器		Seat belt warning light 安全带提醒灯
	Horn 喇叭		Master lighting switch 灯光主开关
	Speaker 扬声器		Hazard warning lamp 危急报警闪光灯
	Interior light 顶灯		充电系统指示灯 Charging system indicator
	Fuse block 熔断丝		Brake system indicator 制动系统指示灯
	High beam indicator 远光指示灯		Parking brake indicator 驻车制动指示灯
	Turn light lamp 转向指示灯		Windshield wiper 前窗刮水器
	Dipped headlight 近光灯		Windshield washer 风挡玻璃冲洗器
	Front fog light 前雾灯		Windshield defroster 前窗除霜器
	Dash-light 仪表板灯		Engine coolant temperature 发动机冷却液温度
	Ventilator 通风机		Door lock 车门钥匙

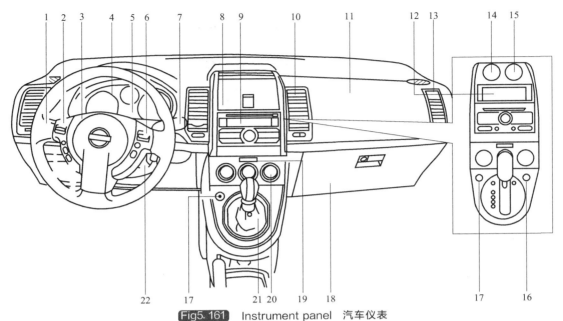

Fig5.161　Instrument panel　汽车仪表

1—Headlight/fog light/turn signal switch;Manual shift paddles　前大灯/雾灯/转向灯开关;2—Steering wheel switch for audio control and Bluetooth Hands-Free Phone System　方向盘音频控制开关及蓝牙免提电话系统;3—Driver's supplemental air bag/Horn　驾驶员安全气囊/喇叭;4—Meters and gauges　仪表和量表;5—Instrument brightness control　仪表照明开关;6—Cruise control main/set switches　巡航控制与设置开关;7—Windshield wiper/washer switch　刮水器及洗涤器开关;8—Storage bin　储物盒;9—Audio system　音频系统;10—Center ventilator　中央出风口;11—Passenger's supplemental air bag　乘客安全气囊;12—Control panel display　控制面板;13—Side ventilator　侧向出风口;14—Engine oil pressure gauge　机油油压表;15—G(gravity)- force gauge　加速度计;16—Hazard warning flasher switch　危险警告灯开关;17—Hazard warning flasher switch;Manual shift mode switch　危险警告灯开关,手动模式开关;18—Glove box　储物箱;19—Passenger air bag status light　乘客安全气囊状态灯;20—Climate control　空调控制开关;21—Shift selector lever　换挡杆;22—Ignition switch　点火开关

5.18　Electronic control system　电子控制系统

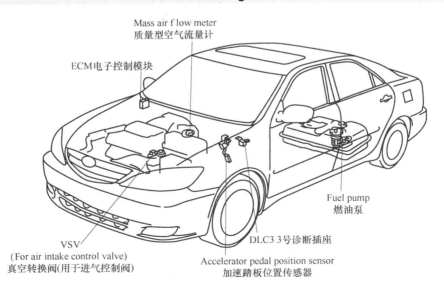

Chapter 5　Functional components　功能部件　197

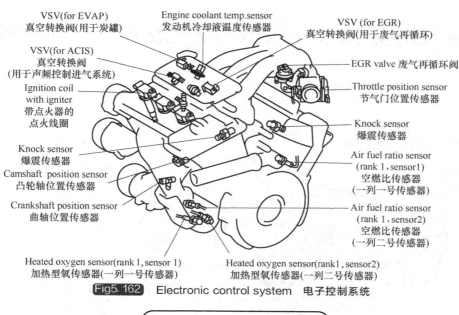

Fig5.162　Electronic control system　电子控制系统

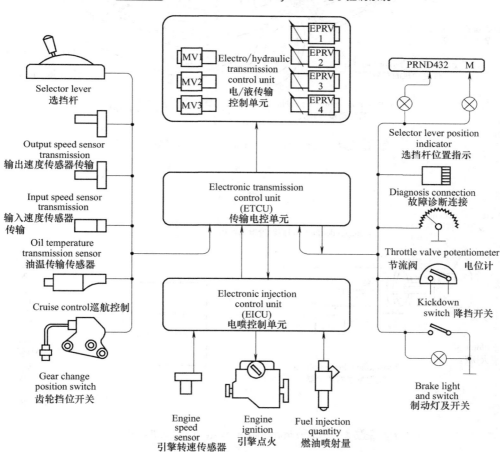

Fig5.163　Basic electronic control system layout　基本电控系统设计

5.19 Door lock control system 门锁控制系统

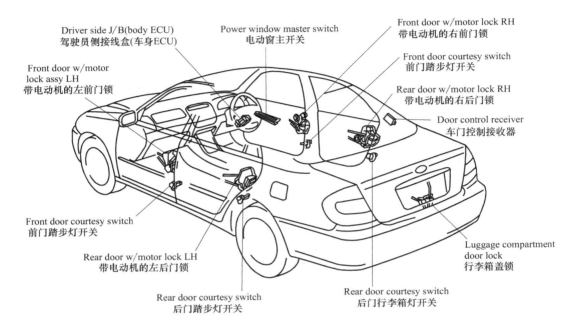

Fig5.164 Door lock control system 门锁控制系统

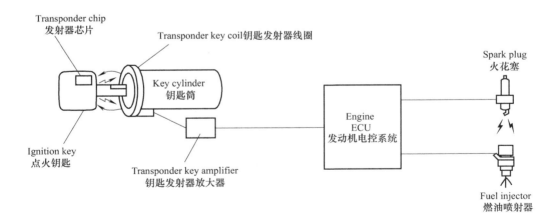

Fig5.165 Engine immoblizer system 发动机停机系统

5.20 ABS and EBD 防抱死与电子动力分配

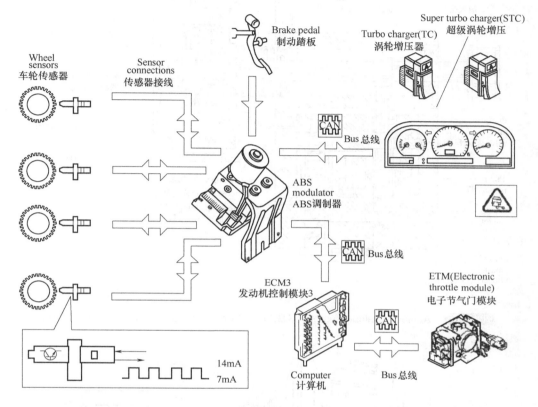

Fig5.166 Elements of a modern ABS system 现代防抱死制动系统的构成元件

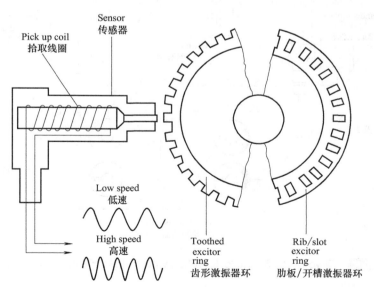

Fig5.167 Magnetic speed sensor and excitor 磁力速度传感器和激振器

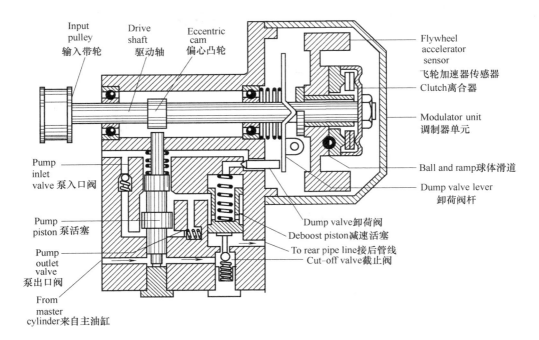

Fig5.168　Antilock braking system (ABS) for front wheel drive　前轮驱动防抱死系统

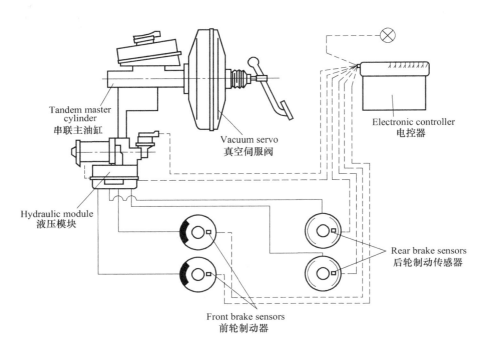

Fig5.169　Teves ABS IV anti-lock brake system　防抱死系统（Teves ABS IV）

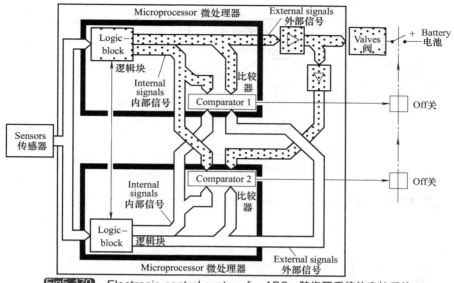

Fig5.170　Electronic control system for ABS　防抱死系统的电控系统

5.21　Airbag　安全气囊

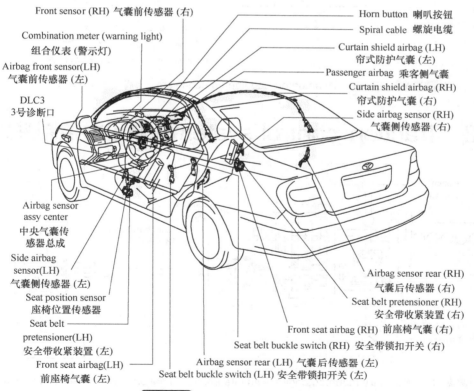

Fig5.171　SRS System　安全气囊系统

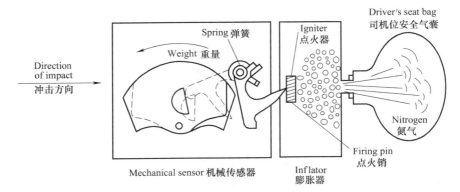

Fig5.172　Mechanically actuated bag firing mechanism　机械启动气囊点火机构

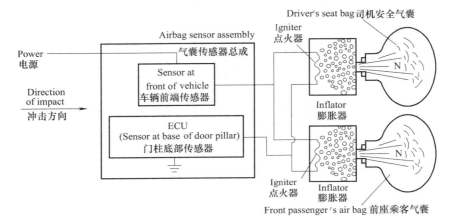

Fig5.173　Electrically actuated bag firing mechanism　电启动气囊点火机构

5.22 Traction control system　牵引力控制系统

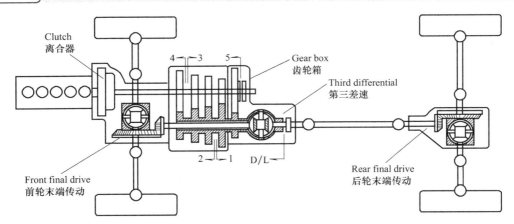

Fig5.174　Longitudinally mounted engine with integral front final drive four wheel drive system
整体前轮末端传动四轮驱动的纵向安装发动机

Chapter 5 Functional components 功能部件

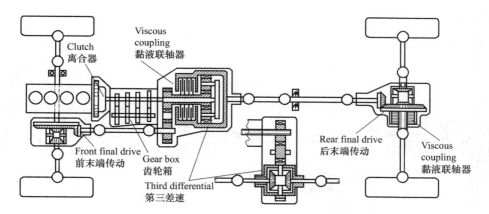

Fig5.175 Longitudinally mounted engine with independent front final drive four wheel drive system
独立前末端驱动四轮驱动系统的纵向安装发动机

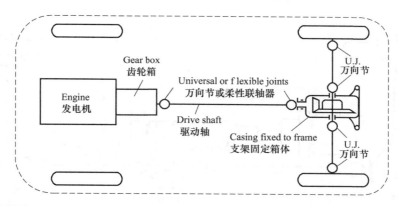

Fig5.176 A front engine and rear-wheel-drive layout with independent suspension
独立悬挂的前置发动机和后轮驱动布局

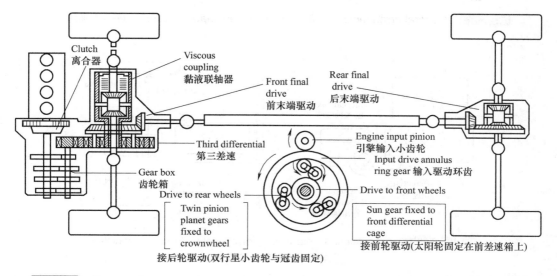

Fig5.177 Traversely mounted engine four wheel drive system 横置安装发动机四轮驱动系统

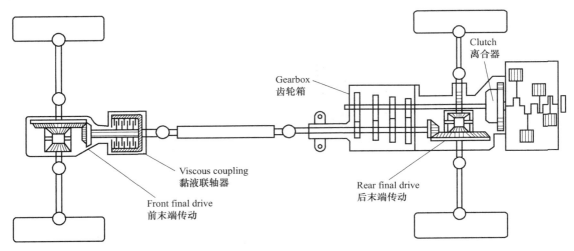

Fig5.178　Rear mounted engine four wheel drive system　后置安装发动机四轮驱动系统

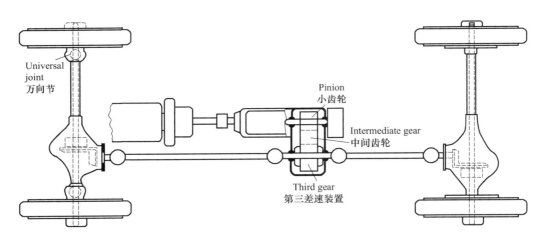

Fig5.179　General arrangement of four-wheel driven chassis　四轮驱动底盘的通用布局

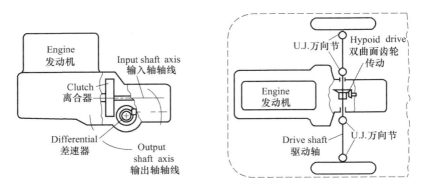

Fig5.180　An axleless transmission for a front-wheel-drive vehicle　前轮驱动车轮的无轴传动

Chapter 5 Functional components 功能部件   205

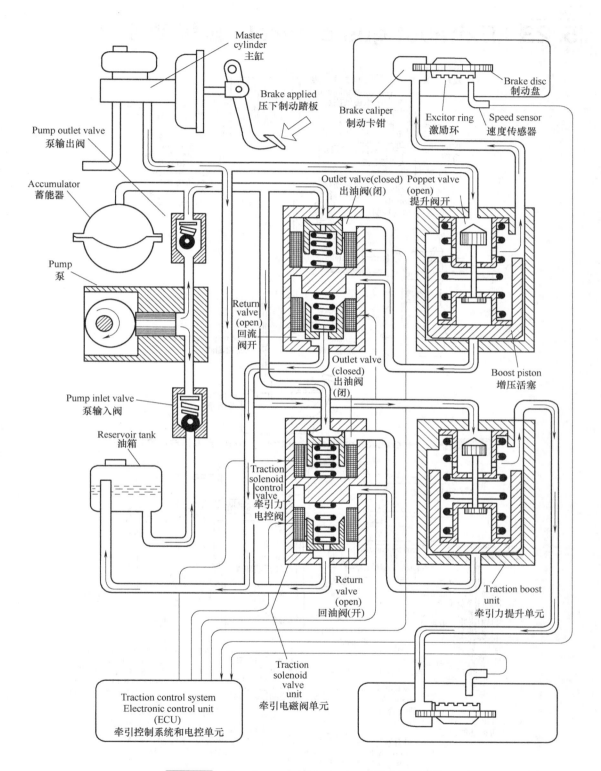

Fig5.181   Traction control system   牵引力控制系统

5.23 Exhaust gas control 废气控制

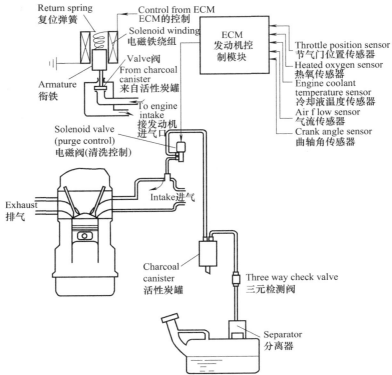

Fig5.182 Evaporative emissions control system 蒸发排放物控制系统

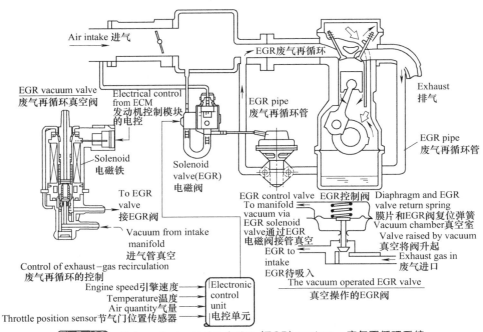

Fig5.183 Exhaust gas recirculation (EGR) system 废气再循环系统

Chapter 5 Functional components 功能部件

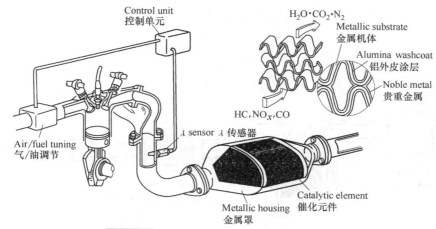

Fig5.184 Catalytic converter 催化转换器

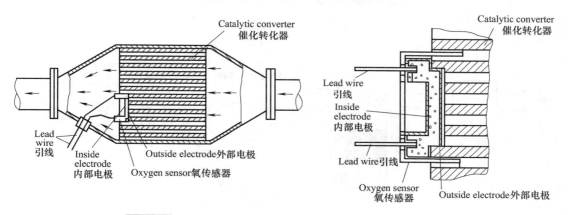

Fig5.185 Monolithic catalytic converter 整体式催化转化器

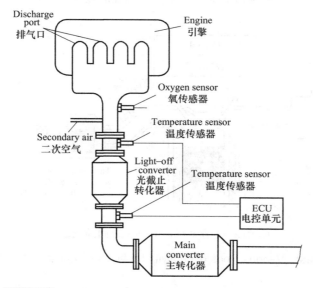

Fig5.186 Light-off catalytic converter 光截止催化转化器

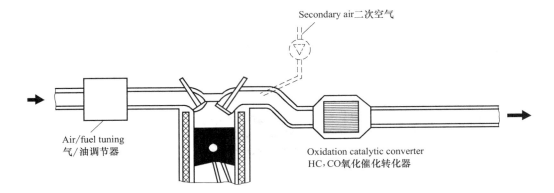

(a) One-way catalytic converter 一元催化转化器

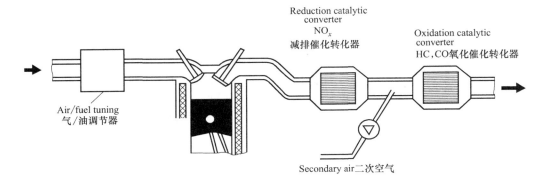

(b) Two-way catalytic converter 二元催化转化器

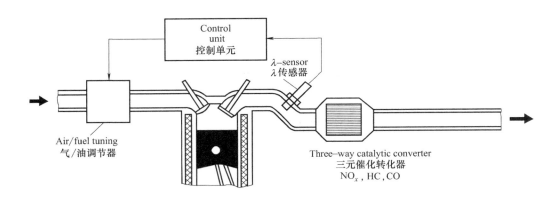

(c) Three-way catalytic converter 三元催化转化器

Fig5.187　Various types of catalytic converters　不同类型的催化转化器

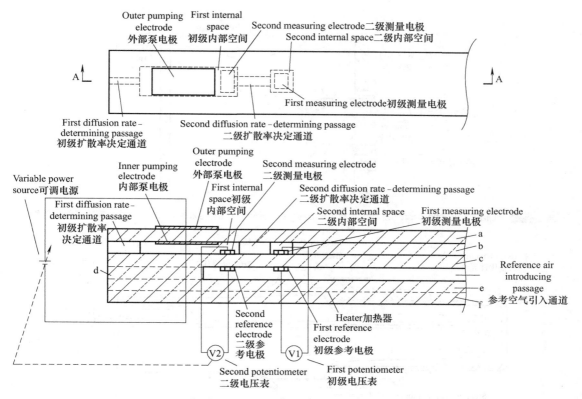

Fig5.188 NOₓ sensors used for monitoring the automotive exhaust gas
用于监测汽车尾气排放的 NOx 传感器
a~f: Solid electrolyte layers 固态电解质层

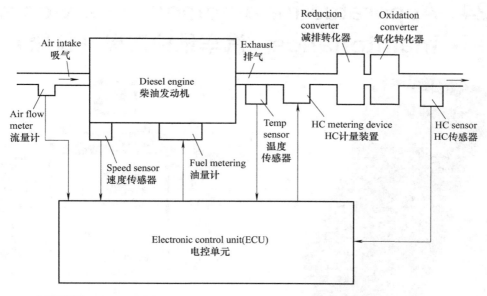

Fig5.189 A Diesel engine with an a exhaust system comprising an oxidation catalytic converter and/or a reduction catalytic converter
排气系统包含氧化和/或减排催化转化器的柴油发动机

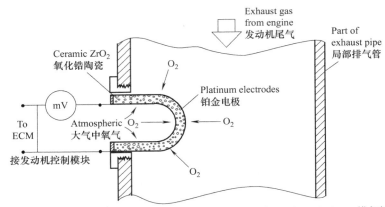

Fig5.190　Diagrammatic representation of the oxygen sensor in the exhaust pipe　排气管的氧传感器图解

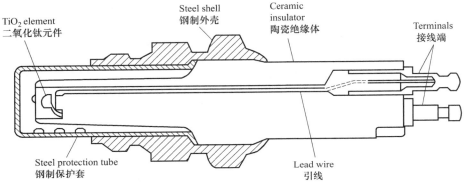

Fig5.191　The titanium dioxide (titania) type EGO sensor　二氧化钛型尾气氧传感器

5.24 Apparatus for automotive service and maintenance　汽车维护工具（仪器）

Fig5.192　Automobile decoder　汽车解码器

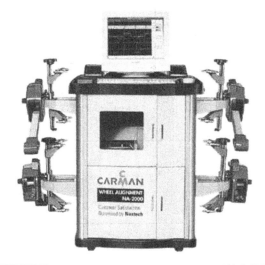

Fig5.193　Automobile 4-wheel aligner　四轮定位仪

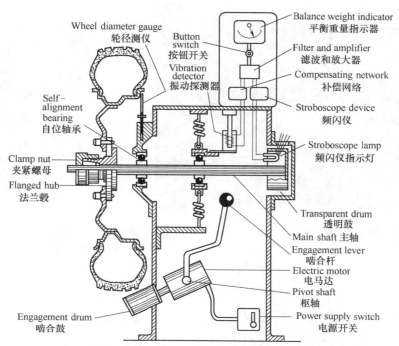

Fig5. 194　Wheel balancing machine which balances statically and dynamically in two different planes
在两个平面里实现静平衡和动平衡的车轮平衡机

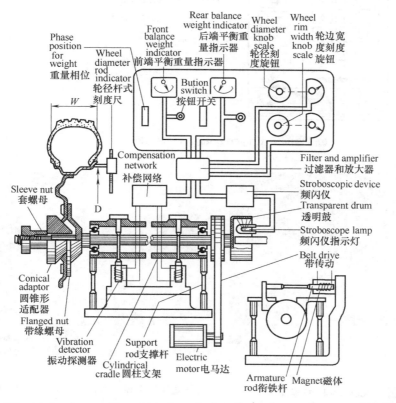

Fig5. 195　Wheel balancing machine which dynamically balances in two planes　两个平面动平衡的车轮平衡机

Fig5.196　Automobile oscilloscope　汽车示波器

Fig5.197　The Bosch PMS 100 portable oscilloscope　博世 PMS 100 袖珍型示波器

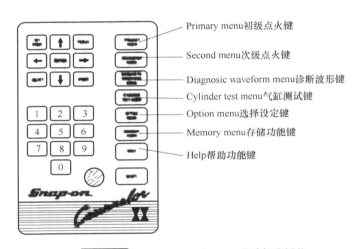

Primary menu 初级点火键
Second menu 次级点火键
Diagnosic waveform menu 诊断波形键
Cylinder test menu 气缸测试键
Option menu 选择设定键
Memory menu 存储功能键
Help 帮助功能键

Fig5.198　Engine analyzer　发动机分析仪

Fig5.199　Scan tool　扫描仪

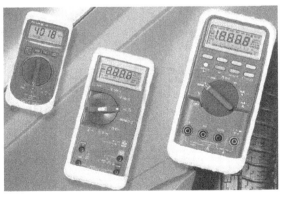

Fig5.200　Fluke digital multimeters　数字万用表

Chapter 5　Functional components　功能部件

Fig5. 201　The Bosch KTS 300 pocket system tester　博世 KTS300 袖珍型系统测试仪

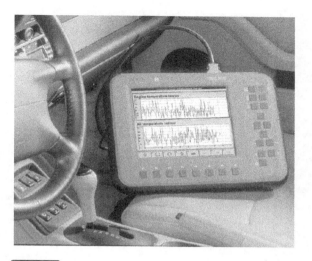

Fig5. 202　The Bosch KTS 500 control unit diagnosis tester 博世 KTS500 控制单元诊断测试仪

Chapter 1
Perspective view
汽车外观

Chapter 2
Engine
发动机

Chapter 3
Body
车身

Chapter 4
Chasis
底盘

Chapter 5
Functional components
功能部件

Chapter 6
Special-purpose vehicles
特种车辆

Chapter 7
Electric vehicles 电动汽车

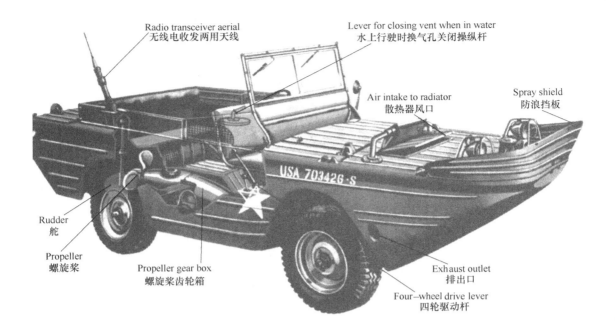

Fig6.1　Amphibian　水陆两用车

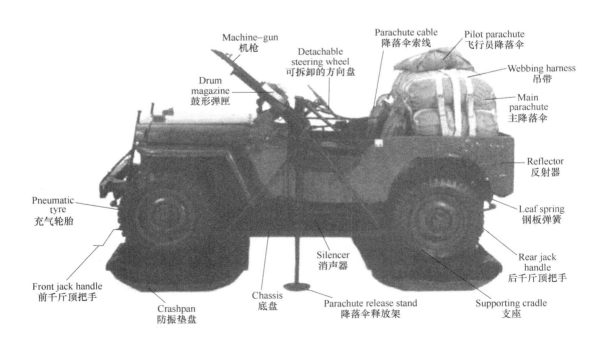

Fig6.2　Jeep　吉普车

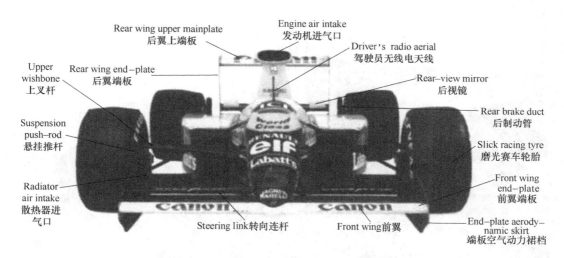

Fig6.3　Formula one racing car　一级方程式赛车

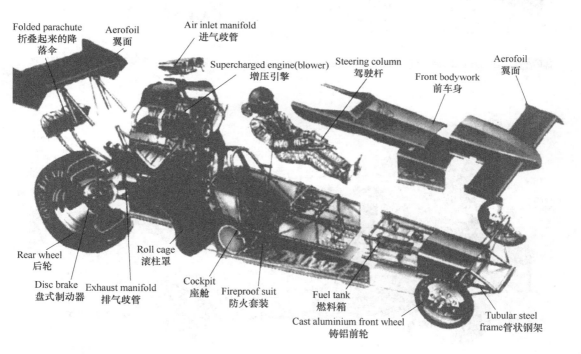

Fig6.4　Exploded view of a top-fuel dragster　高能燃料减重短程高速赛车分解图

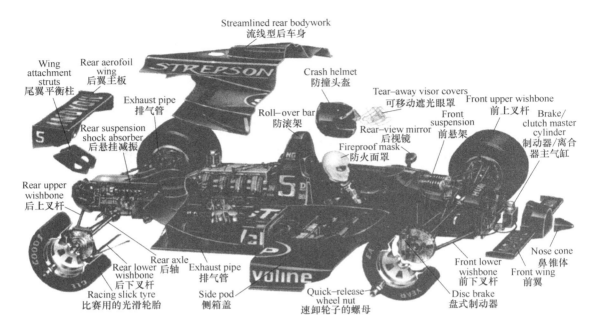

Fig6.5　Exploded view of a turbocharged, V-8 engine Indycar　涡轮增压 V-8 发动机英迪赛车分解图

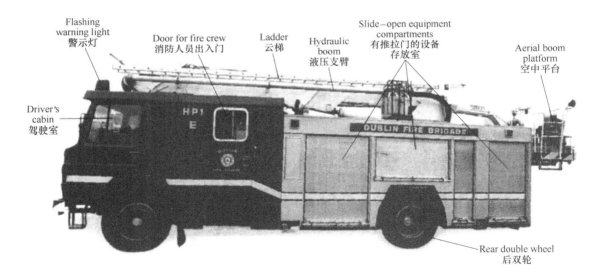

Fig6.6　Fire engine　消防车

Chapter 1
Perspective view
汽车外观

Chapter 2
Engine
发动机

Chapter 3
Body
车身

Chapter 4
Chassis
底盘

Chapter 5
Functional components
功能部件

Chapter 6
Special-purpose vehicles
特种车辆

Chapter 7
Electric vehicles
电动汽车

7.1 Types and structure of EV
电动车类型及其结构

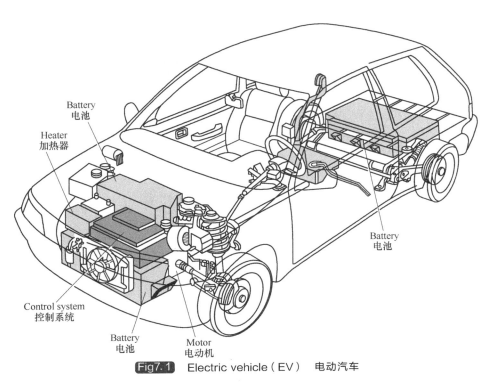

Fig7.1 Electric vehicle (EV) 电动汽车

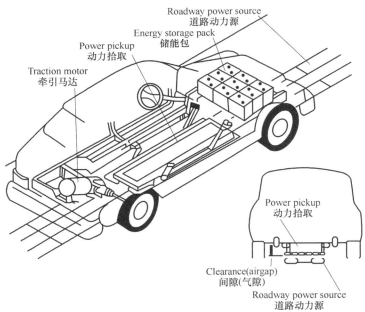

Fig7.2 Road-induced electricity 路面感应电动车

Chapter 7 Electric vehicles 电动汽车

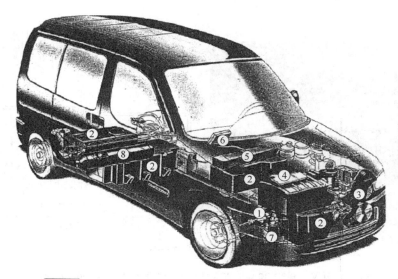

Fig7.3 Citroen Berlingo Dynavolt 雪铁龙 Berlingo 电动车
1—Electric motor and drive 电动车和驱动装置；2—Traction battery pack 牵引电池组；3—Generator set 发电机装置；4—Motor controller 马达控制器；5—Generator controller 发电机控制器；6—Drive programme selector 驱动程序选择面板；7—LPG regulator LPG 调节器；8—LPG storage tank LPG 储存箱

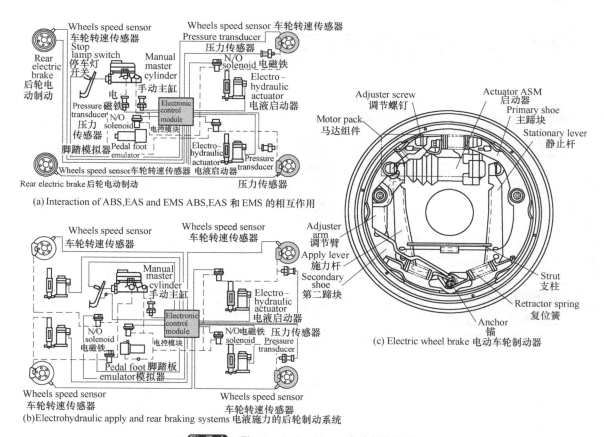

Fig7.4 Electronic braking 电动制动装置

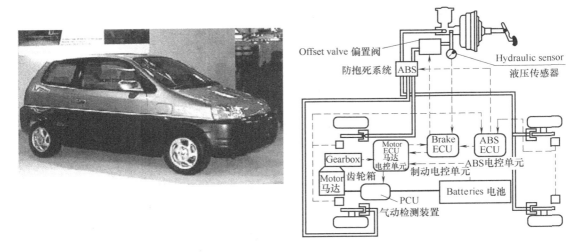

Fig7.5 Honda "EV" electric car and Honda regenerative braking/coasting system
本田电动车和本田再生制动/滑行系统

7.2 Battery system 电池系统

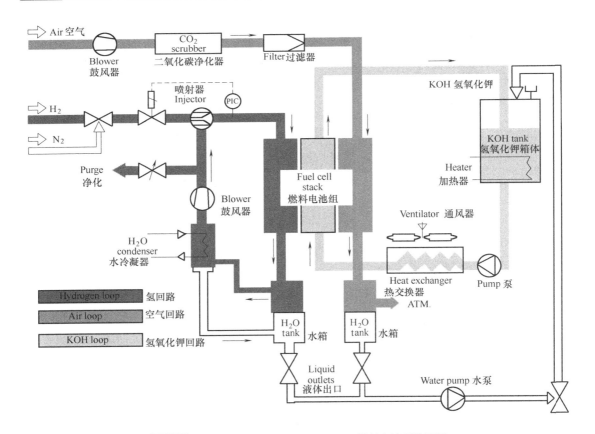

Fig7.6 Fuel-cell system schematic 燃料电池系统图解

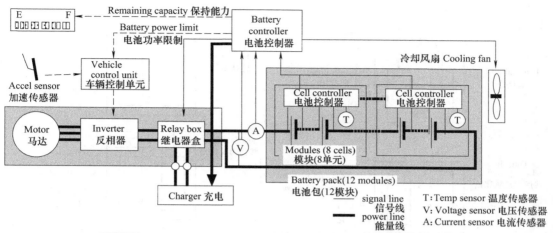

Fig7.7　Overall system configuration of cell　电池系统的总体构造

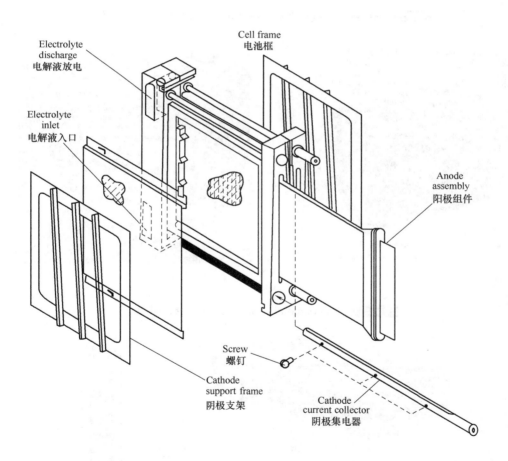

Fig7.8　Exploded view of aluminium/air bipolar battery　铝板/空气双极性电池爆炸图

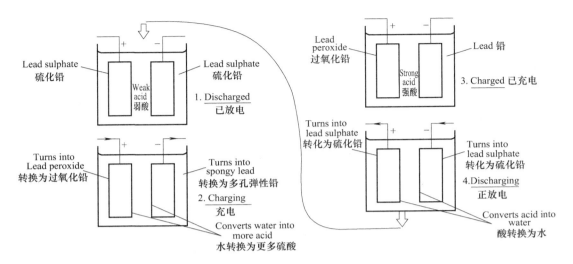

Fig7.9 Battery charge-discharge cycle 电池的充电/放电循环

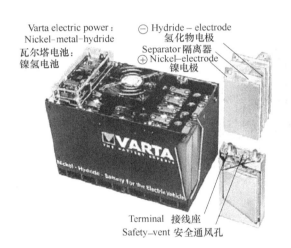

Fig7.10 Nickel-metal hydride battery 镍氢电池

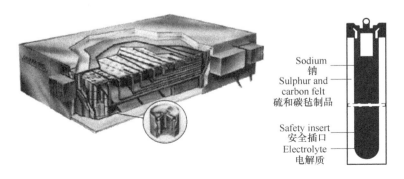

Fig7.11 Sodium-sulphur battery 钠硫电池

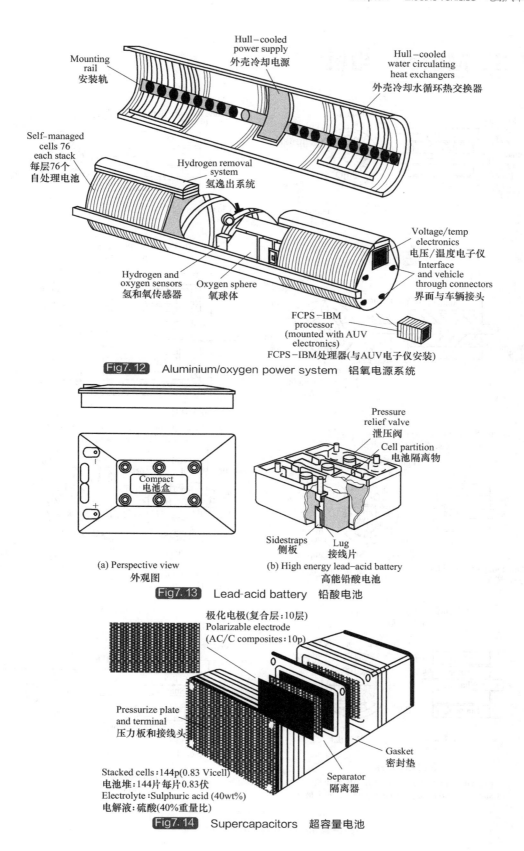

Fig7.12 Aluminium/oxygen power system 铝氧电源系统

(a) Perspective view
外观图

(b) High energy lead-acid battery
高能铅酸电池

Fig7.13 Lead-acid battery 铅酸电池

Fig7.14 Supercapacitors 超容量电池

7.3 Motor 电机

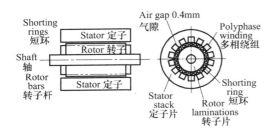

(a) Induction motor
感应电机

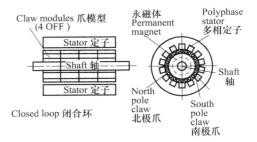

(b) Claw type PM magnet motor
爪形PM永磁电机

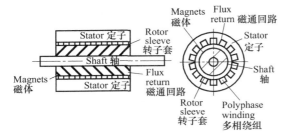

(c) Surface mounted PM magnet motor
端面安装的PM永磁电机

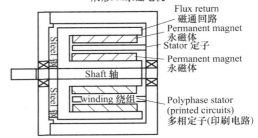

(d) UNIO type motor(Contentional construction)
欧式电机(欧洲大陆构造)

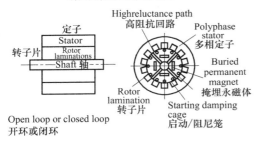

(e) Buried magnet motor(4 pole)
埋磁电机(4级)

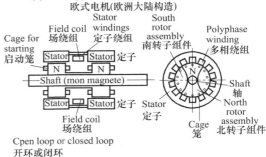

(f) Homopolar machine
同极电机

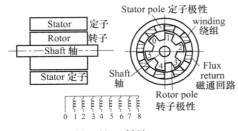

(g) Switched reluctance motor 开关磁阻电机
(8 Stator poles,6 rotor poles)(8定子极性,6转子极性)

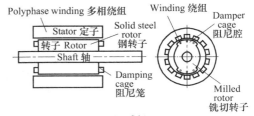

(h) Reluctance motor
磁阻电机

Fig7.15　Types of motors　电机类型

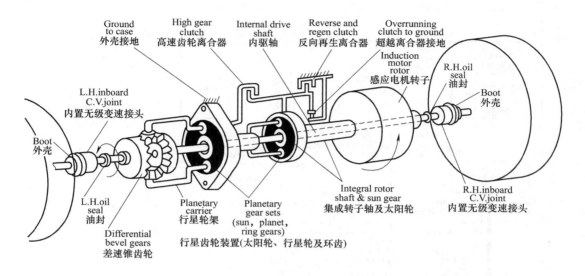

Fig 7.16 Ford EXT11 EV transaxle drive with coaxial motor
福特 EXT11 电动车传输轴驱动及同轴电机

7.4 Hybrid vehicle 混合动力车

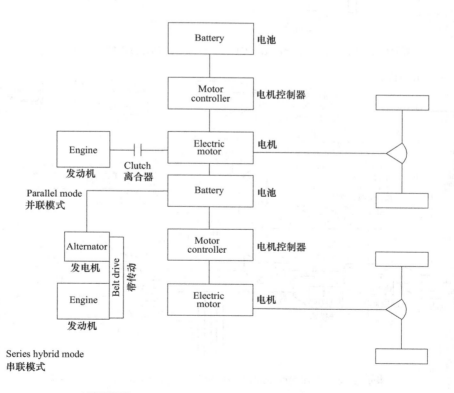

Fig 7.17 Bi-mode drive system 双模式驱动系统

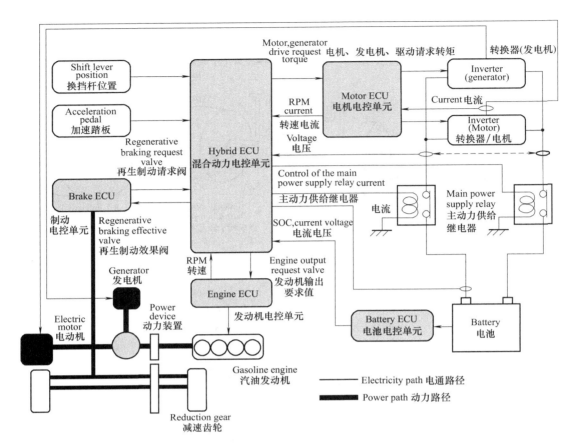

Fig7.18 Power-split control:ECU schematic 动力分离控制：电控单元方案

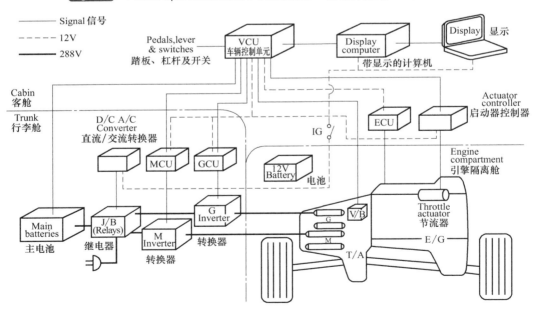

Fig7.19 Dual system:hybrid system 双重系统：混合动力系统

Chapter 7　Electric vehicles　电动汽车

(a) Parallel hybrid drive mechanism
并联混合动力机构

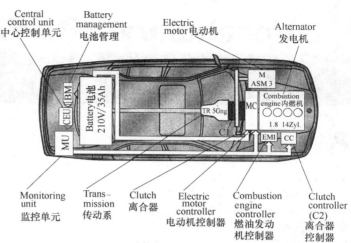

(b) BMW parallel hybrid drive　宝马并联混合动力驱动车

Fig 7.20　Map-controlled drive management　驱动控制管理平面图

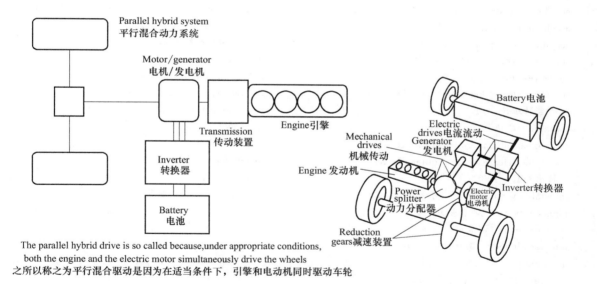

The parallel hybrid drive is so called because, under appropriate conditions, both the engine and the electric motor simultaneously drive the wheels
之所以称之为平行混合驱动是因为在适当条件下，引擎和电动机同时驱动车轮

(a) Structure　结构图　　　　(b) Layout of Toyota parallel hybrid drive vehicle
丰田平行混合动力汽车的布局

Fig 7.21　Parallel hybrid drive　平行混合驱动

Vocabulary with Figure Index
词汇及图形索引（英中对照）

A

ABS modulator ABS 调制器 199
AC oil bath cleaner AC 油池清洁器 42
A/C compressor 空调压缩机 8
A/C compressor clutch 空调压缩机离合器 33
A/C radiator fan switching 空调散热器风扇开关 33
accelerator control arm 加速控制杆 183
accelerator pedal 加速踏板 2, 22, 140, 183
accelerator pedal position sensor 加速踏板位置传感器 34
accelerator pedal switch 加速踏板开关 34
accelerator switch 加速器开关 183
accumulator 蓄电池，蓄能器 8, 90
active iron core 活动铁芯 49
active resistor 有源电阻 50
actuating sleeve dog clutch member 启动套齿形离合器组件 147
actuator 启动器 34
actuator air chamber 启动器气腔 178
adjustable release bearing outer sleeve 可调释放轴承外套 120
adjustable vertical strut 可调立柱 66
adjusted gasket 调整垫片 49
adjuster chain 调节链 180
adjuster plunger 调节柱塞 174
adjusting pawl 调节爪 174
adjustment nut 调节螺母 121
adjustment screw 调节螺钉 30
advance device 前进装置 17
aerial boom platform 空中平台 218
aerofoil 翼面 217
A-frame drawbar A 形架拖杆 108
after flow wake 尾流 60
air absorber 空气缓冲器 188
airbag sensor assembly 气囊传感器总成 202
airbag sensor rear 气囊后传感器 201
air bleed 渗气口 25

air cleaner 空气滤清器 33
air compressor 空气压缩机 51
air connection pipe 空气连接管 89
air cylinder 气缸 122
air drier 空腔干燥器 93
air filter 空气滤清器 8
air-flow meter 空气流量计 26
air-flow sensor flap 空气流量传感器叶片 40
air-flow sensor plate 空气流量传感器板 27
air-fuel control barrel 空气/燃油控制筒 14
air fuel ratio sensor 空燃比传感器 197
air funnel 空气漏孔 27
air inlet camshaft 进气凸轮轴 48
air inlet manifold 进气岐管 217
air inlet pipe 进气管 147
air intake control valve 进气控制阀 40
air intake to radiator 散热器风口 216
airmass 空气量 22
air pistion 空气活塞 122
air pump 空气泵 8
air reservoir tank 储气箱 122
air-temperature sensor 空气温度传感器 40
air thermo sensor 气温传感器 29
aligment hole for assembly 装配定位孔 45
alternator 交流发动机，发电机，发动机 8, 193, 229
aluminium cylinder head 铝缸盖 181
amphibian 水陆两用车 216
anchor block 锚定块 145
anchor pin 支撑销 171
anchor plunger 固定柱塞 174
angle plate 角铁 126
annular cylinder 环形油缸 188
annular gear 环齿 130, 131
annulus carrier 环形支架，环形架 127, 129
annulus ring gear 环形齿轮，环形内齿

127, 129
anti-lock brake system　防抱死系统　200
anti-roll bar　防滚动杆件，防转杆　73，79
anti-roll tube　防转杆　80
anti-stall stop　防止滞后挡块　19
armature　衔铁，电枢　26，49，169
armature rod　衔铁杆　211
armrest　扶手　58
articulating beam　活动梁　87
ascending valve spring seat　上气门弹簧座　48
atmospheric pressure　大气压力　6
atomised fuel　燃油雾化　23
attached flow　附着流体　60
audio system　音频系统　196

automatic belt tensioner　皮带自动张紧轮　8
automatic gearbox control system　自动变速箱控制系统　142
automatic transmission　自动变速器　134
automobile 4-wheel aligner　四轮定位仪　210
automobile decoder　汽车解码器　210
automobile oscilloscope　汽车示波器　212
auxiliary-air device　附属空气装置，空气附属装置　27，28
auxiliary counter gear cluster　附属反向联齿　128
axis of pivot　转枢轴　58
axle modulator　轴模块　186
axle shaft　半轴　68
axle tube　轴管　95

B

back closing valve　回油关闭阀　51
back-leak connection　后泄漏接头　9
back plate　后盖，背板　15，187
back tubing　回油管　31
backup light　倒车灯　141
back-up washer　支撑垫片　35
back window glass　后窗玻璃　58
balance beam　平衡梁　86
balance weight　平衡重　44
balance weight indicator　平衡重量指示器　211
ball-and-socket bearing　球窝轴承　126
ball and socket joint　球座接头　125
ball bearing　球轴承　118，184
ball cage　球体保持架　155
ball pin drive　球销传动　50
ball post　球形柱　122
ball track　球体滚道　157
ball-type selector　球形换挡手把　124
ball valve　球阀　18，129
band clamp　带式夹头　168
bar code label　条形码标签　4
barrel-shaped helical spring　柱形螺旋弹簧　75
barshaft　拉杆轴　192
base plate　垫板　77
battery supply　电源　141
bead core　轮胎胎芯　191
bead wire　胎缘钢丝　189
bead wrap　胎缘束　189
beam plate　梁板　105
bearing and hub carrier　轴承轮毂支架　83
bearing housing　轴承腔　83

bearing housing cover　轴承腔盖　120
bearing pin　轴承销　178，180
bearing support bracket　轴承支撑架　125
bell crank lever　钟形曲柄（杆）　86，90
belleville preload spring　锥形预载弹簧　168
bell housing facing　钟形腔端面　120
below still trundle patch　下止推片　44
belt drive　带传动　211
belt reel　卷带筒　194
bevel gear　锥齿轮　95
bevel pinion　小锥齿轮　106，152
bevel wheel　锥齿轮　106
bias spring　斜弹簧，偏转弹簧　173，187
biconical profile　双锥形结构　9
bi-mode drive system　双模式驱动系统　227
bleed plug　混气塞　24
bleed screw　渗漏螺钉，油口螺钉　122，175
bobweight　摆块　121
bobweight pivot　摆块转枢　121
body　阀体　26
bolt arm　螺栓臂　88
boost controller　增压控制器　19
boost piston　增压活塞　205
boost pressure　涡轮增压，增压　16，22
boot　行李箱，套管　2，122
boot pan　行李箱底板　69
Bosch snubber valve　博世减振阀　11
brace　扣件　74
brake disc　制动（碟）盘　74，83，205
brake applied　压下制动踏板　205
brake caliper　制动卡钳　205

brake drum　鼓式制动器，制动鼓　77，170
brake fluid reservoir　制动液储箱　170
brake light　制动灯　3
brake line　制动管路　170
brake pedal　制动踏板　2，199
brake system indicator　制动系统指示灯　195
brake valve slave cylinder　制动阀从动缸　183
breech plug　尾塞　10
bridge block　连接块　178
bridge pipe　连管　171
Broulhiet suspension　布萝立特悬架　95
brush holder　电刷架　49
brush holder cover　电刷架罩　193
built-up crankshaft　组合式曲轴　45
bulge water swell　膨胀水管　51
bulk head　前挡板　69
bump compression block　冲击压缩块　103
bump housing　冲击腔　103
bump stop　撞击挡块　89
bumper　保险杠　2
bumper bar　保险杠主杆　58
bumper beam　保险杠梁　57
bumper end cap　保险杠端帽　58
buried magnet motor　埋磁电机　226
butterfly brake valve　蝶形制动阀　183
button switch　按钮开关　211
bypass aperture　旁路小孔　38
bypass button　旁路钮　14
bypass groove　旁路通道　103

C

cable　拉绳　188
cable bracket　拉绳支架　188
calibration slide　调节滑块　26
caliper　卡钳，夹钳　170，178
caliper carrier　夹钳支架　180
cam ring　凸轮环　19
cam roller　凸轮滚子　17
camshaft　凸轮轴　8，51，15
camshaft identification sensor　凸轮轴识别传感器　33
camshaft position sensor　凸轮轴位置传感器　197
camshaft timing belt gear wheel　凸轮轴正时齿形带轮　48
cantilever torsion bar　悬臂扭杆　44
cantrail and roof panel　顶盖纵梁　57
capnut　顶部螺母　9
carbon canister　活性炭罐　33
carbon dam seal　碳块密封　12
carburetor　化油器　8
carrier bracket　托架　175
carrier retaining spring　支架复位弹簧　171
carrier strut　支架支柱　171
casing anchor bolt　箱体固定螺栓　80
casing cone clutch member　腔室锥形离合器组件　127
cast trailing arm　铸铁从臂　72
castellated nut　槽形螺母　105
catalytic converter　催化转化器　35，207
catalytic element　催化元件　207
cathode current collector　阴极集电器　223
cathode support frame　阴极支架　223
cell frame　电池框　223
center bolt　中心螺栓　77
center pillar　中柱　56
center ventilator　中央出风口　196
central control unit　中心控制单元　229
central double yoke member　中心双架组件　155
central ring　中心环　89
centre bearing　中间支承　155
ceramic button　陶瓷钮　119
chafer　防擦层　189
chain sprocket wheel　腹板链轮　180
charcoal canister　活性炭罐　206
charging system indicator　充电系统指示灯　195
chassis　机壳，汽车底盘，底盘　49，71，216
chassis bracket　底盘支架　52
chassis sidemember　底盘侧面件　106
check valve　检测阀　30
choke　阻风门　2
circuit opening relay　开路继电器　29
circular disc　圆盘　45
circular disc crankweb　圆盘曲柄臂　45
circular filter gauze　环形过滤纱网　31
circlip　卡圈　155
clasp　卡环　49
claw type PM magnet motor　爪形PM永磁电机　226
climate control　空调控制开关　196
closure cap　封闭盖　101
closure plate　盖板　103
clutch　离合器　3，118，200，229
clutch actuator cylinder　离合器启动缸　133
clutch bell-housing　离合器外罩　123

clutoh controuer 离合器控制器 229
clutch disc 离合器主动盘 118
clutch housing 离合器壳 118
clutch lining 离合器衬垫 140
clutch pedal 离合器踏板 2, 122, 183
clutch release mechanism 离合器脱开机构 136
clutch release rod 离合器分离推放杆 123
clutch slave cylinder 离合器分泵 123
clutch switch 离合器开关 183
coarse nylon filter 粗尼龙过滤 18
cockpit 座舱 217
coil （点火）线圈 8, 26
coil spring 螺栓弹簧，螺旋弹簧 79, 95
cold start injector 冷启动喷嘴 26
collapsible steering tube 可调转向柱 160
collar 颈圈，套 11, 74
combustion engine controller 燃油发动机控制器 229
comet combustion chamber 彗星燃烧室 6
compact trailing arm rear axle 紧凑型纵向臂后轴 72
companion yoke 结合叉 124
compensation flap 补偿翼 38
compensation jet 补偿喷嘴 23
compensation network 补偿网络 211
compensation ring 补偿环 95
compensation flap 补偿叶片 40
compliant mount 适应安装垫 98
compound epicycle gear train 复合行星齿轮轮系 127
compression pressure 压缩压力 6
compressive strain 压缩应变 50
concentrate colander 集滤器 51
condenser 冷凝器，电容器 112, 193
condenser coil 冷凝器蛇形管 115
condenser unit 冷凝器单元 115
cone 锥体 126
cone clutch 锥形离合器 142
conical adaptor 圆锥形适配器 211
conical diffuser 锥形扩散器 16
conical piston 锥形活塞 84
conical portion 锥形口 126
connecting cable 连接缆绳 194
connecting rod 连杆 8
connecting-rod body 连杆体 44, 48
connecting-rod bolt 连杆螺栓 44
connecting-rod top 连杆盖 44, 48
constant gear wheel 恒定齿轮 144
constant mesh gearbox 常啮合齿轮箱 126
constant mesh gear 常啮合齿轮 144~146
constant velocity universal joint 恒速万向节 83

contact plate 接触板 49
control fork 控制叉 15
control lever 控制杠杆，操纵杆 95, 188
control link 控制连杆 156
control panel 控制面板 96
control panel display 控制面板 196
control plunger 控制柱塞 27
control rack 控制齿条 14
control rod 控制杆 13, 15
control rod bracket 控制杆支架 15
control rod travel adjustment screw 控制杆行程调节螺钉 13
control shaft 控制轴 15
control slide 控制滑块 50
control unit 控制单元 36
converter 变矩器 134
converter（housing）cover 变矩器壳 134
convertible 敞篷车 56
coolant 冷却水 8
coolant pump 冷却液泵 8
coolant temperature gauge 冷却液温度表 58
coolant temperature sensor 冷却剂温度传感器 35
cooler duct 冷却器管 59
cooling circuit 冷却回路 158
cooling fan 冷却风扇 8
cooling system 冷却系统 51
core 芯套 26
corner channel 拐角通道 104
corrugated tube 波纹管 160
countershaft 中间轴，反轴 124, 128
coupe 双门小轿车 56
coupling head for brake 制动连接头 186
coupling jaw 连接爪 104
cover drive 驱动端盖 49
cover plate 罩板 118
cover pressing 冲压盖 121
cover sheet 盖板 77
crank angle sensor 曲轴角传感器 206
crankcase 曲轴箱 114
crankcase breather connection 曲轴箱吸气接头 42
cranked cross-pin arm 弯曲横销臂 149
crankshaft 曲轴 8, 44, 114, 121
crankshaft position sensor 曲轴位置传感器 34, 197
crankshaft sensor 曲轴传感器 35
crankshaft speed 曲轴转速 22
crankshaft timing belt gear wheel 曲轴正时齿形带轮 48

crankshaft timing gear 曲轴正时齿轮 44
crash helmet 防撞头盔 218
crashpan 防振垫盘 216
cross-member 横向杆件，横跨件，叉形件 69，73，94
cross member under seat 后座下横梁 56
cross member under windshield 前窗下横梁 56
cross-pin member 十字销组件 85
cross-shaft release lever 交叉轴释放杆 120
crown wheel 冠齿轮盘 148
crown wheel flange 冠齿轮盘法兰 147
crown wheel mounting flange 冠齿安装法兰 150

cruise control 巡航控制 20，197
cup seal 杯形密封 25
cup thrust plate 杯形推力板 149
curtain shield airbag 帘式防护气囊 201
cushioning rubber block 缓冲橡胶块 105
cut-off valve 截止阀 200
cylinder 气缸，筒体 8，147
cylinder block 气缸体 8
cylinder head 气缸盖，缸头 8，114
cylinder test menu 气缸测试键 212
cylinder wall 缸壁 114
cylindrical cradle 圆柱支架 211

D

damper bump valve 阻尼器撞击阀 99
damper cage 阻尼腔 226
damper rebound valve 阻尼反弹阀 99
damper valve assembly 阻尼阀组件 102
damping cage 阻尼笼 226
damping chamber 阻尼室 40
dashboard 仪表板 2
dash-light 仪表板灯 195
dash panel 前围板，仪表板架 57，69
dashpot 冲击口 19
deboost piston 减速活塞 200
decel timing assembly 减速正时组件 40
decel timing chamber 减速正时腔 40
decoupled strut mount 可拆解滑柱座 72
DeDion tube 蒂带管 82
deflected airstream 偏转气流 66
deflector side baffle 偏转板侧隔板 66
delivery valve 供液阀，供气阀 92，181
detachable cover 可拆盖罩 42
detachable steering wheel 可拆卸的方向盘 216
diagnosic waveform menu 诊断波形键 212
diagnostic light 故障灯 141
diagnostic socket 诊断口 35，169
diagonal radius rod 斜置转杆 82
diaphragm 膜片，薄膜 19，30
diaphragm and self seating valve assembly 薄膜-自位阀组件 35
diesel engine 柴油机 115
diesel filter 柴油滤清器 31
diesel tank 柴油箱 31
differential 差速器 68，147
differential assembly 差速器组件 152
differential bevel gear 差速锥齿轮 227

differential casing 差速箱 75
differential gearing 差动齿轮
differential lock mechanism 差速锁止机构 147
differential pressure sampling point 压差采样点 33
differential pressure transducer 压差传感器 33
diffuser 扩散板 59
digital ignition system 数字点火系统 38
dimpled 浅凹 130
dipped headlight 近光灯 3，195
direct-drive engagement 直接驱动啮合 126
direct injection 直喷装置 11，23
direct pad 直接驱动垫 175
direct piston 直接驱动活塞 175
dirt excluder 排脏器 171
dirt shield 脏物防护罩 171
disc brake 盘式制动器 217
disc discharge valve 排气碟阀 182
discharge ball retainer 出油球保持器 25
discharge check ball 出油检测球 25
discharge disc valve 卸荷碟阀 182
discharge line 卸载管，排出管线 114，116
discharge nozzle 卸荷喷嘴 23
discharge passage 出油通道 25
discharge port 排出口 116
discharge valve 排出阀 116
disc inlet valve 进气碟阀 182
DIS coil 直喷火花塞线圈 33
displacer chamber 抽气室 84
distributor 分电器 8，38，193
distributor breaker lead 分电器断路导线 193
distributor cap 分电器盖 193
distributor cover 分配器端盖 38
distributor housing 分电器壳体 193

distributor port 配油口 17
distributor rotor 配油转子 18
dog clutch member 齿形离合器组件 126
dog clutch sliding hub 齿形离合器滑动轮毂 128
dog clutch teeth 齿形离合器轮齿 142，144
door 车门 2
door control receiver 车门控制接收器 198
door lock 车门钥匙 195
door lock control system 门锁控制系统 198
double acting cylinder 双作用缸 170
double acting cylinder expander 双作用缸膨胀器 170
double bulkhead 双重隔板 57
double hooke's type constant velocity joint 双万向节恒速接头 155
double ignition loop 双点火线圈 36
double planetary gears 双行星齿轮 131
double wishbone suspension 双叉形件悬架 77
dowel 销 74
dowel pin 销钉，定位销 13，45
DPA pump DPA 泵 17
drag link ball joint 拉杆球节头 108
drain plug 排漏塞 16
draw beam 受拉梁 105
draw link assembly 拉动组件 171
drawbar eye 拖杆孔 105

drill hole 钻削孔 102
drive block 驱动块 120
drive coupling 传动联轴器 14
drive cover slot 驱动盖槽 120
drive gear 驱动齿轮 124
drive plate 驱动板 119
driver's function switch 司机功能开关 93
driver's seat bag 司机位安全气囊 202
drive shaft 驱动轴，传动轴 17，155，200
drive shaft coupling flang 驱动轴联轴法兰 131
drive spindle 驱动轴 180
driven plate 从动板 121
drop arm 升降臂 160
drum brake 鼓式制动器 171
drum magazine 鼓形弹匣 216
dubonnet suspension 杜蒳悬架 95
duct 分管路 50
dump valve 卸荷阀 200
dump valve lever 卸荷阀杆 200
duration spring 工作弹簧 25
dust bellow 防尘套 101
dust cover 防尘盖 175
dust proof packing 防尘密封垫 193
dust tube 防尘管 73

E

eccentric 偏心件 188
eccentric cam 偏心凸轮 200
eccentric liner 偏心衬套 18
eccentric shaft 偏心轴 167
eccentric shaft peg 偏心轴销 167
eccentric yoke 偏心轮架 129
ECU socket 电控单元插口 38
edge 边缘，边口 104
edge filter 边口过滤器 11
EGR control 废气再循环控制 20
EGR pipe 废气再循环管 206
EGR vacuum valve 206
EGR valve 废气（再）循环阀 33，34
elastic rear bearing 后部弹性轴承 76
elastic ring 弹簧环 101
elastomer spring 弹性体弹簧 74
elastomer tube 弹性管 100
electric eddy current type retarder 电涡流类缓速器 185
electric fuel pump 电动燃油泵 26，27，36

electric motor 电马达，电机，电动机 211，227，229
electric motor controller 电动机控制器 229
electric servo unit 电伺服单元 169
electric vehicle 电动汽车 220
electric wheel brake 电动车轮制动器 221
electrical connection 电接头，电气接头 22，40，194
electrically actuated bag firing mechanism 电启动气囊点火机构 202
electrically adjustable steering column 电动可调节转向柱 162
electrical power steering system 电动转向系统 169
electrical supply 电源 13
electrolyte 电解质 224
electromagnetic switch 电磁开关 49
electronic clock 电子时钟 58
electronic controlled transmission system 电子控制变速系统 141
electronic controller 电控器 200

electronic control unit　电子控制单元　20
electronic fuel injection system　电子燃油喷射系统　29
electronic module　电子模导体　141
electronic transmission control　电子传动控制　33
electronic transmission control unit　传动电控单元　133
electronic vacuum regulator　电子真空调节器　33
emission control label　排放控制标签　4
emulsion block　乳化囡　24
end cover　端盖　49
end float spring and plunger　端部浮动弹簧柱塞　163
end of the striking arm　接触臂末端　124
end plate　端盘，边板，尾板　18，59
end seal cover　端部密封盖　25
energy absorber　吸能元件　57
energy storage pack　储能包　220
engagement lever　啮合杆　211
engagement striking finger　拨挡杆　125
engine analyzer　发动机分析仪　212
engine bonnet　发动机罩　2
engine compartment　发动机舱，引擎隔离舱　112，228
engine coolant temperature　发动机冷却液温度　195
engine coolant temperature sensor　引擎冷剂温度传感器　33，197
engine cover　发动机盖罩　59
engine flywheel　发动机飞轮　37
engine front end panel　发动机罩前支撑板　56
engine foot　发动机地脚　52
engine immoblizer system　发动机停机系统　198
engine load　引擎加载　37
engine load sensor　发动机载荷传感器　141
engine mount arm　引擎安装臂　53
engine oil cleaner　机油滤清器　51
engine oil cooler　机油冷却器　51
engine oil pressure gauge　机油油压表　196
engine oil pump　引擎润滑油泵　183
engine revolution counter　发动机转速表　2
engine speed sensor　发动机速度传感器，引擎速度传感器　34，93，133，197

engine support cross member　发动机支撑横梁　56
engine unit　引擎单元　133
enhancer　提升器　194
epicyclic rear steering box　行星齿轮后转向盒　167
equalization chamber　平衡腔　100
equalizer　平衡臂　188
estate car　旅行车　56
estate wagon　客货两用轿车　56
evaporator coil　蒸发器蛇形管　115
evaporator unit　蒸发器单元　115
excess fuel delivery piston　额外供油活塞　19
excess fuel linkage pin　过油连接销　19
excess fuel shaft　额外燃油轴　13
excess fuel solenoid　额外燃油电磁铁　13
excitor ring　激励环　205
exhaust valve　出口阀　122
exhaust bypass valve　排气旁路阀　43
exhaust camshaft　排气凸轮轴　48
exhaust gas recirculation system　废气再循环系统　206
exhaust manifold　排气（岐）管　183，217
exhaust outlet　排出口　216
exhaust pipe　排气管　9，218
exhaust port　排气口　7
exhaust pressure　排气压力　6
exhaust solenoid valve unit　排气电磁阀　93
exhaust valve　排气门　8，48
expander band　膨胀器带　145
expander housing　膨胀器腔体　173
expansion element　膨胀元件　14
expansion valve　膨胀阀　113
explosion pressure　爆炸压力　6
extended side panel　侧板延伸板　66
extension arm　延展臂　75
external teeth　外齿　126
extra air tank　补气腔　89
eye bolt　穿孔销　105
eye bolt adjuster　眼孔调节螺栓　79
eye bolt pin　螺栓孔销　121
eye-type joint　眼孔接头　100

F

face cam　端面凸轮　109
fan　风扇　8
fan belt　风扇皮带　8
fascia　罩面　57
fastback configuration　快速后背构形　64

feed port　进油口　11
field frame　磁场框架　49
filler plug　加油塞　134
filter paper element　滤纸件　16
filter screen　过滤网　14

fin 鳍板 116
final drive casing 末端驱动箱体 95
final drive crown wheel gear 末端传动冠齿轮 131
final drive 主减速器 3，68
final reduction gear 末端减速齿轮 152
fine wire 细丝 42
finger 凸出齿 126
fire engine 消防车 218
fireproof suit 防火套装 217
firing pin 点火销 202
fixed annular ring gear 固定周边环齿 167
fixed calliper 固定弯脚器 74
fixed detector block 固定探测块 168
fixed dog clutch member 固定啮合齿组件 147
fixed outboard joint 固定外置接头 192
fixed pivot 固定转枢 22
fixing point 固定点 73
flange 法兰 74
flanged dog clutch teeth member 边缘齿形离合器轮齿 147
flanged hub 法兰毂 211
flanged nut 带缘螺母 211
flanged universal joint coupling 法兰万向节联轴器 148
flap 侧板，副翼 59
flashing warming light 警示灯 218
flexible-ring joint 柔性环接头 156
flexible stabilizer 柔性稳定器 128
flipper 鳍边 191
floating adjuster link 浮动调节器杆 170
floating calliper 浮动夹钳 187
floating mainshaft 浮动主轴 128，132
floating shuttle valve 浮动梭形阀 109
floor pan 地板盘 69
floor valve 底部阀口 99
flow control valve 流量控制阀 165
flow reattachment 流体附着 60
flow separation 流体分离，气流分离 60
fluid 流体 52
fluid coupling 液力偶合器 134
fluid friction coupling 流体摩擦偶合器 135
fluke digital multimeter 数字万用表 212
flux plate 流出板 184
flux return 磁通回路 226
flyweight 飞轮重物块 15
flywheel 飞轮 8，44，118，134
flywheel accelerator sensor 飞轮加速器传感器 200
flywheel bolt 飞轮螺栓 44

flywheel drum 飞轮鼓 135
fog lamp 雾灯 3
foot brake switch 脚刹开关 93
foot control valve 脚控阀 183，185
foot-operated parking brake 脚动驻车制动器 188
foot wheel 脚轮 106
fork arm 叉臂 147
fork control lever 叉形控制杆 15
fork operating lever 叉形操作杆 122
fork prong 叉耙 180
formula one racing car 一级方程式赛车 217
forward clutch 前行离合器 130
forward multiplate clutch 前行多盘离合器 130
forward planetary gear set 前行行星齿轮装置 137
four-cylinder in-line engine 四缸直列发动机 7
four-door saloon 四门轿车 56
four-wheel drive lever 四轮驱动杆 216
four-wheel drive vehicle 四轮驱动多用汽车 56
friction lining 摩擦片，耐摩擦衬垫 171，188
friction thrust washer 摩擦推力垫片 181
friction washer 摩擦垫片 119
front actuator 前启动器 96
front axle 前轴 71
front bearing 前轴承 49，124
front brake sensor 前制动传感器 200
front cross member 前横梁 56
front door courtesy switch 前门踏步灯开关 198
front final drive 前轮末端传动 202
front fog light 前雾灯 195
front height and levelling strut actuator 前高度水平支柱启动器 92
front jack handle 前千斤顶把手 216
front levelling control solenoid valve 前水平控制电磁阀 92
front light 前照灯 3
front lower wishbone 前下叉杆 218
front pillar 前柱 56
front roof bow 顶盖前横梁 56
front screen pillar 前风挡立柱 57
front seat airbag 前座椅气囊 201
front side member 前纵梁 56
front spring shackle pin 前弹簧固锁销 108
front stiffening solenoid valve 前刚性电磁阀 92
front suspension 前悬架，前悬挂 3，84，218
front upper wishbone 前上叉杆 218
front wheel 前车轮 3
front wheel arrester 前轮制动器 3
front wing assy 前翼组件 59

fuel 燃油 195
fuel accumulator 燃油蓄能器 26
fuel adjustment plate 燃油量调节板 18
fuel control 燃油控制 20
fuel cut-off slave cylinder 燃油截止从动缸 183
fuel delivery 燃油喷出 11
fuel distributor 燃油分配器 26
fuel enter 油入口 10
fuel filter 燃油过滤器，油滤 27，33
fuel gauge 油量表 2
fuel injector 燃油喷嘴 33
fuel inlet 燃料（油）入口 9，14
fuel metering 油量计 209
fuel pressure regulator 燃油压力调节器，燃油调压器 26，30，32
fuel pressure regulator assembly 燃油压力调节器组件 35
fuel pump relay 油泵继电器 33
fuel rail 燃油轨道 33
fuel tank 燃油箱 27，217
fuel temperature sensor 燃油温度传感器 34
fuse block 熔断丝 195

gaiter 套管 159
gallery duct 主管路 50
Gardner injector 加德纳喷油器 10
garter spring 自紧弹簧 135
gas main spring 气体主阀 99
gas-filled equalization chamber 充气平衡腔 99
gasoline pump 汽油泵 9
gasoline tank 汽油箱 9
gauze filter washer 薄过滤垫 10
gauze strainer 薄网过滤器 50
gearbox assembly 变速器总成 155
gearbox casing 变速箱盒 123
gearbox mainshaft 齿轮箱主轴 185
gearbox splined output shaft 齿轮箱花键输出轴 184
gear bush bearing 齿轮套轴承 145
gear change position switch 齿轮挡位开关 197
gear knob 换挡杆手柄 123
gear lever 变速杆，换挡杆，齿轮（操纵）杆 2，123，126
gear pump 齿轮泵 14
gear selector fork 变速叉 123
gear shift lever 齿轮换挡杆，齿轮换挡手把 125
gear stick 齿轮操纵杆 129
gear type pump 齿轮泵 50
generator 发电机 8
generator controller 发电机控制器 221
generator set 发电机装置 221
gimbat bracket 万向支架 86
Girling suspension 格林悬架 95
glove box 储物箱 196
glove compartment 手套箱 2
governor 调节器 31
governor arm 调节臂 17
governor assembly 调节器组件 22
governor cage 调节器壳体 15
governor link rod 调节器连杆 183
governor plunger 调节柱塞 14
governor plunger tube 调速柱塞管 182
governor spring 调节器弹簧 15，17
governor valve 调节阀 181
governor weight 调节器配重 14，17
grease fitting 润滑脂嘴 77
grip spring 夹紧弹簧 177
groove 沟槽 101，125
guide 气门导管 39
guide arm 导引臂 90
guide core 导芯 134
guide pin bolt 导销螺栓 176
guide roller 导向滚子 163
guide slot 导（向）槽 163，174

half band expander 半圆带状膨胀器 145
half eccentric 局部离心块 178
half socket housing 半座腔 168
hand brake expander housing 手刹膨胀腔 171
hand brake lever 手动制动杆 173，187
hand brake switch 手刹开关 93
handbrake 驻车制动器（手刹） 2，68
handle 车门把手，手闸 2，170
hand-operated parking brake 手动驻车制动器 188
hardened steel plate 淬硬钢板 98
harness connector 电气配线接头 37
hatchback 仓门式后背车身小客车 56

hatchback configuration 天窗背式构形 64
hazard warning flasher 危险警告灯 196
hazard warning lamp 危急报警闪光灯 195
head location fitting 头部固定配件 18
headrest 头枕 59
heat exchanger 热交换器 184
heat shield 绝热垫 171
heated oxygen sensor 加热型氧传感器 197
heater 加热器 2
heater machine 暖风机 51
heater machine penstock 暖风机进水管 51
heavy-duty drum brake 重载鼓式制动器 171
HEGO sensor 排气氧传感器 33
height sensor 高度传感器 92
helical grease groove 螺旋润滑槽 168
hexagonal bolt 六角螺栓 74
hexagonal nut 六角螺母 101
high beam indicator 远光指示灯 195
high gear clutch 高速齿轮离合器 227
high pressure pipeline 高压油管 31
high pressure valve jumper 高压阀跳开器 129
highreluctancepath 高阻抗回路 226
hinge 铰链 66
hinge joint 铰接头 125
hinge pin 转销 176

hole type nozzle 孔式喷油器 10
hollow worm 空心蜗杆轴 149
homopolar machine 同极电动 226
hoop bolt 加箍螺栓 77
horn 喇叭 2，195
horn button 喇叭按钮 201
hourglass worm 沙漏形蜗杆 161
housing 壳体 124
housing cover 腔盖 120
hubcap 轮毂罩 2
hybrid system 混合动力系统 228
hybrid vehicle 混合动力车 227
hydraulic boom 液压支臂 218
hydraulic control unit 油压控制单元 131
hydraulic cylinder 液压缸 127
hydraulic damper 液压减振器 53
hydraulic head 液压头 18
hydraulic module 液压模块 200
hydraulic pipeline 液压管件 96
hydraulic pistion 液压活塞 122
hydraulic pump 液压泵 92，96
hydraulic switch 油压开关 51
hydraulic type retarder 液压式缓速器 185
hydraullc annulus seal 油压环形密封圈 147

IC regulator IC 调节器 193
idle air control valve 急速空气控制阀 35
idle by-pass valve actuator 急速旁路阀启动器 26
idle fuelling adjustment screw 急速燃油调节螺钉 39
idle gear 惰轮 49
idle shaft 惰轴 28
idle speed actuator 急速启动器 36
idle speed adjusting screw 急速调节螺钉 27
idle speed control valve 急速控制阀 33
idle spring pack 急速弹簧壳体 14
idling air passage 急速空气通道 38
idling spring 惰簧 17
ignition coil 点火线圈 35，193
ignition key 点火钥匙 198
ignition loop 点火线圈 8
ignition switch 点火开关 8，33
impeller 泵轮，叶轮 134，135
impeller member 叶轮组件 136
impeller shaft 叶轮轴 135
inboard epicyclic double reduction final drive axle 内置行星双级减速末端传动轴 153
inboard epicyclic double reduction axle 内置行星齿轮双级减速轴 153
inclined guide link 倾斜导杆 98
inclining adjuster release handle （靠背）倾角调节器释放手柄 59
indicator 转弯信号灯 3
indicator light 指示灯 2
indirect pad 反向驱动垫 175
indirect piston 反向驱动活塞 175
indoor handle 门锁内手柄 58
induction motor 感应电机 226
inductive sensor 感应式传感器 36
inertia reel 惯性卷轴 194
inertia switch 惯性开关 33
inflator 膨胀器 202
initiator 引爆器 194
injection advancer 喷油推进器 31
injection controller 喷射控制器 14
injection pump calibration unit 喷射泵计量单元 34

injection pump 喷油泵，喷射泵，注射泵 7，14，51，183
injection timing piston 喷射正时活塞 22
injector 喷油器，喷射器，喷嘴 7
injector cam 喷射器凸轮 183
injector electrical terminal 喷射器电接头 35
injector fuel filter 喷射器燃油过滤器 35
injector rocker 喷射摇杆 183
inlet bolt 入口螺栓 12
inlet port 进气口 7
inlet solenoid valve 进气电磁阀 93
inlet valve 进气门，进口阀 8，122
inner drum 内鼓轮 118
inner hub 内轮毂，内部轮毂 142，144，145
inner tongue on link plate 连板内舌 19
input flange coupling 输入法兰联轴器 151
input pulley 输入带轮 200
input reduction gear 输入减速齿轮 152
input shaft 输入轴 118，124
input shaft bearing 输入轴轴承 124
input speed sensor 输入速度传感器 197
inside electrode 内部电极 207
instrument brightness control 仪表照明开关 196
instrument panel 仪表盘 2
intake air temperature sensor 进气温度传感器 34
intake heater 进气加热器 34
intake manifold 进气歧管 9，31
intake shutter 进气百叶窗 34
intake tube 进气软管 9
integral bearer 整体支撑 74
integral dog tooth portion 整体齿轮轮齿 126
integral gear 整体齿轮 126
interconnecting pipe 互联管 84
intercooler 互冷器 34
interior light 顶灯 195
intermediate pinion 中间轴齿轮 162
intermediate plate 中间板 120
intermediate reduction gear 中间减速齿轮 152
intermediate shaft 中间轴 75
intermediate tube 中间管 99
internal bevelled dog teeth 内锥形齿
internal dog clutch 内齿离合器 126
internal drive shaft 内驱轴 227
inverter 转换器 229
involute bellow spring 渐开空腔弹簧 89
isolator valve 隔离阀 88

J

jaw 卡爪 74
jaw pivot pin 钩爪转销 104
jet cap 喷嘴盖罩 23
jet carrier 喷嘴支座 23
jet needle 喷嘴阀针 32
jet orifice 喷嘴小孔 23
jet tube 喷嘴管 23
joint 对接头 12
jointed ball 球体铰接 124
jounce stop 颠簸挡块 101
journal 轴颈 45

K

key cylinder 钥匙筒 198
kickdown switch 降挡开关 197
knife edge link 刀口连杆 121
knife edge strut 刀口支柱 121
knock sensor 爆燃传感器，爆震传感器 37，197

L

ladder 云梯 218
laminated spring 层片弹簧 99
large pinion gear 大齿轮 127
latch valve 闭锁阀 18
lateral acceleration sensor 侧向加速传感器 92
layshaft gear 副轴轮 123
lead wire 引线 207
lead-acid battery 铅酸电池 225
leading shoe 领蹄 170
leaf spring 片弹簧，板弹簧，钢板弹簧 15，89，216
leakage valve 泄漏阀 10
leak-off housing 泄漏套 12
left hand height actuator 左端高度启动器 90

Vocabulary with Figure Index 词汇及图形索引（英中对照） 241

left track 左滑轨 59
levelling air control valve 空气平衡控制阀 89
levelling control valve 水平控制阀 90
levelling rod 平衡杆 99
levelling valve 平衡阀 88
lever arm 杆臂 178
lift adjustment screw 提升量调节螺钉 12
lift bellow 抬升空腔 90
lift stop 提升挡块 11
lift yoke 抬升架 90
lighter 点烟器 195
light-off catalytic converter 光截止催化转化器 207
limiting stopper 限位块 77，119
limousine 豪华轿车 56
link arm 连接臂 79
link plate 连接板 15
link plate torsion-spring 连板扭簧 19
linkage hook 连接钩 17
linkage member 连杆件 95
lip oil seal 唇形油封 160
lip seal 唇形密封 134
liquid window 液窗 113
live axle 动轴 68
load plate 加载板 180
load sensor 载荷传感器 92
load transfer member 载荷传输件 87

locating pin 定位销 44
locating tag 定位凸耳 42
location washer 定位垫片 145
lock nut 锁紧螺母 120
locking piece 锁片 49
lock-up clutch 锁止离合器 136
lock-up torque converter 锁止式液力变矩器 140
longitude acceleration sensor 纵向加速传感器 92
longitudinal link 纵向连杆 73
longitudinal member 纵向件 69
longitudinal spring arm 纵向弹簧臂 80
longitudinal wishbone arm 纵向叉形杆臂 80
lower compression 下气环 44
lower control piston 下控制柱塞 186
lower rubber diaphram 下部橡胶膜垫 52
lower transverse control arm 下横向控制臂 73，77
lower transverse link 下横杆，下部横向连杆 74
lower wishbone arm 下部叉形杆臂 79
low friction ring 低摩擦环 101
low-spring injector 小刚度弹簧喷油器 10
lubricant 润滑油 8
lubrication nipple 润滑嘴 120
lubrication system oil route 润滑系统油路 51
Lucas engine 卢卡斯发动机 7
luggage compartment door lock 行李箱盖锁 198
lugged thrust washer 凸耳推力垫片 119

machine-gun 机枪 216
Macpherson strut 麦弗逊支柱 83，96
magnetic clutch 磁性离合器 41，115
main beam headlight 远光灯 3
main beam indicator light 远光指示灯 2
main bleed 主渗流 103
main clutch 主离合器 127
main parachute 主降落伞 216
main plate 主板 59
main plate table 主板台 107
main relay 主继电器 29
main shaft 主轴 14，145
main shaft auxiliary input gear 主轴附属输入齿轮 128
main supply jet 主喷嘴 23
manifold air temperature sensor 增压空气温度传感器 35
manifold pressure 管内压力 30
manifold pressure sensor 管压传感器 35

manifold vacuum 管路真空 41
manual valve 手动阀 140
mass air flow meter 空气质量流量计 33，196
master cylinder 主缸，制动总泵 122，170
master lighting switch 灯光主开关 195
master piston 主活塞 183
max. fuel adjuster 最大燃油量调节器 15
max. fuel stop lever 最大燃油量挡杆 15
maximum fuel adjustment screw 最大燃油量调整螺钉 19
measuring flap 测量翼 38
mechanical governor 机械调节器 17
mechanically actuated bag firing mechanism
mechanical sensor 机械传感器 202
median ring 中间环 88
memory menu 存储功能键 212
metallic housing 金属罩 207
metering valve 计量阀，测量阀 17，18
microjector 微喷油器 11

mileometer 里程表 2
milled rotor 铣切转子 226
minimec governor 微机械调节器 15
mirror 反光镜 2
mixture control unit 混合控制单元 27
mixture flow 混合气流 23
model number plate 车型号码标牌 4
modulator unit 调制器单元 200
molding 装饰条 58
monitoring unit 监控单元 229
monolithic catalytic converter 整体式催化转化器 207
motor controller 马达（电机）控制器 221
moulded deflector 模具成形偏转板 66

mounting subframe bracket 安装下架支架 53
mounting 安装口，安装座 30，187
mounting plate 安装板 59
mounting point 安装点 69
mounting rail 安装轨 225
muliple clutch 复式离合器 140
multifunction contactor 多功能接触器 141
multihole injector 多孔式微喷油器 10
multilink rear axle 多连杆后轴 71
multiplate clutch 多片离合器 118
multiplate friction type retarder 多块摩擦片式缓速器 184
multi-point injection 多点喷射 32
multistage torque converter 多级液力变矩器 136

N

nailing 穿钉 49
needle roller 滚针滚子 144
nickel-metal hydride battery 镍氢电池 224
nonlockable differential 非锁死型差速器 75
non-return valve 单向阀 40，129
nonrotating part 非回转件 188
nose cabin 鼻头舱 59
nose cone 鼻锥体 218

notchback configuration 凹口背部构形 65
nozzle 喷嘴 9
nozzle body 喷嘴本体 11
nozzle cap 喷嘴套 10
nozzle holder 喷嘴夹套，喷嘴固定座 11
number plate 牌照 2
number plate light 牌照灯 3

oil drain plug 放油塞 123
oil filter 机油滤清器 8
oil level indicator 油面指示器 50
oil passage 油道 45
oil press switch 油压开关 35
oil pressure warning light 机油压力警报灯 195
oil pump 输油泵，机油泵 31，51
oil pump lock-up clutch 油泵锁止离合器 137
oil seal assembly 油封组件 95
oil separator 油分离器 116
oil sump tank 油底壳 51
oil temperature 油温 14
oil temperature transmission sensor 油温传输传感器 197
oil unloader valve 放油阀 109
oil-water separator 油水分离器 31
one-way clutch 单向离合器 49，134
one-way roller clutch 滚子单向离合器 129
open cabriolet 开式敞篷车 65
operating cam 工作凸轮 109

opposed twin engine 双缸相对排列发动机 7
option menu 选择设定键 212
optoelectronic sensor 光电传感器 37
outboard epicylic spur double reduction axle 外置行星直齿轮双级减速轴 153
outer hub sleeve 外轮毂套 142
outer hub thrust plate 外毂推板 181
outer sliding sleeve hub 外部滑动套轮毂 145
outer yoke 外部支架 155
outlet solenoid valve 出流电磁阀 93
output flange 输出法兰 134
output propeller shaft 输出叶轮轴 184
output shaft 输出轴 124
output shaft flanged coupling 输出轴法兰接头 184
output shaft pinion gear 输出轴小齿轮 130
output shaft auxiliary gear 输出轴附属齿轮 128
output speed sensor 输出速度传感器 197
outrigger 悬臂支架 75
outside electrode 外部电极 207
overdrive planetary gear set 超速行星齿轮装置 137

over press valve 过压阀 51
override clutch 超越离合器 179
oxygen sensor 氧传感器 207
oxygen sphere 氧球体 225

P

panel 门护板 58
Panhard rod 潘哈杆 75
paper air cleaner 纸质空滤器 42
parachute cable 降落伞索线 216
parachute release stand 降落伞释放架 216
parallel hybrid drive mechanism 并联混合动力机械 229
parallel hybrid drive 平行混合驱动 229
parallel hybrid system 平行混合动力系统 229
parking brake 驻车制动器 188
parking brake indicator 驻车制动指示灯 195
parking brake lever 驻车制动器拉杆 188
parking brake strut 驻车制动器撑杆 188
parking pawl 锁止爪 137
parking ring 驻车环齿轮 137
part throttle by-pass slot 局部节流旁路槽 25
passenger airbag 乘客侧气囊 201
passenger's supplemental air bag 乘客安全气囊 196
passive resistor 无源电阻 50
pedestal member 踏板件 98
peg 栓钉 160
pencil nozzle 铅笔式喷油嘴 12
pendulum mass 振摆质量 50
peripheral gap 周边空隙 42
peripheral pump 周边泵 30
permanent magnet 永磁体 37，226
permanent magnet slowdown starter 永磁式减速启动机 49
petrol tank (u. s. gas tank) 油箱 68
photodiode 光电二极管 37
phototransistor 光敏管 168
pickup coil 拾取线圈 199
pickup pipe 拾取管 129
pickup truck 敞篷小型载货卡车（皮卡） 56
pilot bearing 导向轴承 118
pilot parachute 飞行员降落伞 216
pilot solenoid vale 先导电磁阀 116
pin dust cover 导销防尘盖 176
pinch clamp 拧紧夹头 168
pinion 小齿轮 74
pinion carrier 小齿轮托架 129
pinion carrier pin 小齿轮托架销 127
pinion spline 小齿轮花键 148

pinion steering 小齿轮转向器 76
pinion support bearing 齿轮支撑轴承 169
pintaux type nozzle 轴针式喷嘴，轴针式喷油器 9
pintle 柱销 26
piston 活塞 8
pistion diaphragm 活塞膜片 84
piston valve 活塞阀口 99
pivot 转枢 187
pivot ball joint 转动球节头 125
pivot beam 转枢梁 87
pivot pin 转枢销 85
pivot stop post 转枢挡柱 119
plain bush bearing 轴套滑动轴承 163
planet carrier 行星齿轮托架 127
planet pinion abutment shoulder 行星小齿轮接触轴肩 149
planetary carrier 行星齿轮（托）架 130，131
planetary gear 行星齿轮 41，130
planetary gear machine 行星齿轮机构 49
plate terminal 扁平端子 193
pleated paper filter element 折叠纸质过滤元件 42
plectrum 拨叉 49
plunger-injector 柱塞式喷油器 31
plunger seal 柱塞密封 173
plunging inboard joint 内置柱塞接头 192
pneumatic tyre 充气轮胎 216
pole piece 磁极 184
polyphase winding 多相绕组 226
positive baulk pin synchromesh unit 增力锁销式同步离合器 144
pot member 壳形件 102
power relay 电源继电器 33
power-split control 动力分离控制 228
power steering pressure switch 动力转向压力开关 33
power steering pump 动力转向泵 8
power window master switch 电动窗主开关 198
pre-combustion chamber 预燃烧的燃烧室 6
preload shim 预紧垫片 160
presser plate 承压板 48
pressure adjustment screw 压力调节螺钉 12
pressure control valve 压力控制阀 22
pressure holding valve 压力保持阀 22

pressure limiting valve　限压阀　51
pressure plate　压力板　120，127
pressure regulating valve　调压阀　140，177
pressure relief assembly　压力释放组件　40
pressure spring　压力弹簧　30，120
pretensioner cable　预张紧绳　194
primary governor valve　主控阀　140
primary menu　初级点火键　212
primary pulley　主动轮　130
primary pulley servo cylinder　主动轮伺服缸　131
primary reservoir　初级储气罐　181
primary shoe　主蹄块　170
priming spring　启动弹簧　18
pronged yoke　分叉轭架　156
propellant grain　推进粒　194
propeller　螺旋桨　216
propeller gear box　螺旋桨齿轮箱　216
propeller shaft　传动轴　68
proportional relay valve　比例延时阀　186
proportional solenoid valve　电磁比例阀　99
proportional valve　比例阀　186

pulley　带轮　92
pulley position sensor　带轮位置传感器　131
pull-off spring　截止弹簧　178，180
pulsation damper　脉冲阻尼　14
pulsator　脉冲器　35
pulse air solenoid valve　脉冲空气电磁阀　33
pump blade　泵叶片　18
pump body　泵体　13
pump cylinder　泵缸体　99，200
pump jet　泵喷头　25
pump lever　泵杠杆　25
pump mounting flange　泵安装法兰　13
pump outlet valve　泵出阀　99，200
pump piston　泵活塞　200
pump plunger　泵柱塞　25，99
pump relay　泵继电器　35
pump return spring　泵复位弹簧　25
pump suction breaker　泵吸入截止器　25
purge solenoid valve　清污电磁阀　33
push rod　推杆　8，122

R

racing slick tyre　比赛用的光滑轮胎　218
rack　齿条　14
rack and pinion power steering　齿轮齿条动力转向器　74
rack nut　齿条螺母　163
radial packing seal　径向填料密封　134
radial ply tyre　子午线轮胎　190
radiator pod　散热箱　59
radio transceiver aerial　无线电收发两用天线　216
radius arm　转臂，可转（支撑）杆　73，80
ramp　斜坡块　15
ratchet　棘爪　188
ratchet pawl　棘爪　109
reaction piston　作用活塞　186
reaction plunger　作用柱塞　122
reaction rod　作用杆　125
reactor　导轮　134
reactor plate　作用板　121
rear actuator　后启动器　96
rear aerofoil wing　后翼主板　218
rear axle　后轴　71，218
rear bearing　后轴承　49，124
rear brake sensor　后轮制动传感器　200
rear differential　后差速器　77

rear door courtesy switch　后门踏步灯开关，后门行李箱灯开关　198
rear door pillar　后门立柱　57
rear double wheel　后双轮　218
rear drive axle　后驱动桥　155
rear electric brake　后轮电动制动　221
rear end cover　后端罩　193
rear end panel　后围板　56
rear final drive　后轮末端传动　202
rear height and levelling strut actuator　后高度水平支柱启动器　92
rear jack handle　后千斤顶把手　216
rear levelling control solenoid valve　后水平控制电磁阀　92
rear light　尾灯，后照灯　2，3
rear lower wishbone　后下叉杆　218
rear mounting　后安装座　73
rear pillar　后柱　56
rear road wheel　后路面轮　106
rear roof bow　顶盖后横梁　56
rear soft ride spring　后软驱弹簧　92
rear stiffening solenoid valve　后硬驱电磁阀　92
rear suspension-independent　后独立悬架　95
rear suspension shock absorber　后悬挂减振　218

rear suspension 后悬架,后悬挂 3,84
rear upper wishbone 后上叉杆 218
rear-view mirror 后视镜 218
rear wheel 后轮 3
rear wheel arrester 后轮制动器 3
rear window backlight rail 后窗尾灯梁 57
rear wing assembly 后翼组件 59
rebound 反弹 103
rebound compression block 反弹压缩块 103
rebound housing 反弹腔 103
rebound valve cover plate 反弹阀盖板 102
rebound valve spring 反弹阀弹簧 102
rebound valve washer 反弹阀垫圈 102
recirculating ball 循环滚珠 163
rectifier 整流器 193
rectifier end frame 后端盖 193
redundancy valve 冗余阀 186
reflector 反射器 216
regulating piston 调节活塞 18
regulating sleeve 调节套 18
regulating spring 调节弹簧 18
regulating screw 调节螺钉 35
relay lever 中继杆 183
relay set 延时装置 28
relay switch 继电器开关 93
relay valve 延时阀 186
release bearing 分离轴承,释放轴承,脱开轴承 118,121,136
release bearing assembly 释放轴承组件 122
release bearing housing 释放轴承腔 120
release bearing inner sleeve 释放轴承内套 120
release button 释放按钮 188
release hand lever 释放手把 106
release lever 分离杆,释放杆 118,120
release piston 卸压活塞 181
release plate 释放板 121
relief spill valve 溢流阀 185
reluctance motor 磁阻电动机 226
remote control rod 遥控杆 125
remote control tube 遥控管 125
remote feeler bulb 遥感灯 116
remote linkage 联动装置 123
reserve liquid dryer 储液干燥器 113
reservoir tank 油箱 88
reservoir 油池,储液器 104,113
reset button 归零按钮 58
restricted orifice 节流小孔 22
restriction damper 限流阻尼器 90,92

retainer 保持器 25
retaining (snap) ring 挡圈 44
retaining spring 保持弹簧 18
retarder output shaft 缓速器输出轴 184
retarder support bracket 缓速器支座 184
retraction spring 回位弹簧 121,135,170
return flow restrictor valve 回流节制阀 11
return guide 回珠导向器 163
return spring 复位弹簧,回位弹簧 26,49,130,147
reverse brake 倒挡制动 131
reverse-flow scavenge DKW Engine DKW 逆流扫气发动机 7
reverse gear 倒挡,倒挡齿轮 123,124
reverse gear engaged 倒挡齿轮啮合 131
reverse lever 倒挡杆 125
reverse multiplate brake 倒挡多盘制动器 130
reverse planetary gear set 倒车行星齿轮装置 137
reverse servo piston 倒挡伺服活塞 130
reverse shaft 倒挡轴 124
reversing light 倒车灯
right hand height actuator 右端高度启动器 90
right track 右滑轨 59
rigid axle casing 刚性轴壳 75
rigid axle suspension 刚性轴悬架 77
ring chamber 活塞环腔 99
ring channel 环槽 103
ring gear 环齿 120
ring gear teeth 环状轮齿 37
rivet 铆钉 171
road-induced electricity 路面感应电动车 220
road speed 路面速度 93
roadway power source 道路动力源 220
rocker arm 摇杆臂 160
rocker-arm shaft 摇臂轴 51
rocker fork 摇臂叉架 163
rocker shaft 摇臂轴,摇杆轴 160
rocking lever 摇杆 15
rocking lever pin 摇杆销钉 15
roll cage 滚柱罩 217
roller 滚子 15
roller follower pin 滚针从动件销 161
rolling diaphragm spring 可翻转膜片弹簧 89
roll over bar 翻折杆,防滚架 65,218
roof 车顶 2
roof rack 车顶行李架 2
roof rail 上边梁 56
rotary coupler 回转连接器 194

rotating part　回转件　188
rotor　转子，分火头　17
rotor arm　旋转臂　38
rotor hub internally splined　内带花键转子毂　184
rotor lamination　转子片　226
rotor sleeve　转子套　226
rotor vent switch valve　转子通风开关阀　18，28
rubber bearing　橡胶轴承　80
rubber bearing and clamp　橡胶支撑及其夹套　79
rubber bearing point　橡胶支承点　77
rubber bush　橡胶套，橡胶轴衬　94，123
rubber flap valve　橡胶止回阀　102
rubber grommet　橡胶环　171
rubber insulator　橡胶绝缘块　193
rubber joint ring　橡胶连接环　42
rubber mounting　橡胶安装垫　53，73
rubber seal　橡胶密封条　58
rubber sealing ring　橡胶密封　18
rub strip　防擦条　57
rudder　舵　216
rzeppa universal joint　球笼式等速万向节　156

S

safety certification label　安全认证标签　4
Saurer combustion chamber　索雷尔燃烧室　6
scan tool　扫描仪　212
screwed retainer cap　螺纹保持盖　168
screw-type oil baffle　螺杆型油挡　50
scroll plate　滚盘　19
scuttle　车颈，天窗　69，112
seal　密封　12
sealing edge　密封边口　102
sealing washer　密封垫圈　11
seat back　靠背　59
seatback frame　靠背骨架　59
seat belt　安全带　2
seat belt warning light　安全带提醒灯　195
seat belt buckle switch　安全带锁扣开关　201
seat belt pretensioner　安全带收紧装置　201
seat belt tensioner　安全带张紧器　194
seat cushion　座垫　59
seat cushion frame　座垫骨架　59
secondary fixed half pulley　从动轮固定半轮　130，131
secondary governor valve　辅控阀　140
secondary pulley servo cylinder　从动轮伺服缸　130，131
secondary pully shaft　从动带轮轴　130
secondary shoe　次蹄块　170
secondary sliding half pulley　从动轮滑动半轮　130，131
second menu　次级点火键　212
sector gear　扇形齿　163
sector shaft　扇形齿轴　163
sector shaft bearing　扇形齿轴轴承　163
securing bolt　安全螺栓　42
sedimenter chamber　沉积室　16
sedimenter head　沉积头　16
selector rod　选挡杆　129
selector fork　拨叉，选挡拨叉　124，125
selector fork sleeve　换挡叉套　144
selector gate　选挡口　125
selector rod　选挡杆　125
self aligning bearing　自位轴承　125，211
self-levelling hydropneumatic suspension　自平衡液气悬挂　99
self-test connector　自检接头　33
semi-active hydro/gas suspension　半主动液气悬挂　90
semi-cylindrical flange　半柱形法兰　95
sensor　传感器　34
sensor signal　传感器信号　36
sensor wheel　传感器轮盘　36
separation bubble　分离泡　60
separation diaphragm　隔离膜片　84
servo cylinder　伺服缸　130
servomotor　伺服电机　161
servo piston　伺服活塞　130
servo valve　伺服阀　96
set pin sleeve　限位销套　77
shackle pin　锁固销　109
shackle plate　固定板　86
shaft lock button　锁止按钮　134
shallow recess　浅坑　124
shift bell crank lever　钟形曲柄转换杆　183
shift lever　换挡杆　124
shift position indicator　挡位指示器　134
shift rail　变速杆　123
shift selector lever　换挡杆　196
shift valve　换向阀　140
shim　垫片　12

shock absorber 减振器 72, 75
shock absorber cartridge 减振杆 101
shock damper piston 减振活塞 95
shock damper relieve valve plug 减振溢流阀塞 95
shock damper return piston spring 减振回流活塞
 弹簧 95
shod abutment 蹄块结合块 170
shoe and roller assemblies 蹄块滚子组件 18
shoe carrier 蹄块支架 135
shoe pivot 蹄块转枢 135
shoe retainer 蹄块保持架 174
shoe return spring 蹄块复位弹簧 171
shoe web 蹄块腹板 173
short upper transverse control arm 短上横向控制
 臂 77
shouldered adjustment screw and nut 轴肩调整丝
 杠螺母 161
shut-down valve 截止阀 14
shut-off bar 截止杆 17
shut-off solenoid 截止电磁铁 28
side airbag sensor 气囊侧传感器 201
side-by-side twin engine 双缸并列发动机 7
side light 侧灯 2
side member 纵梁 56
side plate 侧板 119
side plate notch 侧板槽 119
side pod 侧柱，侧箱盖 59, 218
side screen 侧挡风玻璃 65
side ventilator 侧向出风口 196
silencer (u. s. muffler) 消声器 68
sill 门槛 69
single acting cylinder 单作用缸 170
single cylinder air compressor 单缸空气压缩机 181
single plate dry clutch 单板干式离合器 133
single-point injection 单点喷射 31
slave piston 从动活塞 129, 183
sleeve fork 套叉 180
sleeve nut 套螺母 211
sleeve output port 套式输出口 17
slide cylinder body brake caliper 缸体滑动型制动
 夹钳 175
slide pin 导向销 170
slide pin type brake caliper 滑柱型制动夹钳 176
sliding dog clutch member 滑动啮合齿组件 147
sliding hub 滑移轮毂 146
sliding member 滑动部件 93
sliding pillar suspension 侧柱悬挂 96
sliding plate 滑板 77

sliding sleeve dog clutch 滑套齿形离合器 154
sliding sleeve hub 滑套壳 145
sliding yoke type brake caliper 轭架滑动型制动
 夹钳 175
slipper block 滑块 86
slit 开槽 80
slit disc 开槽盘 168
slot 拨槽，槽 124, 126
small pinion gear 小齿轮 127
small plunger 小柱销 124
smaller clutch 小型离合器 127
snap ring 卡圈 74
socket joint 座口接头 73
sodium-sulphur battery 钠硫电池 224
solenoid 电磁铁 32, 39, 206
solenoid coil 电磁铁线圈 39
solenoid return spring 电磁铁回程弹簧 13
solenoid winding 电磁铁绕组 184
sound-deadening rib 消声柱 123
spacer 隔套 12, 188
sparking plug 火花塞 8
spark plug 火花塞 38
speaker 扬声器 195
speed change lever 变速杆 183
speed out valve 速度截止阀 140
speed selector eccentric 偏心速度选挡杆 154
speedometer 速度表 2
speedometer gear 车速表齿轮 124
spherical enlargement 球形扩口 156
spherical grease seal 环形润滑脂密封 155
spherical member 球形件 98
spherical spring chamber 球形环腔 84
spigot bearing 插入轴承 120, 134
spigot needle roller 插入滚针轴承 144
spigot roller 插入滚子 142
spill control valve 溢流控制阀 34
spill hole 溢油孔 21
spiral cable 螺旋电缆 201
spiral gear 螺旋齿轮 50
spiral spring 螺旋弹簧 38
spline 花键 147
splined drive shaft 花键传动轴 181
splined half shaft hub 花键半轴毂 150
splined hub 花键轮毂 119
splined input hub 花键输入轮毂 184
splined input shaft 花键输入轴 120
split baulk pin synchromesh unit 开合锁销式同
 步离合器 146

split baulk ring synchromesh unit 开合摩擦环式同步离合器 145
split collet 开合套 39
split crankwed 部分式曲柄臂 45
split ring 开合环 145
split synchronizingring 开合同步环 145
spool valve 绕轴阀 164
sports car 跑车 56
spray shield 防浪挡板 216
spring 弹簧 11，74
spring bracket 弹簧座 19
spring bushing 弹簧销衬套 77
spring clamp 弹簧压头，钢板弹簧 12，77
spring laded disc 弹簧加载盘 118
spring-loaded ball 弹簧加载球体 126
spring pin 弹簧销 77
spring seat 弹簧座 9，12
spring shock absorber 弹簧减振器 77
spring strut 弹簧滑柱 74
spring tower 弹簧座 69
spur gear 直齿轮 147
spur gear oil pump 直齿油泵 130
spur gear pin 直齿销 147
spur-type differential wheel 直齿差动齿轮 95
squareback configuration 方形后背盖构形 64
SRS warning light 安全气囊警示灯 194
SRS wiring harness 安全气囊引线套 194
stabilizer 稳定器 74
standard clutch 标准离合器 127
standby electric motor 旁设电动机 115
starter clutch 启动机离合器 49
starter housing 启动机壳体 49
starting engine 启动机
startup ring gear 启动齿圈 134
stationary cone clutch member 静止锥形离合器构件 129
stationary lever 静止杆 221
stator 定子 135
stator hub 定子毂 140
stator pin 定子销 185
stator plate lug 静止板凸耳 184
stator support plate 定子支撑板 184
steady post 稳定柱 171
steel bead 钢珠 102
steel casing 钢盒 52
steer angle transducer 转向角度传感器 96
steering arm 转向臂 72，101
steering ball unit 转向滚子单元 168

steering column 转向杆 168
steering column jacket 转向柱外套 74
steering damper 转向阻尼 73
steering gear 转向器 158
steering sensor 转向传感器 168
steering valve 转向阀 158
steering wheel 转向盘 2
stepper motor 步进电机 39
stop 停止杆，挡销 14，121
stop control shaft 挡杆控制轴 13
stop lever 挡杆 13
stop shaft 挡轴 13
storage bin 储物盒 196
streamline 流线 59
strike pin 插销 180
striking arm 接触臂 126
striking finger 接触杆 125
stroboscope device 频闪仪 211
stroboscope lamp 频闪仪指示灯 211
strub shaft 短轴 83
strut 支柱 76
strut and cam brake shoe expander 支柱凸轮制动蹄膨胀器 173
strut link 柱连杆 173，187
stub axle hub 短轴毂 83
subframe 下架，副车架 53
submit still trundle patch 上止推片 44
suction line 吸管 114
suction pressure 吸入压力 6
suction valve 吸入阀 99
sump 油底壳 8，114
sun gear 太阳轮 127
sun gear cone clutch 太阳轮锥形离合器 127
supercapacitor 超容量电池 225
supercharged engine 增压引擎 217
super charger 增压器 51
super turbo charger 超级涡轮增压 199
supplementary spring 附加弹簧 101
supply plunger 供油柱塞 109
supply poppet valve 供油提升阀 109
support block 支撑块 50
support disc 支撑板 100
support rod 支撑杆 211
support sleeve 支撑套 147
supporting cradle 支座 216
suspension housing 悬架座 94
suspension lower swing arm 悬架下部摆杆 93
swing arm 摇臂 87

swing yoke 摆动轭架 176
swing yoke type brake caliper 轭架摆动型制动夹钳 176
swivel ball joint 旋转球节头 125
swivel pin 转销 83
synchromesh device 同步啮合装置 126
synchromesh drive hub 同步啮合驱动轮毂 128
synchronizer 同步（离合）器 124，142
synchronizer ring 同步环 123
synchronizing cone hub 同步锥形轮毂 146
synchronizing hub 同步轮毂 144
synchronous belt 同步（齿形）带 48

T

tab 挂耳 73
tachometer 转速表，速度表 58，169
tachometer shaft 转速计轴 14
tail housing 尾壳 123
tandem master cylinder 串联主缸，串联主油缸 177，200
taper bearing preload shim 锥形轴承预紧垫片 163
tapered seat 锥形座 163
tapered skirt 锥形裙部 84
tapper roller bearing 圆锥滚子轴承 83
tappet 凸轮从动件 171
tappet head 挺杆头 173
tappet plunger 挺杆柱塞 173
tappet strut 挺杆 173
tax disc 税牌 2
tdc sensor 上止点传感器 37
tear-away visor cover 可移动遮光眼罩 218
Teflon gas seal 特氟龙气体密封圈 12
temperature gauge 水温表 2
temperature sensor 温度传感器 28
tensioning lever stop 张紧杆挡块 22
terminal 接线端，接线座 50，224
terminal C kit part 端子C套件 49
terminal energy output pole 终极能量输出极 36
terminal insulator 端子绝缘体 49，193
thermostat 恒温器 51，112
thermostat regulator 恒温调节器 112
thermo-time switch 温度/时间开关 27
threaded adjustment barrel 螺纹调节筒 180
threaded eye bolt sleeve 螺纹孔螺栓套 120
three-port two-stroke engine 三口两冲程发动机 7
throttle actuator 节流器 228
throttle link 节流连杆 17
throttle plate 节流板 27，32
throttle plate control motor 节流板控制马达 32
throttle position sensor (TPS) 节气门位置传感器，节流阀位置传感器 32，33，35，197
throttle potentiometer 节气门电压表 39
throttle shaft 节流轴 13，28
throttle stop screw 节气门挡钉 39
throttle valve 节流阀 140
throttle valve potentiometer 节流阀电位计 197
thrust ballrace 推力球轴承滚道 129
thrust block 推力块 145
thrust pad 推垫，推力肩盘 15
thrust pin 推销 15，144
thrust plate 推力板 129
thrust roller 推力滚子 144
thrust sleeve 推力套 15
thrust spring 推力弹簧 129
thrust washer 止推垫圈，推力垫片，推力挡圈 49，119，142，144
tie rod 转向横拉杆，拉杆 74
tilt lever 斜杆 90
timing belt 正时皮带 8
timing chain 正时链 8
timing control 正时控制 20
timing control valve 正时控制阀 34
timing gear 正时齿轮 51
tip 端部 12
tire information label 轮胎信息标签 4
tongue groove 榫舌槽 175
toothed excitor ring 齿形激振器环 199
toothed pawl 齿爪 173
toothed sector lever 扇形齿轮杆 173
top windscreen rail 风挡顶部横梁 57
torque convertor 液力偶合器 136
torque plate 支撑板 171
torque rod 力矩杆 86
torque spring 扭矩弹簧 14
torque tube 扭转杆 80
torsional damper spring 扭转减振弹簧 119
torsionally elastic bearing 扭转弹性轴承 72
torsion bar 扭转杆 72，165
torsion damper 扭矩阻尼器 140
torsion shaft 扭转轴 95
torsion tube 扭矩管 95
torus guide core 环形导芯 135

track handle 滑轨手柄 59
track rod ball joint 轮距杆球节头 108
traction battery pack 牵引电池组 221
traction boost unit 牵引力提升单元 205
traction control system 牵引力控制系统 202
traction motor 牵引马达 220
traction solenoid valve unit 牵引电磁阀单元 205
tractor chassis 牵引底盘 104
trailing arm 从臂, 纵向臂 71, 77, 87
trailing arm anchor bolt 纵臂固定螺栓 80
trailing edge 从边 172
trailing shoe 从蹄 171
trailing vortex cone 尾部涡流锥 61
trailor chassis 拖车底盘 104
trailor platform 拖车平台 104
transfer channel tube 传输通道管 163
transfer hole 传输孔 52
transfer port 传输口 7
transfer pressure adjuster 传输压力调节器 18
transfer pump rotor 传输泵转子 18
transfer tube 滚珠传输管 163
transmission 变速器, 传动系 3, 68, 229
transmission housing 传动箱体 141
transmission shaft 传动轴 3
transparent drum 透明鼓 211
transpatent bowl 透明筒 16
transponder chip 发射器芯片 198
transponder key amplifier 钥匙发射器放大器 198
transponder key coil 钥匙发射器线圈 198
transverse arm 横臂 73, 95
transverse control arm 横向控制臂 71
transverse groove 横槽 101
transverse leaf spring 横向板弹簧 96
transverse link 横杆 76
transverse link mounting point 横杆安装点 74
transverse screw 横向螺杆 72
transverse Watt linkage 横向瓦特杆 80

travel sensor 里程传感器 186
tread 胎面 189
trigger vane 触发片 38
trim lever 调整杆 79
trip mileometer 短距离里程表 2
tripot flexible coupling 三叉柔性联轴器 73
tripot type universal joint 三球销式万向节 157
trip pin 行程销 106
tripronged type universal joint 三叉架型万向节 157
trough 边槽 50
true-stop brake 驻车制动器 188
trunnion 耳轴 86
trunnion bearing 耳轴轴承 104
trunnion block 耳轴座 98
T-shaped axle casing T形轴外壳 74
tubular axle beam 管式轴梁 80
tubular casing 管形腔体 80
tubular cross-member 管件横向件 106
tubular steel frame 管状钢架 217
tumtable 转台 108
tunnel 通道 69
turbine 涡轮 43, 134
turbine member 涡轮组件 136
turbine shaft bearing 涡轮轴轴承 134
turbo charger (TC) 涡轮增压器 199
turbo pressure 涡轮压力 34
turbulent volume 涡流卷团 60
turn light lamp 转向指示灯 195
twin cylinder compressor 双缸压缩机 182
twin drive plate 双驱动盘 120
twintube shock absorber 双管减振器 74
two row angular (contact) ball bearing 双列角接触轴承 74
two speed double reduction helical gear axle 两速双级减速螺旋齿轮轴 154
tyre 车胎 2

U-bolt U形螺栓 77
uncoupling handle 脱扣手把 105
undertray 底托板 59
universal joint 万向节 68, 125, 155
universal joint flange 万向节法兰盘 184
unloader plunger 卸荷柱塞 182
unloader valve 卸载阀 122
upper centre pillar 上部中心立柱 57

upper compression 上气环 44
upper control arm 上控制臂 73
upper control piston 上控制活塞 186
upper reinforcement (保险杠)上加强梁 57
upper rubber diaphram 上部橡胶膜垫 52
upper seal 上部密封条 58
upper spring seat 上弹簧座 101
upper transverse link 上横杆 74

upper wishbone arm 上部叉形杆臂 79

vacuum hose diagram label 真空管路图标签 4
vacuum power booster 真空助力器 170
vacuum pump 真空泵 34
vacuum regulating valve 真空调节阀 34
vacuum servo 真空伺服阀 177，200
vacuum tank 真空箱 29
valance 帷幔 69
valve 阀，气门 8，12
valve disc 阀盘 102
valve guide 气门导管 48
valve head 阀头 39
valve locker 气门锁夹 48
valve needle 阀针 26
valve oil seal 气门油封 48
valve plate 阀板 181
valve push rod 阀推杆 9
valve seat 阀座，气门座 12，26，48
valve spindle 阀轴 25
valve spring 气门弹簧 48
valve train 配气机构 48
vane pump 叶片泵 158
vane switch 片状开关 38

variable resistor 可变电阻 29
Vauxhall front suspension 氟斯霍前悬架 95
ventilated disc 通气碟 172
Vee cylinder compressor V形缸体压缩机 115
Vee helper V形辅助块 87
Vee slot ramp V形槽坡面 149
vehicle control unit 车辆控制单元 223
vehicle speed sensor 车辆速度传感器，车速传感器 29，35
ventilated disc 通风盘，通风碟 178，180
ventilator 通风机 195
vent orifice 通气小孔 18
Venturi 文丘里管 24
Venturi effect 文丘里效应 61
vertically adjustable torque support 立式可调转矩支架 74
vertical slot 立槽 109
vibration detector 振动探测器 211
visco clutch 黏性离合器 77
viscous coupling 黏液联轴合器 203
vortex combustion chamber 涡流燃烧室 6

wake 尾流 60
wall rubber 外层橡胶 189
warm-up regulator 加热调节器 27
warning light 报警灯 2
water pump transmission belt gear wheel 水泵传动齿形带轮 48
water thermo sensor 水温传感器 29
Watt linkage 瓦特杆 82
wave washer 波形垫圈 49
webbing harness 吊带 216
wedge lever 楔块杠杆 105
wedge profile 楔形件 149
wedge roller assembly 楔块滚子组件 174
weight carrier assembly 承重组件 15
wet clutch 湿式离合器 127
wheel carrier arm 车轮支撑臂 95
wheel arch 车轮拱板 69
wheel cylinder 制动分泵，轮缸 170，171
wheel diameter gauge 轮径测仪 211

wheel fastening bolt 车轮紧固螺栓 170
wheel hub carrier 轮毂架 73
wheel sensor 车轮传感器 199
wheel speed sensor 车轮转速传感器 221
wheel well 轮室 56
winding 绕组 26
window regulator handle 玻璃升降器手柄 58
window winder 玻璃窗摇把 2
windscreen 风窗玻璃 2
windshield defroster 前窗除霜器 195
windshield glass 前窗玻璃 58
windshield washer 风挡玻璃冲洗器 195
windshield wiper 前窗刮水器 195
wing attachment strut 尾翼平衡柱 218
wing beam 翼梁 59
worm and roller type steering gearbox 蜗杆滚子类转向齿轮箱 161
worm gear 蜗杆 148
worm taper roller bearing 蜗杆锥形滚子轴承 163

worm wheel　蜗轮　147

Y

yaw gyro　偏航陀螺仪　96

yoke　束套　10

Z

zigzag spring　锯齿形弹簧　59

Vocabulary with Figure Index
词汇及图形索引（中英对照）

A

A 形架拖杆　A-frame drawbar　108
ABS 调制器　abs modulator　199
AC 油池清洁器　AC oil bath cleaner　42
安全带　seat belt，safety belt　2
安全带收紧装置　seat belt pretensioner　201
安全带锁扣开关　seat belt buckle switch　201
安全带提醒灯　seat belt warning light　195
安全带张紧器　seat belt tensioner　194
安全螺栓　securing bolt　42
安全气囊警示灯　SRS warning light　194
安全气囊引线套　SRS wiring harness　194
安全认证标签　safety certification label　4
安装口　mounting　30
安装板　mounting plate　59
安装点　mounting point　69
安装轨　mounting rail　225
安装下架支架　mounting subframe bracket　53
安装座　mounting　187
按钮开关　button switch　211
凹口背部构形　notchback configuration　65

B

摆动轭架　swing yoke　176
摆块　bobweight　121
摆块转枢　bobweight pivot　121
板弹簧　leaf spring　89
半圆带状膨胀器　half band expander　145
半轴　axle shaft　68
半主动液气悬挂　semi-active hydro/gas suspension　90
半柱形法兰　semi-cylindrical flange　95
半座腔　half socket housing　168
保持弹簧　retaining spring　18
保持器　retainer　25
保险杠　bumper　2
保险杠端帽　bumper end cap　58
保险杠梁　bumper beam　57
（保险杠）上加强梁　upper reinforcement　57
保险杠主杆　bumper bar　58
报警灯　warning light　2
爆燃传感器　knock sensor　37
爆炸压力　explosion pressure　6
爆震传感器　knock sensor　197
杯形密封　cup seal　25
杯形推力板　cup thrust plate　149
背板　back plate　187
泵安装法兰　pump mounting flange　13
泵出阀　pump outlet valve　99
泵出口阀　pump outlet valve　200
泵复位弹簧　pump return spring　25
泵缸体　pump cylinder　99
泵杠杆　pump lever　25
泵活塞　pump piston　200
泵继电器　pump relay　35
泵轮　impeller　134
泵喷头　pump jet　25
泵入口阀　pump inlet valve　200
泵体　pump body　13
泵吸入截止器　pump suction breaker　25
泵叶片　pump blade　18
泵柱塞　pump plunger　25，99
鼻头舱　nose cabin　59
鼻锥体　nose cone　218
比例阀　proportional valve　186
比例延时阀　proportional relay valve　186
比赛用的光滑轮胎　racing slick tyre　218
闭锁阀　latch valve　18
边板　end plate　59
边槽　trough　50

边口　edge　104
边口过滤器　edge filter　11
边缘　edge　104
边缘齿形离合器轮齿　flanged dog clutch teeth member　147
扁平端子　plate terminal　193
变矩器　converter　134
变矩器壳　converter (housing) cover　134
变速叉　gear selector fork　123
变速杆　gear lever, shift rail, speed change lever 2, 123, 183
变速器　transmission　3, 68
变速器总成　gearbox assembly　155
变速箱盒　gearbox casing　123
标准离合器　standard clutch　127
并联混合动力机械　parallel hybrid drive mechanism　229
拨槽　slot　124
拨叉　plectrum, selector fork　49, 124
拨挡杆　engagement striking finger　125

波纹管　corrugated tube　160
波形垫圈　wave washer　49
玻璃窗摇把　window winder　2
玻璃升降器手柄　window regulator handle　58
博世减振阀　Bosch snubber valve　11
薄过滤垫　gauze filter washer　10
薄膜　diaphragm　30
薄膜-自位阀组件　diaphragm and self seating valve assembly　35
薄网过滤器　gauze strainer　50
补偿环　compensation ring　95
补偿喷嘴　compensation jet　23
补偿网络　compensation network　211
补偿叶片　compensation flap　40
补偿翼　compensation flap　38
补气腔　extra air tank　89
布萝立特悬架　Broulhiet suspension　95
步进电机　stepper motor　39
部分式曲柄臂　split crankwed　45

C

仓门式后背车身小客车　hatchback　56
操纵杆　control lever　188
槽　slot　126
槽形螺母　castellated nut　105
侧板　flap, side plate　59, 119
侧板槽　side plate notch　119
侧板延伸板　extended side panel　66
侧挡风玻璃　side screen　65
侧灯　side light　2
侧箱盖　side pod　218
侧向出风口　side ventilator　196
侧向加速传感器　lateral acceleration sensor　92
侧柱　side pod　59
侧柱悬挂　sliding pillar suspension　96
测量阀　metering valve　18
测量翼　measuring flap　38
层片弹簧　laminated spring　99
叉臂　fork arm　147
叉耙　fork prong　180
叉形操作杆　fork operating lever　122
叉形件　cross member　94
叉形控制杆　forked control lever　15
插入滚针轴承　spigot needle roller　144
插入滚子　spigot roller　142
插入轴承　spigot bearing　120, 134
插销　strike pin　180

差动齿轮　differential gearing　131
差速器　differential　68, 147
差速器组件　differential assembly　152
差速锁止机构　differential lock mechanism　147
差速箱　differential casing　75
差速锥齿轮　differential bevel gear　227
柴油机　diesel engine　115
柴油滤清器　diesel filter　31
柴油箱　diesel tank　31
常啮合齿轮　constant mesh gear　145
常啮合齿轮箱　constant-mesh gearbox　126
敞篷车　convertible　56
敞篷小型载货卡车（皮卡）　pickup truck　56
超级涡轮增压　super turbo charger　199
超容量电池　supercapacitor　225
超速行星齿轮装置　overdrive planetary gear set　137
超越离合器　override clutch　179
车顶　roof　2
车顶行李架　roof rack　2
车颈　scuttle　69
车辆控制单元　vehicle control unit　223
车辆速度传感器　vehicle speed sensor　29
车轮传感器　wheel sensor　199
车轮拱板　wheel arch　69
车轮紧固螺栓　wheel fastening bolt　170
车轮支撑臂　wheel carrier arm　95

车轮转速传感器　wheel speed sensor　221
车门　door　2
车门把手　handle　2
车门控制接收器　door control receiver　198
车门钥匙　door lock　195
车速表齿轮　speedometer gear　124
车速传感器　vehicle speed sensor　35
车胎　tyre　2
车型号码标牌　model number plate　4
沉积室　sedimenter chamber　16
沉积头　sedimenter head　16
承压板　presser plate　48
承重组件　weight carrier assembly　15
乘客安全气囊　passenger's supplemental air bag　196
乘客侧气囊　passenger airbag　201
齿轮泵　gear pump, gear type pump　14，50
齿轮操控杆　gear lever　126
齿轮操纵杆　gear stick　129
齿轮齿条动力转向器　rack and pinion power steering　74
齿轮挡位开关　gear change position switch　197
齿轮杆　gear lever　124
齿轮换挡杆　gear shift lever　125
齿轮换挡手把　gear shift lever　125
齿轮套轴承　gear bush bearing　145
齿轮箱花键输出轴　gearbox splined output shaft　184
齿轮箱主轴　gearbox mainshaft　185
齿轮支撑轴承　pinion support bearing　169
齿条　rack　14
齿条螺母　rack nut　163
齿形激振器环　toothed excitor ring　199
齿形离合器滑动轮毂　dog clutch sliding hub　128
齿形离合器轮齿　dog clutch teeth　142，144
齿形离合器组件　dog clutch member　126
齿爪　toothed pawl　173
充电系统指示灯　charging system indicator　195
充气轮胎　pneumatic tyre　216
充气平衡腔　gas-filled equalization chamber　99
冲击口　dashpot　19
冲击腔　bump housing　103
冲击压缩块　bump compression block　103
冲压盖　cover pressing　121
抽气室　displacer chamber　84
出口阀　exhaust valve　122
出流电磁阀　outlet solenoid valve　93
出油检测球　discharge check ball　25
出油球保持器　discharge ball retainer　25
出油通道　discharge passage　25

初级储气罐　primary reservoir　181
初级点火键　primary menu　212
储能包　energy storage pack　220
储气箱　air reservoir tank　122
储物盒　storage bin　196
储物箱　glove box　196
储液干燥器　reserve liquid dryer　113
储液器　reservoir　113
触发片　trigger vane　38
穿钉　nailing　49
穿孔销　eye bolt　105
传动电控单元　electronic transmission control unit　133
传动联轴器　drive coupling　14
传动系　transmission　229
传动箱体　transmission housing　141
传动轴　transmission shaft, propeller shaft, drive shaft　3，68，155
传感器　sensor　34
传感器轮盘　sensor wheel　36
传感器信号　sensor signal　36
传输泵转子　transfer pump rotor　18
传输孔　transfer hole　52
传输口　transfer port　7
传输通道管　transfer channel tube　163
传输压力调节器　transfer pressure adjuster　18
串联主（油）缸　tandem master cylinder　177，200
唇形密封　lip seal　134
唇形油封　lip oil seal　160
磁场框架　field frame　49
磁极　pole piece　184
磁通回路　flux return　226
磁性离合器　magnetic clutch　41，115
磁阻电动　reluctance motor　226
次级点火键　second menu　212
次蹄块　secondary shoe　170
从臂　trailing arm　71，87
从边　trailing edge　172
从动板　driven plate　121
从动带轮轴　secondary pully shaft　130
从动活塞　slave piston　129，183
从动轮固定半轮　secondary fixed half pulley　130，131
从动轮滑动半轮　secondary sliding half pulley　130，131
从动轮伺服缸　secondary pulley servo cylinder　130，131

从蹄　trailing shoe　171
粗尼龙过滤　coarse nylon filter　18
催化元件　catalytic element　207
催化转化器　catalytic converter　35，207
淬硬钢板　hardened steel plate　98
存储功能键　memory menu　212

D

DKW 逆流扫气发动机　reverse-flow scavenge dkw engine　7
DPA 泵　dpa pump　17
大齿轮　large pinion gear　127
大气压力　atmospheric pressure　6
带传动　belt drive　211
带轮　pulley　92
带轮位置传感器　pulley position sensor　131
带啮合齿轮　constant mesh gear　144，146
带式夹头　band clamp　168
带缘螺母　flanged nut　211
急速弹簧壳体　idle spring pack　14
急速调节螺钉　idle-speed adjusting screw　27
急速空气控制阀　idle air control valve　35
急速空气通道　idling air passage　38
急速控制阀　idle speed control valve　33
急速旁路阀启动器　idle by-pass valve actuator　26
急速启动器　idle speed actuator　36
急速燃油调节螺钉　idle fuelling adjustment screw　39
单板干式离合器　single plate dry clutch　133
单点喷射　single-point injection　31
单缸空气压缩机　single cylinder air compressor　181
单向阀　non-return valve　40，129
单向离合器　one-way clutch　49，134
单作用缸　single acting cylinder　170
挡杆　stop lever　13
挡杆控制轴　stop control shaft　13
挡圈　retaining (snap) ring　44
挡位指示器　shift position indicator　134
挡销　stop　121
挡轴　stop shaft　13
刀口连杆　knife edge link　121
刀口支柱　knife edge strut　121
导槽　guide slot　174
导轮　reactor　134
导向槽　guide slot　163
导向滚子　guide roller　163
导向销　slide pin　170
导向轴承　pilot bearing　118
导销防尘盖　pin dust cover　176
导销螺栓　guide pin bolt　176
导芯　guide core　134，136

导引臂　guide arm　90
倒车灯　reversing light, backup light　3，141
倒车行星齿轮装置　reverse planetary gear set　137
倒挡　reverse gear　123
倒挡齿轮　reverse gear　124
倒挡齿轮啮合　reverse gear engaged　131
倒挡多盘制动器　reverse multiplate brake　130
倒挡杆　reverse lever　125
倒挡伺服活塞　reverse servo piston　130
倒挡制动　reverse brake　131
倒挡轴　reverse shaft　124
道路动力源　roadway power source　220
灯光主开关　master lighting switch　195
低摩擦环　low friction ring　101
底部阀口　floor valve　99
底盘　chassis　216
底盘侧面件　chassis sidemember　106
底盘支架　chassis bracket　52
底托板　undertray　59
地板盘　floor pan　69
蒂带管　DeDion tube　82
颠簸挡块　jounce stop　101
点火开关　ignition switch　8，33
点火线圈　coil, ignition loop, ignition coil　8，35，193
点火销　firing pin　202
点火钥匙　ignition key　198
点烟器　lighter　195
电池框　cell frame　223
电磁比例阀　proportional solenoid valve　99
电磁开关　electromagnetic switch　49
电磁铁　solenoid　32，39，183，206
电磁铁回程弹簧　solenoid return spring　13
电磁铁绕组　solenoid winding　184
电磁铁线圈　solenoid coil　39
电动车轮制动器　electric wheel brake　221
电动窗主开关　power window master switch　198
电动机　electric motor　229
电动机控制器　electric motor controller　229
电动可调节转向柱　electrically adjustable steering column　162
电动汽车　electric vehicle　220

电动燃油泵　electric fuel pump　26，36
电动转向系统　electrical power steering system　169
电机　electric motor　227
电机控制器　motor controller　227
电接头　electrical connection　22，40
电解质　electrolyte　224
电控单元插口　ECU socket　38
电控器　electronic controller　200
电马达　electric motor　211
电气接头　electrical connection　194
电气配线接头　harness connector　37
电启动气囊点火机构　electrically actuated bag firing mechanism　202
电容器　condenser　193
电枢　armature　49
电刷架　brush holder　49
电刷架罩　brush holder cover　193
电伺服单元　electric servo unit　169
电涡流类缓速器　electric eddy current type retarder　185
电源　electrical supply, battery supply　13，141
电源继电器　power relay　33
电子传动控制　electronic transmission control　33
电子控制变速系统　electronic controlled transmission system　141
电子控制单元　electronic control unit　20
电子模导体　electronic module　141
电子燃油喷射系统　electronic fuel injection system　29
电子时钟　electronic clock　58
电子真空调节器　electronic vacuum regulator　33
垫板　base plate　77
垫片　shim　12
吊带　webbing harness　216
蝶形制动阀　butterfly brake valve　183
顶部螺母　capnut　9
顶灯　interior light　195
顶盖后横梁　rear roof bow　56
顶盖前横梁　front roof bow　56
顶盖纵梁　cantrail and roof panel　57

定位垫片　location washer　145
定位凸耳　locating tag　42
定位销　locating pin, dowelpin　44，45
定子　stator　135
定子毂　stator hub　140
定子销　stator pin　185
定子支撑板　stator support plate　184
动力分离控制　power-split control　228
动力转向泵　power steering pump　8
动力转向压力开关　power steering pressure switch　33
动轴　live axle　68
杜蛘悬架　Dubonnet suspension　95
端部　tip　12
端部浮动弹簧柱塞　end float spring and plunger　163
端部密封盖　end seal cover　25
端盖　end cover　49
端面凸轮　face cam　109
端盘　end plate　18
端子C套件　terminal C kit part　49
端子绝缘体（套）　terminal insulator　49，193
短距离里程表　trip mileometer　2
短上横向控制臂　short upper transverse control arm　77
短轴　strub shaft　83
短轴毂　stub axle hub　83
对接头　joint　12
多点喷射　multi-point injection　32
多功能接触器　multifunction contactor　141
多级液力变矩器　multistage torque converter　136
多孔式微喷油器　multi-hole injector　10
多块摩擦片式缓速器　multiplate friction type retarder　184
多连杆后轴　multi-link rear axle　71
多片离合器　multi plate clutch　118，181
多相绕组　polyphase winding　226
舵　rudder　216
惰簧　idling spring　17
惰轮　idle gear　49
惰轴　idle shaft　28

额外供油活塞　excess fuel delivery piston　19
额外燃油电磁铁　excess fuel solenoid　13
额外燃油轴　excess fuel shaft　13
轭架摆动型制动夹钳　swing yoke type brake caliper　176

轭架滑动型制动夹钳　sliding yoke type brake caliper　175
耳轴　trunnion　86
耳轴轴承　trunnion bearing　104
耳轴座　trunnion block　98

F

发电机　generator，alternator　8，193
发电机控制器　generator controller　221
发电机装置　generator set　221
发动机舱　engine compartment　112
发动机地脚　engine foot　52
发动机飞轮　engine flywheel　37
发动机分析仪　engine analyzer　212
发动机盖罩　engine cover　59
发动机冷却液温度　engine coolant temperature　195
发动机冷却液温度传感器　engine coolant temp. sensor　197
发动机速度传感器　engine speed sensor　34
发动机停机系统　engine immoblizer system　198
发动机载荷传感器　engine load sensor　141
发动机罩　engine bonnet　2
发动机罩前支撑板　engine front end panel　56
发动机支撑横梁　engine support cross member　56
发动机转速表　engine revolution counter　2
发动机转速传感器　engine speed sensor　93
发射器芯片　transponder chip　198
阀　valve　12
阀板　valve plate　181
阀盘　valve disc　102
阀体　body　26
阀头　valve head　39
阀推杆　valve push rod　9
阀针　valve needle　26
阀轴　valve spindle　25
阀座　valve seat　12，26
法兰　flange　74
法兰毂　flanged hub　211
法兰万向节联轴器　flanged universal joint coupling　148
翻折杆　roll over bar　65
反弹　rebound　103
反弹阀弹簧　rebound valve spring　102
反弹阀垫圈　rebound valve washer　102
反弹阀盖板　rebound valve cover plate　102
反弹腔　rebound housing　103
反弹压缩块　rebound compression block　103
反光镜　mirror　2
反射器　reflector　216
反向驱动垫　indirect pad　175
反向驱动活塞　indirect piston　175
反轴　countershaft　128
方向灯指示灯　indicator light　2

方形后背盖构形　squareback configuration　64
防抱死系统　anti-lock brake system　200
防擦层　chafer　189
防擦条　rub strip　57
防尘盖　dust cover　175
防尘管　dust tube　73
防尘密封垫　dust proof packing　193
防尘套　dust bellow　101
防滚动杆件　anti-roll bar　73
防滚架　roll over bar　218
防火套装　fireproof suit　217
防浪挡板　spray shield　216
防振垫盘　crashpan　216
防止滞后挡块　anti-stall stop　19
防转杆　anti-roll bar，anti-roll tube　79，80
防撞头盔　crash helmet　218
放油阀　oil unloader valve　109
放油塞　oil drain plug　123
飞轮　flywheel　8，44，118，134
飞轮鼓　flywheel drum　135
飞轮加速器传感器　flywheel accelerator sensor　200
飞轮螺栓　flywheel bolt　44
飞轮重物块　flyweight　15
飞行员降落伞　pilot parachute　216
非回转件　nonrotating part　188
非锁死型差速器　nonlockable differential　75
废气再循环阀　EGR valve　33，34
废气再循环管　EGR pipe　206
废气再循环控制　EGR control　20
废气再循环系统　exhaust gas recirculation system　206
废气再循环真空阀　EGR vacuum valve　206
分叉轭架　pronged yoke　156
分电器　distributor　8，193
分电器断路导线　distributor breaker lead　193
分电器盖　distributor cap　193
分电器壳体　distributor housing　193
分管路　duct　50
分火头　rotor　193
分离杆　release lever　118
分离泡　separation bubble　60
分离轴承　release bearing　118
分配器　distributor　38
分配器端盖　distributor cover　38
风窗玻璃　windscreen　2
风挡玻璃冲洗器　windshield washer　195

风挡顶部横梁　top windscreen rail　57
风扇　fan　8
风扇皮带　fan belt　8
封闭盖　closure cap　101
扶手　armrest　58
氟斯霍前悬架　Vauxhall front suspension　95
浮动调节器杆　floating adjuster link　170
浮动夹钳　floating calliper　187
浮动梭形阀　floating shuttle valve　109
浮动主轴　floating mainshaft　128，132
辅控阀　secondary governor valve　140

附加弹簧　supplementary spring　101
附属反向联齿　auxiliary counter gear cluster　128
附属空气装置　auxiliary-air device　27
附着流体　attached flow　60
复合行星齿轮轮系　compound epicycle gear train　127
复式离合器　muliple clutch　140
复位弹簧　return spring　26，130，147
副车架　sub-frame　3
副翼　flap　59
副轴轮　layshaft gear　123
腹板链轮　chain sprocket wheel　180

盖板　cover sheet，closure plate　77，103
杆臂　lever arm　178
感应电机　induction motor　226
感应式传感器　inductive sensor　36
刚性轴壳　rigid axle casing　75
刚性轴悬架　rigid axle suspension　77
钢板弹簧　spring clamp，leaf spring　77，216
钢盒　steel casing　52
钢珠　steel bead　102
缸壁　cylinder wall　114
缸体滑动型制动夹钳　slide cylinder body brake caliper　175
缸头　cylinder head　114
高度传感器　height sensor　92
高速齿轮离合器　high gear clutch　227
高压阀跳开器　high pressure valve jumper　129
高压油管　high-pressure pipeline　31
高阻抗回路　highreluctancepath　226
格林悬架　Girling suspension　95
隔离阀　isolator valve　88
隔离膜片　separator diaphragm　84
隔套　spacer　12，188
工作弹簧　duration spring　25
工作凸轮　operating cam　109
供气阀　delivery valve　181
供液阀　delivery valve　92
供油提升阀　supply poppet valve　109
供油柱塞　supply plunger　109
沟槽　groove　101，125
钩爪转销　jaw pivot pin　104
鼓式制动器　brake drum，drum brake　77，171
鼓形弹匣　drum magazine　216
固定板　shackle plate　86
固定点　fixing point　73

固定啮合齿组件　fixed dog clutch member　147
固定探测块　fixed detector block　168
固定外置接头　fixed outboard joint　192
固定弯脚器　fixed calliper　74
固定周边环齿　fixed annular ring gear　167
固定柱塞　anchor plunger　174
固定转枢　fixed pivot　22
故障灯　diagnostic light　141
挂耳　tab　73
拐角通道　cornet channel　104
冠齿安装法兰　crownwheel mounting flange　150
冠齿轮盘　crownwheel　148
冠齿轮盘法兰　crown wheel flange　147
管件横向件　tubular cross-member　106
管路真空　manifold vacuum　41
管内压力　manifold pressure　30
管式轴梁　tubular axle beam　80
管形腔体　tubular casing　80
管压传感器　manifold pressure sensor　35
管状钢架　tubular steel frame　217
惯性卷轴　inertia reel　194
惯性开关　inertia switch　33
光电传感器　optoelectronic sensor　37
光电二极管　photodiode　37
光截止催化转化器　light-off catalytic converter　207
光敏管　phototransistor　168
归零按钮　reset button　58
滚盘　scroll plate　19
滚针　needle roller　146
滚针从动件销　roller follower pin　161
滚针滚子　needle roller　144
滚珠传输管　transfer tube　163
滚柱罩　roll cage　217
滚子　roller　15

滚子单向离合器　one-way roller clutch　129
过滤网　filter screen　14
过压阀　over press valve　51
过油连接销　excess fuel linkage pin　19

豪华轿车　limousine　56
恒定齿轮　constant gear wheel　144
恒速万向节　constant velocity universal joint　83
恒温器　thermostat　51，112
恒温调节器　thermostat regulator　112
横臂　transverse arm　73，95
横槽　transverse groove　101
横杆　transverse link　76
横杆安装点　transverse link mounting point　74
横跨件　cross member　73
横向板弹簧　transverse leaf spring　96
横向杆件　cross-member　69
横向控制臂　transverse control arm　71
横向螺杆　transverse screw　72
横向瓦特杆　transverse Watt linkage　80
后安装座　rear mounting　73
后部弹性轴承　elastic rear bearing　76
后差速器　rear differential　77
后窗玻璃　back window glass　58
后窗尾灯梁　rear window backlight rail　57
后独立悬架　rear suspension-independent　95
后端盖　rectifier end frame　193
后端罩　rear end cover　193
后盖　back plate　15
后高度水平支柱启动器　rear height and levelling strut actuator　92
后路面轮　rear road wheel　106
后轮　rear wheel　3
后轮电动制动　rear electric brake　221
后轮末端传动　rear final drive　202
后轮制动传感器　rear brake sensor　200
后轮制动器　rear wheel arrester　3
后门立柱　rear door pillar　57
后门踏步灯开关　rear door courtesy switch　198
后门行李箱灯开关　rear door courtesy switch　198
后启动器　rear actuator　96
后千斤顶把手　rear jack handle　216
后驱动桥　rear drive axle　155
后软驱弹簧　rear soft ride spring　92
后上叉杆　rear upper wishbone　218
后视镜　rear-view mirror　218
后双轮　rear double wheel　218
后水平控制电磁阀　rear levelling control solenoid valve　92
后围板　rear end panel　56
后下叉杆　rear lower wishbone　218
后泄漏接头　back-leak connection　9
后悬挂　rear suspension　84
后悬挂减振　rear suspension shock absorber　218
后悬架　rear suspension　3
后翼主板　rear aerofoil wing　218
后翼组件　rear wing assembly　59
后硬驱电磁阀　rear stiffening solenoid valve　92
后照灯　rear light　3
后轴　rear axle　71，218
后轴承　rear bearing　49，124
后柱　rear pillar　56
后座下横梁　cross member under seat　56
互冷器　intercooler　34
互联管　interconnecting pipe　84
花键　spline　147
花键半轴毂　splined half shaft hub　150
花键传动轴　splined drive shaft　181
花键轮毂　splined hub　119
花键输入轮毂　splined input hub　184
花键输入轴　splined input shaft　120
滑板　sliding plate　77
滑动部件　sliding member　93
滑动啮合齿组件　sliding dog clutch member　147
滑轨手柄　track handle　59
滑块　slipper block　86
滑套齿形离合器　sliding sleeve dog clutch　154
滑套壳　sliding sleeve hub　145
滑移轮毂　sliding hub　146
滑柱型制动夹钳　slide pin type brake caliper　176
化油器　carburetor　8
环槽　ring channel　103
环齿　annular gear, ring gear　120，130
环形齿轮　annulus ring gear　127
环形导芯　torus guide core　135
环形过滤纱网　circular filter gauze　31
环形架　annulus carrier　129
环形内齿　annulus ring gear　129
环形润滑脂密封　spherical grease seal　155
环形油缸　annular cylinder　188
环形支架　annulus carrier　127

Vocabulary with Figure Index 词汇及图形索引（中英对照） 261

环状轮齿　ring gear teeth　37
缓冲橡胶块　cushioning rubber block　105
缓速器输出轴　retarder output shaft　184
缓速器支座　retarder support bracket　184
换挡叉套　selector fork sleeve　144
换挡杆　gear lever，shift selector lever，shift lever　123，124，196
换挡杆手柄　gear knob　123
换向阀　shift valve　140
回流节制阀　return flow restrictor valve　11
回位弹簧　return spring　49，121，135，170
回油关闭阀　back closing valve　51
回油管　back tubing　31
回珠导向器　return guide　163
回转件　rotating part　188

回转连接器　rotary coupler　194
彗星燃烧室　comet combustion chamber　6
混合动力车　hybrid vehicle　227
混合动力系统　hybrid system　228
混合控制单元　mixture control unit　27
混合气流　mixture flow　23
混气塞　bleed plug　24
活动梁　articulating beam　87
活塞　piston　8
活塞阀口　piston valve　99
活塞环腔　ring chamber　99
活塞膜片　pistion diaphragm　84
活性炭罐　carbon canister，charcoal canister　33，206
火花塞　sparking plug，spark plug　8，38

IC 调节器　IC regulator　193

机壳　chassis　49
机枪　machine-gun　216
机械传感器　mechanical sensor　202
机械调节器　mechanical governor　17
机械启动气囊点火机构　mechanically actuated bag firing mechanism　202
机油泵　oil pump　51
机油冷却器　engine oil cooler　51
机油滤清器　oil filter，engine oil cleaner　8，51
机油压力警报灯　oil pressure warning light　195
机油油压表　engine oil pressure gauge　196
激励环　excitor ring　205
棘爪　ratchet pawl，ratchet　109，188
集滤器　concentrate colander　51
计量阀　metering valve　17
继电器开关　relay switch　93
加德纳喷油器　Gardner injector　10
加箍螺栓　hoop bolt　77
加热调节器　warm-up regulator　27
加热器　heater　2
加热型氧传感器　heated oxygen sensor　197
加速控制杆　accelerator control arm　183
加速器开关　accelerator switch　183
加速踏板　accelerator pedal　2，22，140，183
加速踏板开关　accelerator pedal switch　34
加速踏板位置传感器　accelerator pedal position sensor　34

加油塞　filler plug　134
加载板　load plate　180
夹紧弹簧　grip spring　177
夹钳　caliper　178
夹钳支架　caliper carrier　180
监控单元　monitoring unit　229
检测阀　check valve　30
减速活塞　deboost piston　200
减速正时腔　decel timing chamber　40
减速正时组件　decel timing assembly　40
减振杆　shock absorber cartridge　101
减振回流活塞弹簧　shock damper return piston spring　95
减振活塞　shock damper piston　95
减振器　shock absorber　72，75
减振溢流阀塞　shock damper relieve valve plug　95
渐开空腔弹簧　involute bellow spring　89
降挡开关　kickdown switch　197
降落伞释放架　parachute release stand　216
降落伞索线　parachute cable　216
交叉轴释放杆　cross-shaft release lever　120
交流发动机　alternator　8
角铁　angle plate　126
铰接头　hinge joint　125
铰链　hinge　66

脚动驻车制动器　foot-operated parking brake　188
脚控阀　foot control valve　183，185
脚轮　foot wheel　106
脚刹开关　foot brake switch　93
接触板　contact plate　49
接触臂　striking arm　126
接触杆　striking finger　125
接触臂末端　end of the striking arm　124
接线端　terminal　50
接线座　terminal　224
节流板　throttle plate　27，32
节流板控制马达　throttle plate control motor　32
节流阀　throttle valve　140
节流阀电位计　throttle valve potentiometer　197
节流阀位置传感器　throttle position sensor　35
节流连杆　throttle link　17
节流器　throttle actuator　228
节流小孔　restricted orifice　22
节流轴　throttle shaft　13，28
节气门挡钉　throttle stop screw　39
节气门电压表　throttle potentiometer　39
节气门位置传感器　throttle position sensor　32，197
结合叉　companion yoke　124
截止弹簧　pull-off spring　178，180
截止电磁铁　shut-off solenoid　28
截止阀　shut-down valve, cut-off valve　14，200
截止杆　shut-off bar　17
金属罩　metallic housing　207

紧凑型纵向臂后轴　compact trailing arm rear axle　72
进口阀　inlet valve　122
进气百叶窗　intake shuttter　34
进气电磁阀　inlet solenoid valve　93
进气碟阀　disc inlet valve　182
进气管　air inlet pipe　147
进气加热器　intake heater　34
进气控制阀　air intake control valve　40
进气口　inlet port　7
进气门　inlet valve　8
进气歧管　intake manifold, air-inlet manifold　9，31，217
进气软管　intake tube　9
进气凸轮轴　air inlet camshaft　48
进气温度传感器　intake air temperature sensor　34
进油口　feed port　11
近光灯　dipped headlight　3，195
颈圈　collar　11
警示灯　flashing warming light　218
径向填料密封　radial packing seal　134
静止板凸耳　stator plate lugs　184
静止杆　stationary lever　221
静止锥形离合器构件　stationary cone clutch member　129
局部节流旁路槽　part throttle by-pass slot　25
局部离心块　half eccentric　178
锯齿形弹簧　zigzag spring　59
卷带筒　belt ree　194
绝热垫　heat shield　171

K

卡环　clasp　49
卡钳　caliper　170
卡圈　snap ring, circlip　74，155
卡爪　jaw　74
开槽　slit　80
开槽盘　slit disc　168
开合环　split ring　145
开合摩擦环式同步离合器　split baulk ring synchromesh unit　145
开合锁销式同步离合器　split baulk pin synchromesh unit　146
开合套　split collet　39
开合同步环　split synchronizingring　145
开路继电器　circuit opening relay　29
开式敞篷车　open cabriolet　65
靠背　seat back　59

靠背骨架　seatback frame　59
（靠背）倾角调节器释放手柄　inclining adjuster release handle　59
壳体　housing　124
壳形件　pot member　102
可变电阻　variable resistor　29
可拆盖罩　detachable cover　42
可拆解滑柱座　decoupled strut mount　72
可拆卸方向盘　detachable steering wheel　216
可调立柱　adjustable vertical struts　66
可调释放轴承外套　adjustable release bearing outer sleeve　120
可调转向柱　collapsible steering tube　160
可翻转膜片弹簧　rolling diaphragm spring　89
可移动遮光眼罩　tear-away visor cover　218
可转（支撑）杆　radius arm　80

Vocabulary with Figure Index 词汇及图形索引（中英对照）

客货两用轿车　estate wagon　56
空调控制开关　climate control　196
空调散热器风扇开关　A/C radiator fan switching　33
空调压缩机　A/C compressor　8
空调压缩机离合器　A/C compressor clutch　33
空气泵　air pump　8
空气附属装置　auxiliary-air device　28
空气缓冲器　air absorber　188
空气活塞　air pistion　122
空气连接管　air connection pipe　89
空气量　airmass　22
空气流量传感器板　air-flow sensor plate　27
空气流量传感器叶片　air-flow sensor flap　40
空气流量计　air-flow meter　26
空气漏孔　air funnel　27
空气滤清器　air filter，air cleaner　8，33
空气平衡控制阀　levelling air control valve　89
空气/燃油控制筒　air-fuel control barrel　14
空气温度传感器　air-temperature sensor　40
空气压缩机　air compressor　51
空气质量流量计　mass air flow meter　33
空腔干燥器　air drier　93

空燃比传感器　air fuel ratio sensor　197
空心蜗杆轴　hollow worm　149
空中平台　aerial boom platform　218
孔式喷油器　hole type nozzle　10
控制叉　control fork　15
控制齿条　control rack　14
控制单元　control unit　36
控制杆　control rod　13
控制杆行程调节螺钉　control rod travel adjustment screw　13
控制杆支架　control rod bracket　15
控制杠杆　control lever　95
控制滑块　control slide　50
控制连杆　control link　156
控制面板　control panel，control panel display　96，196
控制轴　control shaft　15
控制柱塞　control plunger　27
扣件　brace　74
快速后背构形　fastback configuration　64
扩散板　diffuser　59

拉动组件　draw link assembly　171
拉杆　tie rod　74
拉杆球节头　drag link ball joint　108
拉杆轴　barshaft　192
拉绳　cable　188
拉绳支架　cable bracket　188
喇叭　horn　2，195
喇叭按钮　horn button　201
冷凝器　condenser　112
冷凝器单元　condenser unit　115
冷凝器蛇形管　condenser coil　115
冷启动喷嘴　cold start injector　26
冷却风扇　cooling fan　8
冷却回路　cooling circuit　158
冷却剂温度传感器　coolant temperature sensor　35
冷却器管　cooler duct　59
冷却水　coolant　8
冷却系统　cooling system　51
冷却液泵　coolant pump　8
冷却液温度表　coolant temperature gauge　58
离合器　clutch　3，118，200，229
离合器衬垫　clutch lining　140
离合器分泵　clutch slave cylinder　123

离合器分离推放杆　clutch release rod　123
离合器开关　clutch switch　183
离合器壳　clutch housing　118
离合器启动缸　clutch actuator cylinder　133
离合器踏板　clutch pedal　2，122，183
离合器脱开机构　clutch release mechanism　136
离合器外罩　clutch bell-housing　123
离合器主动盘　clutch disc　118
离合器控制器　clutch controller　229
里程表　mileometer　2
里程传感器　travel sensor　186
力矩杆　torque rod　86
立槽　vertical slot　109
立式可调转矩支架　vertically adjustable torque support　74
连板内舌　inner tongue on link plate　19
连板扭簧　link plate torsion-spring　19
连杆　connecting rod　8
连杆盖　connecting-rod top　44，48
连杆件　linkage member　95
连杆螺栓　connecting-rod bolt　44
连杆体　connecting-rod body　44，48
连管　bridge pipe　171

连接板　link plate　15，19
连接臂　link arm　79
连接钩　linkage hook　17
连接块　bridge block　178
连接缆绳　connecting cable　194
连接爪　coupling jaw　104
帘式防护气囊　curtain shield airbag　201
联动装置　remote linkage　123
梁板　beam plate　105
两速双级减速螺旋齿轮轴　two speed double reduction helical gear axle　154
领蹄　leading shoe　170
流出板　flux plate　184
流量控制阀　flow control valve　165
流体　fluid　52
流体分离　flow separation　60
流体附着　flow reattachment　60
流体摩擦偶合器　fluid friction coupling　135
流线　streamline　59
六角螺母　hexagonal nut　101
六角螺栓　hexagonal bolt　74
卢卡斯发动机　Lucas engine　7
路面感应电动车　road-induced electricity　220
路面速度　road speed　93

滤纸件　filter paper element　16
旅行车　estate car　56
铝缸盖　aluminium cylinder head　181
轮缸　wheel cylinder　171
轮毂架　wheel hub carrier　73
轮毂罩　hubcap　2
轮径测仪　wheel diameter gauge　211
轮距杆球节头　track rod ball joint　108
轮室　wheel well　56
轮胎胎芯　bead core　191
轮胎信息标签　tire information label　4
螺杆型油挡　screw-type oil baffle　50
螺栓臂　bolt arm　88
螺栓弹簧　coil spring　79
螺栓孔销　eye bolt pin　121
螺纹保持盖　screwed retainer cap　168
螺纹调节筒　threaded adjustment barrel　180
螺纹孔螺栓套　threaded eye bolt sleeve　120
螺旋齿轮　spiral gear　50
螺旋弹簧　spiral spring，coil spring　38，95
螺旋电缆　spiral cable　201
螺旋桨　propeller　216
螺旋桨齿轮箱　propeller gear box　216
螺旋润滑槽　helical grease groove　168

M

马达控制器　motor controller　221
埋磁电机　buried magnet motor　226
麦弗逊支柱　Macpherson strut　83，96
脉冲空气电磁阀　pulse air solenoid valve　33
脉冲器　pulsator　35
脉冲阻尼　pulsation damper　14
锚定块　anchor block　145
铆钉　rivet　171
门护板　panel　58
门槛　sill　69
门锁控制系统　door lock control system　198
门锁内手柄　indoor handle　58

密封　seal　12
密封边口　sealing edge　102
密封垫圈　sealing washer　11
模具成形偏转板　moulded deflector　66
膜片　diaphragm　19
摩擦垫片　friction washer　119
摩擦片　friction lining　171
摩擦推力垫片　friction thrust washer　181
末端传动冠齿轮　final drive crown wheel gear　131
末端减速齿轮　final reduction gear　152
末端驱动箱体　final drive casing　95

N

钠硫电池　sodium-sulphur battery　224
耐摩擦衬垫　friction lining　188
内部电极　inside electrode　207
内部轮毂　inner hub　145
内齿离合器　internal dog clutch　126
内带花键转子毂　rotor hub internally splined　184

内鼓轮　inner drum　118
内轮毂　inner hub　142，144
内驱轴　internal drive shaft　227
内置行星齿轮双级减速轴　inboard epicylic double reduction axle　153
内置行星双级减速末端传动轴　inboard epicyclic

double reduction final drive axle 153
内置柱塞接头 plunging inboard joint 192
内锥形内齿 internal bevelled dog teeth 145
黏性离合器 visco clutch 77
黏液联轴器 viscous coupling 203
啮合杆 engagement lever 211
镍氢电池 nickel-metal hydride battery 224
拧紧夹头 pinch clamp 168
扭矩弹簧 torque spring 14

扭矩杆 torsion bar 165
扭矩管 torsion tube 95
扭矩阻尼器 torsion damper 140
扭转弹性轴承 torsionally elastic bearing 72
扭转杆 torsion bar, torque tube 72, 80
扭转减振弹簧 torsional damper spring 119
扭转轴 torsion shaft 95
暖风机 heater machine 51
暖风机进水管 heater machine penstock 51

P

排出阀 discharge valve 116
排出管线 discharge line 116
排出口 discharge port, exhaust outlet 116, 216
排放控制标签 emission control label 4
排漏塞 drain plug 16
排气电磁阀 exhaust solenoid valve unit 93
排气碟阀 disc discharge valve 182
排气管 exhaust pipe 9, 218
排气口 exhaust port 7
排气门 exhaust valve 8, 48
排气旁路阀 exhaust bypass valve 43
排气岐管 exhaust manifold 183, 217
排气凸轮轴 exhaust camshaft 48
排气压力 exhaust pressure 6
排气氧传感器 HEGO sensor 33
排脏器 dirt excluder 171
牌照 number plate 2
牌照灯 number plate light 3
潘哈杆 Panhard rod 75
盘式制动器 disc brake 217
旁路钮 bypass button 14
旁路通道 bypass groove 103
旁路小孔 bypass aperture 38
旁设电动机 standby electric motor 115
跑车 sports car 56
配气机构 valve train 48
配油口 distributor port 17
配油转子 distributor rotor 18
喷射泵 injection pump 14
喷射泵计量单元 injection pump calibration unit 34
喷射控制器 injection controller 14
喷射器 injector 20
喷射器电接头 injector electrical terminal 35
喷射器燃油过滤器 injector fuel filter 35
喷射器凸轮 injector cam 183
喷射摇杆 injector rocker 183

喷射正时活塞 injection timing piston 22
喷油泵 injection pump 7, 51
喷油器 injector 7
喷油推进器 injection advancer 31
喷嘴 nozzle, injector 9, 26
喷嘴本体 nozzle body 11
喷嘴阀针 jet needle 32
喷嘴盖罩 jet cap 23
喷嘴固定座 nozzle holder 26
喷嘴管 jet tube 23
喷嘴夹套 nozzle holder 11
喷嘴套 nozzle cap 10
喷嘴小孔 jet orifice 23
喷嘴支座 jet carrier 23
膨胀阀 expansion valve 113
膨胀器 inflator 202
膨胀器带 expander band 145
膨胀器腔体 expander housing 173
膨胀水管 bulge water swell 51
膨胀元件 expansion element 14
皮带自动张紧轮 automatic belt tensioner 8
片弹簧 leaf spring 15
片状开关 vane switch 38
偏航陀螺仪 yaw gyro 96
偏心衬套 eccentric liner 18
偏心件 eccentric 188
偏心轮架 eccentric yoke 129
偏心速度选挡杆 speed selector eccentric 154
偏心凸轮 eccentric cam 200
偏心轴 eccentric shaft 167
偏心轴销 eccentric shaft peg 167
偏转板侧隔板 deflector side baffle 66
偏转弹簧 bias spring 187
偏转气流 deflected airstream 66
频闪仪 stroboscope device 211
频闪仪指示灯 stroboscope lamp 211

平衡臂　equalizer　188
平衡阀　levelling valve　88
平衡杆　levelling rod　99
平衡梁　balance beam　86
平衡腔　equalization chamber　100
平衡重　balance weight　44
平衡重量指示器　balance weight indicator　211
平行混合动力系统　parallel hybrid system　229
平行混合驱动　parallel hybrid drive　229

Q

鳍板　fin　116
鳍边　flipper　191
气缸　cylinder, air cylinder　8，122
气缸测试键　cylinder test menu　212
气缸盖　cylinder head　8
气缸体　cylinder block　8
气流分离　flow separation　60
气门　valve　8
气门弹簧　valve spring　48
气门导管　guide, valve guide　39，48
气门锁夹　valve locker　48
气门油封　valve oil seal　48
气座　valve seat　48
气囊侧传感器　side airbag sensor　201
气囊传感器总成　airbag sensor assembly　202
气囊后传感器　airbag sensor rear　201
气体主阀　gas main spring　99
气温传感器　air thermo sensor　29
汽车底盘　chassis　71
汽车解码器　automobile decoder　210
汽车示波器　automobile oscilloscope　212
汽油泵　gasoline pump　9
汽油箱　gasoline tank　9
启动齿圈　startup ring gear　134
启动弹簧　priming spring　18
启动机　starting engine　8
启动机壳体　starter housing　49
启动机离合器　starter clutch　49
启动器　actuator　34
启动器气腔　actuator air chamber　178
启动套齿形离合器组件　actuating sleeve dog clutch member　147
牵引底盘　tractor chassis　104
牵引电池组　traction battery pack　221
牵引电磁阀单元　traction solenoid valve unit　205
牵引力控制系统　traction control system　202
牵引力提升单元　traction boost unit　205
牵引马达　traction motor　220
铅笔式喷油嘴　pencil nozzle　12
铅酸电池　lead-acid battery　225

前车轮　front wheel　3
前窗玻璃　windshield glass　58
前窗除霜器　windshield defroster　195
前窗刮水器　windshield wiper　195
前窗下横梁　cross member under windshield　56
前弹簧固锁销　front spring shackle pin　108
前挡板　bulk head　69
前风挡立柱　front screen pillar　57
前刚性电磁阀　front stiffening solenoid valve　92
前高度水平支柱启动器　front height and levelling strut actuator　92
前横梁　front cross member　56
前进装置　advance device　17
前轮末端传动　front final drive　202
前制动传感器　front brake sensor　200
前轮制动器　front wheel arrester　3
前门踏步灯开关　front door courtesy switch　198
前启动器　front actuator　96
前千斤顶把手　front jack handle　216
前上叉杆　front upper wishbone　218
前水平控制电磁阀　front levelling control solenoid valve　92
前围板　dash panel　57
前雾灯　front fog light　195
前下叉杆　front lower wishbone　218
前行多盘离合器　forward multiplate clutch　130
前行离合器　forward clutch　130
前行行星齿轮装置　forward planetary gear set　137
前悬挂　front suspension　84，218
前悬架　front suspension　3
前翼组件　front wing assy　59
前照灯　front light　3
前轴　front axle　71
前轴承　front bearing　49，124
前柱　front pillar　56
前纵梁　front side member　56
前座椅气囊　front seat airbag　201
浅凹　dimpled　130
浅坑　shallow recess　124
腔盖　housing cover　120

腔室锥形离合器组件 casing cone clutch member 127
倾斜导杆 inclined guide link 98
清污电磁阀 purge solenoid valve 33
球阀 ball valve 18, 129
球笼式等速万向节 rzeppa universal joint 156
球体保持架 ball cage 155
球体滚道 ball track 157
球体铰接 jointed ball 124
球窝轴承 ball-and-socket bearing 126
球销传动 ballpin drive 50
球形环腔 spherical spring chamber 84
球形换挡手把 ball-type selector 124
球形件 spherical member 98
球形扩口 spherical enlargement 156
球形柱 ball post 122
球轴承 ball bearing 118, 184
球座接头 ball and socket joint 125
曲轴 crankshaft 8, 44, 114, 121

曲轴传感器 crankshaft sensor 35
曲轴角传感器 crank angle sensor 206
曲轴位置传感器 crankshaft position sensor 34, 197
曲轴箱 crankcase 114
曲轴箱吸气接头 crankcase breather connection 42
曲轴正时齿轮 crankshaft timing gear 44
曲轴正时齿形带轮 crankshaft timing belt gear wheel 48
曲轴转速 crankshaft speed 22
驱动板 drive plate 119
驱动齿轮 drive gear 124
驱动端盖 cover drive 49
驱动盖槽 drive cover slot 120
驱动块 drive block 120
驱动轴 drive shaft, drive spindle 17, 180, 200
驱动轴联轴法兰 drive shaft coupling flange 131

R

燃料入口 fuel inlet 9
燃料箱 fuel tank 217
燃油 fuel 195
燃油调压器 fuel pressure regulator 33
燃油发动机控制器 combustion engine controller 229
燃油分配器 fuel distributor 26
燃油轨道 fuel rail 33
燃油过滤器 fuel filter 27
燃油截止从动缸 fule cut-off slave cylinder 183
燃油控制 fuel control 20
燃油量调节板 fuel adjustment plate 18
燃油喷出 fuel delivery 11
燃油喷嘴 fuel injector 33
燃油入口 fuel inlet 14
燃油温度传感器 fuel temperature sensor 34
燃油雾化 atomised fuel 23
燃油箱 fuel tank 27
燃油蓄能器 fuel accumulator 26

燃油压力调节器 fuel pressure regulator 26, 32
燃油压力调节器组件 fuel pressure regulator assembly 35
绕轴阀 spool valve 164
绕组 winding 26
热交换器 heat exchanger 184
冗余阀 redundancy valve 186
熔断丝 fuse block 195
柔性环接头 flexible-ring joint 156
柔性稳定器 flexible stabilizer 128
乳化团 emulsion block 24
入口螺栓 inlet bolt 12
润滑系统油路 lubrication system oil route 51
润滑油 lubricant 8
润滑油压力开关 oil press switch 35
润滑脂嘴 grease fitting 77
润滑嘴 lubrication nipple 120

三叉架型万向节 tripronged type universal joint 157
三叉柔性联轴器 tripot flexible coupling 73
三口两冲程发动机 three-port two-stroke engine 7
三球销式万向节 tripot type universal joint 157
散热器风口 air intake to radiator 216
散热箱 radiator pod 59

扫描仪 scan tool 212
沙漏形蜗杆 hourglass worm 161
扇形齿 sector gear 163
扇形齿轮杆 toothed sector lever 173
扇形齿轴 sector shaft 163
扇形齿轴轴承 sector shaft bearing 163

上边梁　roof rail　56
上部叉形杆臂　upper wishbone arm　79
上部密封条　upper seal　58
上部橡胶膜垫　upper rubber diaphram　52
上部中心立柱　upper centre pillar　57
上弹簧座　upper spring seat　101
上横杆　upper transverse link　74
上控制臂　upper control arm　73
上控制活塞　upper control piston　186
上气环　upper compression　44
上气门弹簧座　ascending valve spring seat　48
上止点传感器　tdc sensor　37
上止推片　submit still trundle patch　44
渗漏螺钉　bleed screw　122
渗气口　air bleed　25
升降臂　drop arm　160
湿式离合器　wet clutch　127
十字销组件　cross-pin member　85
拾取管　pickup pipe　129
拾取线圈　pick up coil　199
适应安装垫　compliant mount　98
释放按钮　release button　188
释放板　release plate　121
释放杆　release lever　120
释放手把　release hand lever　106
释放轴承　release bearing　121
释放轴承内套　release bearing inner sleeve　120
释放轴承腔　release bearing housing　120
释放轴承组件　release bearing assembly　122
手动阀　manual valve　140
手动制动杆　hand brake lever　173，187
手动驻车制动器　hand-operated parking brake　188
手刹开关　hand brake switch　93
手刹膨胀腔　handbrake expander housing　171
手套箱　glove compartment　2
手闸　handle　170
受拉梁　draw beam　105
输出法兰　output flange　134
输出速度传感器　output speed sensor　197
输出叶轮轴　output propeller shaft　184
输出轴　output shaft　124
输出轴法兰接头　output shaft flanged coupling　184
输出轴附属齿轮　output shaft auxiliary gear　128
输出轴小齿轮　output shaft pinion gear　130
输入带轮　input pulley　200
输入法兰联轴器　input flange coupling　151
输入减速齿轮　input reduction gear　152
输入速度传感器　input speed sensor　197

输入轴　input shaft　118，124
输入轴轴承　input shaft bearing　124
输油泵　oil pump　31
束套　yoke　10
数字点火系统　digital ignition system　38
数字万用表　fluke digital multimeter　212
栓钉　peg　160
双叉形件悬架　double wishbone suspension　77
双点火线圈　double ignition loop　36
双缸并列发动机　side-by-side twin engine　7
双缸相对排列发动机　opposed twin engine　7
双缸压缩机　twin cylinder compressor　182
双管减振器　twintube shock absorber　74
双列角接触轴承　two row angular（contact）ball bearing　74
双门小轿车　coupe　56
双模式驱动系统　bi-mode drive system　227
双驱动盘　twin drive plate　120
双万向节恒速接头　double hooke's type constant velocity joint　155
双行星齿轮　double planetary gear　131
双重隔板　double bulkhead　57
双锥形结构　biconical profile　9
双作用缸　double acting cylinder　170
双作用缸膨胀器　double acting cylinder expander　170
水泵传动齿形带轮　water pump transmission belt gear wheel　48
水陆两用车　amphibian　216
水平控制阀　levelling control valve　90
水温表　temperature gauge　2
水温传感器　water thermo sensor　29
税牌　tax disc　2
司机功能开关　driver's function switch　93
司机位安全气囊　driver's seat bag　202
四缸直列发动机　four-cylinder in-line engine　7
四轮定位仪　automobile 4-wheel aligner　210
四轮驱动多用汽车　four-wheel drive vehicle　56
四轮驱动杆　four-wheel drive lever　216
四门轿车　four-door saloon　56
伺服电机　servomotor　161
伺服阀　servo valve　96
伺服缸　servo cylinder　130
伺服活塞　servo piston　130
速度表　speedometer，tachometer　2，169
速度截止阀　speed out valve　140
榫舌槽　tongue groove　175
索雷尔燃烧室　Saurer combustion chamber　6
锁固销　shackle pin　109

锁紧螺母　lock nut　120
锁片　locking piece　49
锁止按钮　shaft lock button　134
锁止离合器　lock-up clutch　136
锁止式液力变矩器　lock-up torque converter　140
锁止爪　parking pawl　137

T

T 形轴外壳　T-shaped axle casing　74
踏板件　pedestal member　98
胎面　tread　189
胎缘钢丝　bead wire　189
胎缘束　bead wrap　189
抬升架　lift yoke　90
抬升空腔　lift bellow　90
太阳轮　sun gear　127
太阳轮锥形离合器　sun gear cone clutch　127
弹簧　spring　11，74
弹簧滑柱　spring strut　74
弹簧环　elastic ring　101
弹簧加载盘　spring laded disc　118
弹簧加载球体　spring-loaded ball　126
弹簧减振器　spring shock absorber　77
弹簧销　spring pin　77
弹簧销衬套　spring bushing　77
弹簧压头　spring clamp　12
弹簧座　spring seat，spring bracket，spring tower　9，12，19，69
弹性管　elastomer tube　100
弹性体弹簧　elastomer spring　74
碳块密封　carbon dam seal　12
陶瓷钮　ceramic button　119
套　collar　74
套叉　sleeve fork　180
套管　boot, gaiter　122，159
套螺母　sleeve nut　211
套式输出口　sleeve output port　17
特氟龙气体密封圈　Teflon gas seal　12
提升挡块　lift stop　11
提升量调节螺钉　lift adjustment screw　12
提升器　enhancer　194
蹄块保持架　shoe retainer　174
蹄块复位弹簧　shoe return spring　171
蹄块腹板　shoe web　173
蹄块滚子组件　shoe and roller assemblies　18
蹄块结合块　shod abutment　170
蹄块支架　shoe carrier　135
蹄块转枢　shoe pivot　135
天窗　scuttle　112
天窗背式构形　hatchback configuration　64

调节臂　governor arm　17
调节弹簧　regulating spring　18
调节阀　governor valve　181
调节滑块　calibration slide　26
调节活塞　regulating piston　18
调节链　adjuster chain　180
调节螺钉　adjustment screw, regulator screw　30，35
调节螺母　adjustment nut　121
调节器　governor　31
调节器弹簧　governor spring　15，17
调节器壳体　governor cage　15
调节器连杆　governor link rod　183
调节器配重　governor weight　14，17
调节器组件　governor assembly　22
调节套　regulating sleeve　18
调节柱塞　adjuster plunger, governor plunger　14，174
调节爪　adjusting pawl　174
调速柱塞管　governor plunger tube　182
调压阀　pressure regulating valve　140，177
调整垫片　adjusted gasket　49
调整杆　trim lever　79
调制器单元　modulator unit　200
条形码标签　bar code label　4
停止杆　stop　14
挺杆　tappet strut　173
挺杆头　tappet head　173
挺杆柱塞　tappet plunger　173
通道　tunnel　69
通风碟　ventilated disc　180
通风机　ventilator　195
通风盘　ventilated disc　178
通气碟　ventilated disc　172
通气小孔　vent orifice　18
同步（齿形）带　synchronous belt　48
同步环　synchronizer ring　123
同步（离合）器　synchronizer　124，142
同步轮毂　synchronizing hub　144
同步啮合驱动轮毂　synchromesh drive hub　128
同步啮合装置　synchromesh device　126
同步锥形轮毂　synchronizing cone hub　146

同极电动　homopolar machine　226
筒体　cylinder　147
头部固定配件　head location fitting　18
头枕　headrest　59
透明鼓　transparent drum　211
透明筒　transpatent bowl　16
凸出齿　finger　126
凸耳推力垫片　lugged thrust washer　119
凸轮从动件　tappet　171
凸轮滚子　cam roller　17
凸轮环　cam ring　19
凸轮轴　camshaft　8，15，51
凸轮轴识别传感器　camshaft identification sensor　33
凸轮轴位置传感器　camshaft position sensor　197
凸轮轴正时齿形带轮　camshaft timing belt gear wheel　48
推垫　thrust pad　15
推杆　push rod　8，122

推进粒　propellant grain　194
推力板　thrust plate　129
推力弹簧　thrust spring　129
推力挡圈　thrust washer　144
推力垫片　thrust washer　119，142
推力滚子　thrust roller　144
推力肩盘　thrust pad　15
推力块　thrust block　145
推力球轴承滚道　thrust ballrace　129
推力套　thrust sleeve　15，17
推销　thrust pin　15，144
托架　carrier bracket　175
拖车底盘　trailor chassis　104
拖车平台　trailor platform　104
拖杆孔　drawbar eye　105
脱开轴承　release bearing　136
脱扣手把　uncoupling handle　105

U 形螺栓　U-bolt　77

V 形槽坡面　Vee slot ramp　149
V 形辅助块　Vee helper　87

V 形缸体压缩机　Vee cylinder compressor　115

W

瓦特杆　Watt linkage　82
外部电极　outside electrode　207
外部滑动套轮毂　outer sliding sleeve hub　145
外部支架　outer yoke　155
外层橡胶　wall rubber　189
外齿　external teeth　126
外毂推板　outer hub thrust plate　181
外轮毂套　outer hub sleeve　142
外置行星直齿轮双级减速轴　outboard epicylic spur double reduction axle　153
弯曲横销臂　cranked cross-pin arm　149
万向节　universal joint　68，125，155
万向节法兰盘　universal joint flange　184
万向支架　gimbat bracket　86
危急报警闪光灯　hazard warning lamp　195
危险警告灯　hazard warning flasher　196
微机械调节器　minimec governor　15
微喷油器　microjector　11

帷幔　valance　69
尾板　end plate　59
尾部涡流锥　trailing vortex cone　61
尾灯　rear light　2
尾壳　tail housing　123
尾流　after flow wake，wake　60
尾塞　breech plug　10
尾翼平衡柱　wing attachment strut　218
温度传感器　temperature sensor　28
温度/时间开关　thermo-time switch　27
文丘里管　Venturi　24
文丘里效应　Venturi effect　61
稳定器　stabilizer　74
稳定柱　steady post　171
涡流卷团　turbulent volume　60
涡流燃烧室　vortex combustion chamber　6
涡轮　turbine　43，134
涡轮压力　turbo pressure　34

涡轮增压　boost pressure　16
涡轮增压器　turbo charger (tc)　199
涡轮轴轴承　turbine shaft bearing　134
涡轮组件　turbine member　136
蜗杆　worm gear　148
蜗杆滚子类转向齿轮箱　worm and roller type steering gearbox　161
蜗杆锥形滚子轴承　worm taper roller bearing　163
蜗轮　worm wheel　147
无线电收发两用天线　radio transceiver aerial　216
无源电阻　passive resistors　50
雾灯　fog lamp　3

吸管　suction line　114
吸能元件　energy absorber　57
吸入阀　suction valve　99
吸入压力　suction pressure　6
铣切转子　milled rotor　226
细丝　fine wire　42
下部叉形杆臂　lower wishbone arm　79
下部横向连杆　lower transverse link　94
下部橡胶膜垫　lower rubber diaphram　52
下横杆　lower transverse link　74
下横向控制臂　lower transverse control arm　73，77
下架　subframe　53，73
下控制柱塞　lower control piston　186
下气环　lower compression　44
下止推片　below still trundle patch　44
先导电磁阀　pilot solenoid vale　116
衔铁　armature　26，169
衔铁杆　armature rod　211
限流阻尼器　restriction damper　90
限位块　limiting stopper　77，119
限位销套　set pin sleeve　77
限压阀　pressure limiting valve　51
线圈　coil　26
箱体固定螺栓　casing anchor bolt　80
橡胶安装垫　rubber mounting　53，73
橡胶环　rubber grommet　171
橡胶绝缘块　rubber insulator　193
橡胶连接环　rubber joint ring　42
橡胶密封　rubber sealing ring　18
橡胶密封条　rubber seal　58
橡胶套　rubber bush　94
橡胶支撑及其夹套　rubber bearing and clamp　79
橡胶支承点　rubber bearing point　77
橡胶止回阀　rubber flap valve　102
橡胶轴衬　rubber bush　123
橡胶轴承　rubber bearing　80
消防车　fire engine　218
消声器　silencer (u. s. muffler)　68
消声柱　sound-deadening rib　123
销　dowel　74
销钉　dowel pin　13
小齿轮　pinion, small pinion gear　74，127
小齿轮花键　pinion spline　148
小齿轮托架　pinion carrier　129
小齿轮托架销　pinion carrier pin　127
小齿轮转向器　pinion steering　76
小刚度弹簧喷油器　low-spring injector　10
小型离合器　smaller clutch　127
小柱销　small plunger　124
小锥齿轮　bevel pinion　106，152
楔块杠杆　wedge lever　105
楔块滚子组件　wedge roller assembly　174
楔形件　wedge profile　149
斜弹簧　bias spring　173
斜杆　tilt lever　90
斜坡块　ramp　15
斜置转杆　diagonal radius rod　82
泄漏阀　leakage valve　10
泄漏套　leak-off housing　12
卸荷碟阀　discharge disc valve　182
卸荷阀　dump valve　200
卸荷阀杆　dump valve lever　200
卸荷喷嘴　discharge nozzle　23
卸荷柱塞　unloader plunger　182
卸压活塞　release piston　181
卸载阀　unloader valve　122
卸载管　discharge line　114
芯套　core　26
行程销　trip pin　106
行李箱　boot　2
行李箱底板　boot pan　69
行李箱盖锁　luggage compartment door lock　198
行星齿轮　planetary gear　41，130
行星齿轮后转向盒　epicyclic rear steering box　167
行星齿轮机构　planetary gear machine　49
行星齿轮架　planetary carrier　130
行星齿轮托架　planet carrier　127

行星小齿轮接触轴肩　planet pinion abutment shoulder　149
蓄电池　accumulator　8，90
悬臂扭杆　cantilever torsion bar　44
悬臂支架　outrigger　75
悬架下部摆杆　suspension lower swing arm　93
悬架座　suspension housing　94
旋转臂　rotor arm　38
旋转球节头　swivel ball joint　125
选挡拨叉　selector fork　125
选挡杆　selector rod　125，129
选挡口　selector gate　125
选择设定键　option menu　212
巡航控制　cruise control　20，197
循环滚珠　recirculating ball　163

压差采样点　differential pressure sampling point　33
压差传感器　differential pressure transducer　33
压力板　pressure plate　120，127
压力保持阀　pressure holding valve　22
压力弹簧　pressure spring　30，120，121
压力调节螺钉　pressure adjustment screw　12
压力控制阀　pressure control valve　22
压力释放组件　pressure relief assembly　40
压缩压力　compression pressure　6
压缩应变　compressive strain　50
压下制动踏板　brake applied　205
延时阀　relay valve　186
延时装置　relay set　28
延展臂　extension arm　75
眼孔调节螺栓　eye bolt adjuster　79
眼孔接头　eye-type joint　100
扬声器　speaker　195
氧传感器　oxygen sensor　207
氧球体　oxygen sphere　225
摇臂　swing arm　87
摇臂叉架　rocker fork　163
摇臂轴　rocker-arm shaft，rocker shaft　51，160
摇杆　rocking lever　15
摇杆臂　rocker arm　160
摇杆销钉　rocking lever pin　15
摇杆轴　rocker shaft　160
遥感灯　remote feeler bulb　116
遥控杆　remote control rod　125
遥控管　remote control tube　125
叶轮　impeller　134
叶轮轴　impeller shaft　135
叶轮组件　impeller member　136
叶片泵　vane pump　158
液窗　liquid window　113
液滴　drop　12
液力偶合器　fluid coupling，torque convertor　134，136
液压泵　hydraulic pump　92，96
液压缸　hydraulic cylinder　127
液压管件　hydraulic pipeline　96
液压活塞　hydraulic pistion　122
液压减振器　hydraulic damper　53
液压模块　hydraulic module　200
液压式缓速器　hydraulic type retarder　185
液压头　hydraulic head　18
液压支臂　hydraulic boom　218
一级方程式赛车　formula one racing car　217
仪表板　dashboard　2
仪表板灯　dash-light　195
仪表板架　dash panel　69
仪表盘　instrument panel　2
仪表照明开关　instrument brightness control　196
溢流阀　relief spill valve　185
溢流控制阀　spill control valve　34
溢油孔　spill hole　21
翼梁　wing beam　59
翼面　aerofoil　217
阴极集电器　cathode current collector　223
阴极支架　cathode support frame　223
音频系统　audio system　196
引爆器　initiator　194
引擎安装臂　engine mount arm　53
引擎单元　engine unit　133
引擎隔离舱　engine compartment　228
引擎加载　engine load　37
引擎冷剂温度传感器　engine coolant temperature sensor　33
引擎润滑油泵　engine oil pump　183
引擎速度传感器　engine speed sensor　37
引擎转速传感器　engine speed sensor　197
引线　lead wire　207
永磁式减速启动机　permanent magnet slowdown starter　49
永磁体　permanent magnet　37，226

油泵继电器　fuel pump relay　33
油泵锁止离合器　oil pump lock-up clutch　137
油池　reservoir　104
油道　oil passage　45
油底壳　sump, oil sump tank　8，51，114
油分离器　oil separator　116
油封组件　oil seal assembly　95
油口螺钉　bleed screw　175
油量表　fuel gauge　2
油量计　fuel metering　209
油滤　fuel filter　33
油面指示器　oil level indicator　50
油入口　fuel enter　10
油水分离器　oil-water separator　31
油温传输传感器　oil temperature transmission sensor　197
油温度　oil temperature　14
油箱　petrol tank (u. s. gas tank), reservoir tank　68，88
油压环形密封圈　hydraullc annulus seal　147
油压开关　oil press switch, hydraulic switch　35，51
油压控制单元　hydraulic control unit　131
有源电阻　active resistor　50
右端高度启动器　right hand height actuator　90
右滑轨　right track　59
预紧垫片　preload shim　160
预燃烧的燃烧室　pre-combustion chamber　6
预张紧绳　pretensioner cable　194
圆盘　circular disc　45
圆盘曲柄臂　circular disc crankweb　45
圆柱支架　cylindrical cradle　211
圆锥滚子轴承　tapper roller bearing　83
圆锥形适配器　conical adaptor　211
远光灯　main beam headlight　3
远光指示灯　high beam indicator, main beam indicator light　2，195
钥匙发射器放大器　transponder key amplifier　198
钥匙发射器线圈　transponder key coil　198
钥匙筒　key cylinder　198
云梯　ladder　218

Z

载荷传感器　load sensor　92
载荷传输件　load transfer member　87
脏物防护罩　dirt shield　171
增力锁销式同步离合器　positive baulk pin synchromesh unit　144
增压　boost pressure　22
增压活塞　boost piston　205
增压空气温度传感器　manifold air temperature sensor　35
增压控制器　boost controller　19
增压器　super charger　51
增压引擎　supercharged engine　217
张紧杆挡块　tensioning lever stop　22
单板　cover plate　118
单面　fascia　57
折叠纸质过滤元件　pleated paper filter element　42
诊断波形键　diagnosic waveform menu　212
诊断口　diagnostic socket　35，169
真空泵　vacuum pump　34
真空调节阀　vacuum regulating valve　34
真空管路图标签　vacuum hose diagram label　4
真空伺服阀　vacuum servo　177，200
真空箱　vacuum tank　29
真空助力器　vacuum power booster　170
振摆质量　pendulum mass　50
振动探测器　vibration detector　211
蒸发器单元　evaporator unit　115
蒸发器蛇形管　evaporator coil　115
整流器　rectifier　193
整体齿轮　integral gear　126
整体齿轮轮齿　integral dog tooth portion　126
整体式催化转化器　monolithic catalytic converter　207
整体支撑　integral bearer　74
正时齿轮　timing gear　7，51
正时控制　timing control　20
正时控制阀　timing control valve　34
正时链　timing chain　8
正时皮带　timing belt　8
支撑板　support disc, torque plate　100，171
支撑垫片　back-up washer　35
支撑杆　support rod　211
支撑块　support block　50
支撑套　support sleeve　147
支撑销　anchor pin　171
支架复位弹簧　carrier retaining spring　171
支架支柱　carrier strut　171
支柱　strut　76
支柱连杆　strut link　187

支柱凸轮制动蹄膨胀器　strut and cam brake shoe expander　173
支座　supporting cradle　216
直齿差动齿轮　spur-type differential wheel　95
直齿轮　spur gear　147
直齿销　spur gear pin　147
直齿油泵　spur gear oil pump　130
直接驱动垫　direct pad　175
直接驱动活塞　direct piston　175
直接驱动啮合　direct-drive engagement　126
直喷火花塞线圈　DIS coil　33
直喷装置　direct injection　11，23
止推垫圈　thrust washer　49
纸质空滤器　paper air cleaner　42
指示灯　indicator light　2
制动灯　brake light　3
制动碟盘　brake disc　83
制动阀从动缸　brake valve slave cylinder　183
制动分泵　wheel cylinder　170
制动鼓　brake drum　170
制动管路　brake line　170
制动卡钳　brake caliper　205
制动连接头　coupling head for brake　186
制动盘　brake dise　74，205
制动踏板　brake pedal　2，199
制动系统指示灯　brake system indicator　195
制动液储箱　brake fluid reservoir　170
制动总泵　master cylinder　170
质量型空气流量计　mass air flow meter　196
中继杆　relay lever　183
中间板　intermediate plate　120
中间管　intermediate tube　99
中间环　median ring　88
中间减速齿轮　intermediate reduction gear　152
中间支承　centre bearing　155
中间轴　intermediate shaft, countershaft　75，124
中间轴齿轮　intermediate pinion　162
中心环　central ring　89
中心控制单元　central control unit　229
中心螺栓　center bolt　77
中心双架组件　central double yoke member　155
中央出风口　center ventilator　196
中柱　center pillar　56
终极能量输出极　terminal energy output pole　36
钟形腔端面　bell housing facing　120
钟形曲柄（杆）　bell crank levers　86，90
钟形曲柄转换杆　shift bell crank lever　183

重载鼓式制动器　heavy-duty drum brake　171
周边泵　peripheral pump　30
周边空隙　peripheral gap　42
轴承轮毂支架　bearing and hub carrier　83
轴承腔　bearing housing　83
轴承腔盖　bearing housing cover　120
轴承销　bearing pin　178，180
轴承支撑架　bearing support bracket　125
轴管　axle tube　95
轴肩调整丝杠螺母　shouldered adjustment screw and nut　161
轴颈　journal　45
轴模块　axle modulator　186
轴套滑动轴承　plain bush bearing　163
轴针式喷油器　pintaux type nozzle　10
轴针式喷嘴　pintaux type nozzle　9
主板　mainplate　59
主板台　main plate table　107
主动轮　primary pulley　130
主动轮伺服缸　primary pulley servo cylinder　131
主缸　master cylinder　122
主管路　gallery duct　50
主活塞　master piston　183
主继电器　main relay　29
主减速器　final drive　3，68
主降落伞　main parachute　216
主控阀　primary governor valve　140
主离合器　main clutch　127
主喷嘴　main supply jet　23
主渗流　main bleed　103
主蹄块　primary shoe　170
主轴　main shaft　14，145
主轴附属输入齿轮　mainshaft auxiliary input gear　128
注射泵　injection pump　183
驻车环齿轮　parking ring　137
驻车制动器　handbrake, parking brake, true-stop brake　2，188
驻车制动器撑杆　parking brake strut　188
驻车制动器拉杆　parking brake lever　188
驻车制动器（手刹）　handbrake　68
驻车制动指示灯　parking brake indicator　195
柱连杆　strut link　173
柱塞密封　plunger seal　173
柱塞式喷油器　plunger injector　31
柱销　pintle　26
柱形螺旋弹簧　barrel-shaped helical spring　75
铸铁从臂　cast trailing arm　72
爪形PM永磁电机　claw type PM magnet motor

226
转臂　radius arm　73
转动球节头　pivot ball joint　125
转换器　inverter　229
转枢　pivot　187
转枢挡柱　pivot stop post　119
转枢梁　pivot beam　87
转枢销　pivot pin　15，85
转枢轴　axis of pivot　58
转速表　tachometer　58
转速计轴　tachometer shaft　14
转台　turntable　108
转弯信号灯　indicator　3
转向臂　steering arm　72，101
转向传感器　steering sensor　168
转向阀　steering valve　158
转向杆　steering column　168
转向滚子单元　steering ball unit　168
转向横拉杆　tie rod　74
转向角度传感器　steer angle transducer　96
转向盘　steering wheel　2
转向器　steering gear　158
转向指示灯　turn light lamp　195
转向柱外套　steering column jacket　74
转向阻尼　steering damper　73
转销　swivel pin, hinge pin　83，176
转子　rotor　17
转子片　rotor lamination　226
转子套　rotor sleeve　226
转子通风开关阀　rotor vent switch valve　18，28
装配定位孔　aligment holes for assembly　45
装饰条　molding　58
撞击挡块　bump stop　89
锥齿轮　bevel gear, bevel wheel　95，106
锥体　cone　126
锥形活塞　conical piston　84
锥形口　conical portion　126
锥形扩散器　conical diffuser　16
锥形离合器　cone clutch　144
锥形离合器　cone clutch　142
锥形裙部　tapered skirt　84
锥形预载弹簧　belleville preload spring　168

锥形轴承预紧垫片　taper bearing preload shim　163
锥形座　tapered seat　163
子午线轮胎　radial ply tyre　190
自动变速器　automatic transmission　134
自动变速箱控制系统　automatic gearbox control system　142
自检接头　self-test connector　33
自紧弹簧　garter spring　135
自平衡液气悬挂　self-levelling hydropneumatic suspension　99
自位轴承　self-aligning bearing　125，211
纵臂固定螺栓　trailing arm anchor bolt　80
纵梁　side member　56
纵向臂　trailing arm　77
纵向叉形杆臂　longitudinal wishbone arm　80
纵向弹簧臂　longitudinal spring arm　80
纵向加速传感器　longitude acceleration sensor　92
纵向件　longitudinal member　69
纵向连杆　longitudinal link　73
阻风门　choke　2
阻尼阀组件　damper valve assembly　102
阻尼反弹阀　damper rebound valve　99
阻尼笼　damping cage　226
阻尼器撞击阀　damper bump valve　99
阻尼腔　damper cage　226
阻尼室　damping chamber　40
组合式曲轴　built-up crankshaft　45
钻削孔　drill hole　102
最大燃油量挡杆　max. fuel stop lever　15
最大燃油量调节器　max. fuel adjuster　15
最大燃油量调整螺钉　maximum fuel adjustment screw　19
左端高度启动器　left hand height actuator　90
左滑轨　left track　59
作用板　reactor plate　121
作用杆　reaction rod　125
作用活塞　reaction piston　186
作用柱塞　reaction plunger　122
座舱　cockpit　217
座垫　seat cushion　59
座垫骨架　seat cushion frame　59
座口接头　socket joint　73

参 考 文 献

[1] Ron Hodkinson John Fenton. *Lightweight Electric/Hybrid Vehicle Design*. Oxford Butterworth-Heinemann, 2001.
[2] Marios Sideris. *Methods for Monitoring and Diagnosing the Efficiency of Catalytic Converters*. Amsterdam: Elsevier, 1998.
[3] Prof. Dipl. -Ing. Jörnsen Reimpell, Dipl. -Ing. Helmut Stoll Prof. Dr. -Ing. Jürgen W. Betzler, *The Automotive Chassis: Engineering Principles (2nd Edition)*, Oxford: Butterworth-Heinemann, 2001.
[4] T. K. GARRETT, K. NEWTON, W. STEEDS. *The Motor Vehicle (13th Edition)*. Oxford: Butterworth-Heinemann, 2001.
[5] Heinz Heisler. *Advanced Vehicle Technology (2nd Edition)*. Oxford: Butterworth-Heinemann, 2002.
[6] Allan W. M. Bonnick. *Automotive Computer Controlled Systems: Diagnostic tools and techniques*. Oxford: Butterworth-Heinemann, 2001.
[7] 王海林. 汽车专业英语. 北京: 机械工业出版社, 2008.
[8] 王锦俞. 图解英汉汽车技术词典. 第2版. 北京: 机械工业出版社, 2011.
[9] 英国DK公司. 牛津英汉双解大辞典. 插图版. 北京: 外语教学与研究出版社, 2005.
[10] 吴衡康, 周黎明, 任文. 牛津当代百科大辞典 (英汉·英英·彩色·图解). 北京: 中国人民大学出版社, 2004.
[11] 加拿大QA国际图书出版公司. 学生英汉百科图解词典. 北京: 外语教学与研究出版社, 2005.
[12] 朱派龙. 金属切削刀具与机床. 北京: 化学工业出版社, 2016.
[13] 朱派龙, 赵战峰. 特种加工技术. 北京: 北京大学出版社, 2017.
[14] 朱派龙. 机械工程专业英语图解教程. 第2版. 北京: 北京大学出版社, 2013.
[15] 朱派龙. 图解机械制造专业英语. 增强版. 北京: 化学工业出版社, 2014.